P9-AGS-964

DATE DUE

AG 3 00		
AG 3 00		
OC 23 01		
NO 13 01		
DE 6 01		
SE 3 03		
NO 20 03		
JE 23 08		
MR 17 09		

DEMCO 38-296

DRUMMING FOR THE GODS

• • •

IN THE SERIES

Studies in Latin American and
Caribbean Music,

edited by Peter Manuel

María Teresa Vélez

DRUMMING
FOR
THE GODS

•   •   •

The Life and Times
of Felipe García Villamil,
SANTERO, PALERO, and ABAKUÁ

TEMPLE UNIVERSITY PRESS   PHILADELPHIA

Riverside Community College
Library
4800 Magnolia Avenue
Riverside, CA 92506

Temple University Press, Philadelphia 19122
Copyright © 2000 by Temple University
All rights reserved
Published 2000

ML 419 .G363 V45 2000

V elez, Mar ia Teresa, 1952–

Drumming for the gods

eets the requirements of the
tion Sciences—Permanence
NSI Z39.48–1984

ation Data

Drumming for the gods : the life and times of Felipe García
Villamil, santero, palero, and abakuá / by María Teresa Vélez.
       p.   cm. — (Studies in Latin American and Caribbean music)
    Includes bibliographical references (p.   ) and index.
    ISBN 1-56639-730-8 (cloth: alk. paper). — ISBN 1-56639-731-6
(pbk.: alk. paper)
    1. García Villamil, Felipe, 1931–   . 2. Drummers (Musicians)—
Cuba—Biography.   3. Santeria music—History and criticism.
4. Blacks—Cuba—Religion.   I. Title.   II. Series.
ML419.G363V45   2000
786.9′092
[B]—DC21   99–029450

Frontispiece: Felipe García Villamil playing a batá drum.
(Photo by Adriana Groisman)

CONTENTS

PART TWO: Life as a Musician during the Revolution

PART THREE: Life as a Diasporic Musician

Photographs follow page 104

ACKNOWLEDGMENTS

Customarily, in this section of a book a number of institutions that have contributed to make the research and writing process possible are acknowledged. In my case I have to thank not an institution but a network of wonderful friends who, through many years, have helped me in ways that would take another life history (mine) to describe. Thus, with profound gratitude, I list their names first.

The place of honor in this list belongs to Felipe García Villamil and his wife, Valeria, and to my friends (alphabetically by first name): Adriana Groisman, Ana "Caona" Ellis, Angela María Pérez, Beatriz Smith, Carmen Diaz, David Burrows, Karen Jefferson, Krishna K. Candeth, Linda Pelc, Lyndell Brookhouse-Gil, Michael Smith, Mónica Vélez, Nanette García, Olga Vieira, Oscar Correa, and Rodrigo Henao. *Gracias.*

My gratitude goes also to the many santeros, paleros, and musicians who during these years contributed to make this research possible, and especially to Gregg Askew, Judith Gleason, Louis Bauzo, Milton Cardona, Teddy Holiday, and Jessy Feldman.

I also thank several of my colleagues and teachers for guidance, encouragement, and support: Kay Shelemay, Mark Slobin, Gage Averill, Peter Manuel, and Su Zheng. Robin Moore contributed generously as a reviewer. Special thanks go to Peter Manuel, without whose support this book would have remained unpublished.

To my friend and editor at Temple University Press, Doris Braendel, my warmest gratitude. Thanks also to Joanna Mullins for her careful copyediting.

Finally, I would like to thank Felipe's family in Cuba in their native language: *A la familia Villamil gracias de todo corazón. Quiero agradecer en forma especial a Clarita que me guió a través de las calles de Matanzas y me presentó a todos los miembros de la familia, a Osvaldo por darme generosamente de su tiempo y sus conocimientos, y a Beba y Bertina por compartir sus memorias conmigo.*

A NOTE ON SPELLING

I have chosen to follow the Spanish orthography in transcribing the Lucumí, Abakuá, and Congo words, with a few changes adopted for reasons of clarity. I made this choice because Felipe, with whom I worked closely, is a Cuban whose Lucumí side of the family, like most of the Lucumí speakers in Cuba, are not familiar with written Yoruba and acquired their literacy following the rules of written Spanish. In doing this, I follow the steps of Lydia Cabrera, who, while aware of the relationship between Yoruba and Lucumí, was interested in compiling the language in the way in which it is spoken in Cuba. When quoting the work of other scholars, I use the spelling of the Lucumí terms that they have chosen. However, even within the work of one scholar the spelling of these terms is not always consistent. Accents and sometimes even letters vary. I have chosen one spelling for each term and use it consistently in the text but in no way consider my choice "the right spelling" for these terms.

The pronunciation of the sound /sh/ varies in Lucumí, where many speakers pronounce it like the Spanish *ch,* while others use the softer English *sh* sound. Ortíz and Cabrera fluctuate in the use of *ch* or *sh;* thus, in their writings, one finds the two spellings (e.g., Ochún and Oshún). For simplicity, I have chosen to use only *ch.*

The consonant c in Spanish has a different sound depending on the vowel that follows it. As in English, the sound of c followed by an e or an i varies from when it is followed by a, o, or u. To simplify the spelling, I have chosen to use the letter k when I want to transcribe a c sound like the one found in the word car. An exception to this is the term *Lucumí,* which I consistently spell with a c, following the way in which this term is spelled in most of the literature written in Spanish on the subject.

Considering that in the Spanish spoken in Latin America a phonetic difference rarely appears between v and b or between s and z, I have chosen to use b and s, except when such a difference is clearly distinguishable.

The phoneme /j/, with a sound like the first letter in the English words *jail* or *geometry,* is transcribed as /y/.

The texts of the chants included in this book are transcribed following sung pronunciation. The division of words (when unknown or unclear) also follows the way in which the words are delivered in song. I have kept alternative pronunciations of the same word or expression.

I have chosen to use the phoneme /w/ to convey a sound different from that of the Spanish vowel u and closer to the sound of w in English. However, Felipe alternates between this sound and one that uses a g in front. For example, sometimes he would say *chawala* and other times *chaguala.* Instead of giving a consistent spelling, I have chosen to keep the inconsistencies and to follow the phonetic transcription of the words.

There is a difference between how I chose to transcribe Lucumí words in my texts and how I transcribed them in the chants. For the first type of transcription, I try to be as consistent as possible (leaving nuances and ambiguities on the side) for sake of clarity. However, for the chants, I follow the phonetic transcription of the texts.

I followed the same criteria described for Lucumí in transcribing the Abakuá and Congo words found in the text. Thus, for instance, I use the word *Congo* (with C rather than K), in accordance with Cuban sources.

Spanish, Lucumí, Congo, and Abakuá words appear in italics in the text only if they appear rarely. Words used frequently appear in italics the first time only.

PROLOGUE

I met Felipe García Villamil, a master Afro-Cuban drummer and craftsman, in 1992, several years after I began to do research on the music
of the Afro-Cuban religious traditions, especially Santería. During my
research, I frequently heard Felipe's name mentioned by drummers and
students in the Afro-Cuban dance class I was attending at the Boys Har-
bor in New York. At that time I was struggling with the constraints and
problems posed by research into a corpus of music linked to Santería,
where the tradition of secrecy is still an imperative that many practitioners adhere to, and where musical knowledge is transmitted through
long periods of apprenticeship and through a series of networks that
are not easily accessed, especially by women. I thought that identifying a knowledgeable teacher who would agree to work with me was
the best way to further my research. In January 1992, I went for the first
time to Felipe's house in the Bronx to receive a *chekeré* lesson. This
marked the beginning of weekly trips to the Bronx that lasted, but for
a few breaks, until the end of 1994.

After a month of chekeré lessons, I decided to concentrate on collecting religious chants and to make this repertoire the focus of my dissertation. I explained to Felipe the nature of my work and asked him
if he had any reservations. At that time Felipe's activities as a ritual

drummer were limited; lacking connections with the network through which *batá* drummers customarily get hired to perform at religious rituals, he was quite isolated and had concentrated his musical activities on teaching. His aim was to train a group of drummers in the Matanzas style of batá drumming, a style almost unknown in New York, where all the batá drummers were familiar with the style from Havana. Teaching had also become for him a way to struggle against forgetfulness, a way to remember. He viewed our work together as an opportunity to "let people know the way things were done in Matanzas and back there in Cuba."

Felipe and I conceived these sessions as classes and followed the etiquette of the student-teacher relationship. At the beginning of each session I would turn the tape recorder on, and Felipe would begin to sing. He gradually began to teach me the large body of chants used to praise or address the Santería deities—the *orichas*—in ritual. When he began to sing for a particular oricha, he would tell me some of the myths or legends—*patakís*—that narrate events of the lives of the orichas and tell of their idiosyncrasies, personalities, and demeanors. However, the chants and the music would always bring memories of Cuba back to Felipe, and he would then tell me stories about his family and his life "back there." Sometimes he got so carried away that we would end up not working on the chants, and he spent most of the time reminiscing. He would then apologize and promise to organize "the lesson" better for the next meeting, making sure we went over a large number of chants. Most of the time I would let the train of his thought unwind without interrupting him. However, on some occasions, moved by concern that I would never "get my work done," I would take advantage of a pause between stories to try to bring him back to the chants by asking him politely to sing for me a chant for this or that oricha.

As my work with the chants progressed, my relationship with Felipe and his family—Valeria, his wife, and his children Ajamu, Miguel, Atoyebi, and Tomasa—grew closer. My lessons in some way became part of the family life and were interrupted and enriched according to the unpredictable and sometimes hectic rhythms of Felipe's everyday routines. After several months of working in the repertoire of chants, Felipe, who knew of my desire to learn to play batá drums, invited me to join the lessons he was giving to a woman drummer, Nanette Gar-

Flavell, J. Metacognition and cognitive monito[...] **Psychologist.** 34. 1979. 906-911.

Gardner, H. **The unschooled mind: How chi[...]** 1991.

Glaser, R. Expert knowledge and processes c[...] **sciences and mathematics.** Hillsdale, NJ: E[...]

Gordon, Carol A. Methods for Measuring the [...] **Library Media Research.** Volume 5. 2002. w[...]

Guild, Sandy L. Modeling Recursion in Resea[...] **Library,** edited by Barbara K. Stripling and S[...]

Halpern, D. A cognitive approach to improving[...] **Enhancing thinking skills in the sciences a[...]**

...infrastructure to interactions. In D.R. schools... and Technology. Second Edition. Associatio...

Inquiry and the National Science Educatio... of Sciences, National Research Council, and... Washington, D. C. 2000.

Jakes, D.S., Pennington, M.E., & Knodle, H.A... http://www.biopoint.com/inquiry/ibr.html

Jonassen, D. H., Peck, K.L., & Wilson, B.G. (... Upper Saddle River, NJ: Prentice Hall. 1999

Keller, J. M. Motivational design of instruction... Hillsdale, NJ: Erlbaum. 1983.

Kelly, R. Getting everybody involved: Coopera... Leading with Technology, 27(1), 1999. 10-1...

http://virtualinquiry.com/resources/index.htm

BL 2532.S3 D4 2004

Bl 2532.R37,B37 1988

Bl 2532 S3 ~~D44~~ M27 2002

Bl

cía. He had already explained to me his position with respect to the prohibition that bans women from playing sacred batá drums. He believed that women should never be allowed to play a consecrated set of drums; yet, he saw no harm in teaching to women the music, the rhythms that are played for each oricha, as long as these were performed on unconsecrated drums or on congas. This marked the beginning of my involvement with the drums, which lasted until November 1994, the last time Nanette, Felipe, and I played batá drums together.

The stories that Felipe used to interpolate between chants or after having taught us a batá rhythm constitute the basis for my dissertation and for this book, and they cover Felipe's activities as a musician until 1994. Music carried powerful associations for Felipe, and it was music that triggered his reminiscences. Thus, even after I had decided to use his stories as the main focus of my dissertation, I eschewed formal interviews and limited my questions to clarifying the stories or arguments that arose out of a musical experience, be it a chant, a rhythm, or a performing technique. Yet aside from music, another stimulus would launch Felipe into long monologues and explanations. This happened typically after Valeria read to him from some of the books that began to be published and circulated in New York about the traditions and the music of the Afro-Cuban religions, or after he had an encounter with someone who had in any way questioned his knowledge or his credentials. Aware of the nature of my project, he wanted to explain to me his view about a particular issue, taking this as an opportunity to "set the record straight."

Felipe was not the type of subject who interviews well, and the few times that I "formally interviewed him," his answers lacked the freshness and force of the stories he told while he was drumming or singing. I decided to use the material I had gathered during our music-making sessions by quoting it directly, editing it lightly when necessary. I use my own, authorial voice to incorporate the material I gathered in the interviews and what I learned from and about Felipe during the years I visited his house as a student and as a friend. Although Felipe taught me many things about his religious practices and beliefs, some of it was, according to Felipe, to be kept secret. I have respected his wishes strictly.

I met Felipe again in New York in 1998, where he had returned after spending a couple of years in California. We spent many days talking about what had happened in his life and mine since we had played drums together for the last time in 1994. I had moved to the other side of the Atlantic (Sicily), where I have been living since 1995. During these years, I visited Felipe's family whenever I came back to New York and talked several times with Felipe on the phone; but since we both had left New York, we could not enjoy long conversations. I had sent him a copy of my dissertation and given his sister a copy to bring back to Cuba, but it was clear he had not read it. "You wrote all those things in English" was his comment, although I had given a bilingual version of all his stories, something I knew could not be done for this book. Therefore, I wanted him to be aware of the stories I had included in my narration before they became a published book. Felipe posed no restrictions on the use of any material and information and in fact stated that anything true could be said; which, of course, is not equivalent to saying that everything true *must* be said. Accordingly, I have not included many details about his life that I deemed private, for this is a book about his art (his "trade," as he would refer to it), tightly linked to his religious practices, but not an autobiography or a conventional life history.

Having decided to work on the music of the Afro-Cuban religions in the United States, I did not visit Cuba as part of the fieldwork for my dissertation. However, I did what I jokingly called long-distance fieldwork. Several close friends visited Felipe's family during these years, bringing back videotapes, recordings, photographs, and stories that they shared generously with me. Through them, I got to know Felipe's larger family better and was able to cross-check some of the stories on his personal and family experiences in Cuba. Through sources independent of Felipe, I learned about his reputation as a drummer in Matanzas, listened to tapes of the group he had organized before leaving Cuba, and learned about other aspects of his life in Cuba. I also got to know Felipe's relatives well through reading the correspondence he got from Cuba. Although Felipe's wife, Valeria, spoke some Spanish, she had problems deciphering the letters Felipe received. Felipe's eyesight was very poor, so I was asked frequently to read these letters out loud. As I read, Felipe and Valeria would comment on the person who wrote it and share the family gossip connected to that person. I also met several of Felipe's family members who visited New York as members of Afro-Cuban musical ensembles that toured the United States. After I decided to write this book, I visited

Focusing on an individual and on the particularities of his experiences emerged as a methodological strategy that contributed to correcting generalizations that misrepresented and obscured the complexity and heterogeneity of the practices I was studying. It enabled me also to give a voice (although edited and shaped by my own) to a special individual who, although not a "typical" batá drummer—someone who could be used to represent batá drummers as a group—or a famous or widely successful and well-known one, was nevertheless a master in his trade. Following his stories, we learn something about how an individual musician creatively selects, re-creates, renovates, and modifies the cultural practices considered part of his "heritage" to construct a complex mosaic that is personal and unique. We follow him as he not only lives through history but makes history, as he shapes a fragmented identity that cannot properly be described with generalities such as Cuban immigrant, minority, black, religious drummer, but that nevertheless partakes of all of them.

Naturally, I am aware of the risk of underestimating—or of appearing to underestimate—the formative character of culture. I have thus tried to temper the emphasis on the individual by means of two approaches. The first views the individual as a "carrier of culture" and examines how an individual musician constructs or reconstructs his history. The second examines how this musician has contributed to the diffusion of particular cultural practices (sacred drumming, building of drums, and crafting of religious objects), and how these practices have been accepted and modified in a particular environment (Matanzas in pre- and postrevolutionary Cuba, and New York in the United States) (Fox 1991: 110).

Felipe's story prompts us to examine the interaction between larger social, political, economic, and cultural forces and the specific actions of an individual. His strategies suggest more general themes and problems, for example, the professionalization of musicians after the Cuban Revolution and life as an immigrant in the United States. Through Felipe's story we can gain insights into the musical life of Cuba during and after the revolution and into the lives of immigrant musicians in present-day New York City. By relating his life to its historical contexts, we may understand how history has shaped and given meaning to Felipe's personal experiences and the ways in which his life has contributed to this history.

On another level, Felipe's life history helps us examine the history of a specialized musical trade, sacred batá drumming. It is a demanding musical profession to which serious sacred batá drummers dedicate their whole lives. However, most of these drummers (in Cuba as well as in the United States) are not able to support themselves and their families with the income earned through ritual drumming. Most have to supplement their income through all sorts of jobs or search for alternatives as secular drummers. These "moves" (which vary widely from drummer to drummer) affect and shape their dedication to the batá drums and to ritual drumming. These choices and their outcomes illuminate how actual circumstances and personal experiences are crucial to the "constitution of experience" (Abu-Lughod 1991)—in this case, "musical" experience. An example is Felipe's lack of success in re-establishing himself as a ritual drummer in the United States, even though the Santería community in New York is large enough to offer performing opportunities to sacred drummers. That there are competing regional styles of drumming in Cuba, and that the style that prevails in New York is not the one Felipe practices, only partially explains this outcome. Personal and family constraints have also shaped it.

We also learn how batá drumming is a trade, with apprentices and masters, where the criteria for who is accepted as a member and the rules that judge artistic quality are negotiated constantly according to changing circumstances, and where the rules that govern the construction and transmission of power between sets of batá drums also vary according to specific moments and the needs of a particular locale. Moreover, in following Felipe's activities as a batá drummer, we can give names to a "faceless community." "Naming names" in a tradition where knowledgeable *olúbatás* and *omóañás* and the number of sacred sets of batá drums (in Cuba as well as in the United States) may be counted on the fingers of the hands becomes a way to acknowledge their history and to advance, in part, the historical reconstruction of this tradition.

Following the intricate ceremonies that accompany the construction and consecration of batá drums and the lineages that arise from the process of the transmission of sacred power from one set of drums to another not only adds to the study of musical instruments, in particular batá drums and their history in Cuba and the United States, but at the same time illustrates the way in which musical instruments incorporate layers of history and can be, for a musician, not only a source of income but "life itself."

PART ONE

Learning the Trade

(*Overleaf*) **F**elipe's signature as a palero (his *firma*), which appears in a flag on Felipe's altar. Felipe also uses it in his presentation cards. COLLECTION OF FELIPE GARCÍA VILLAMIL.

*It is—or would like to be—a microhistory [microstory], the
history [story] of a trade and its defeats, victories, and miseries,
such as everyone wants to tell when he feels close to concluding
the arc of his career, and art ceases to be long.*

PRIMO LEVI, *The Periodic Table*

*In certain societies at least (for example the Yoruba and the
Akan) drumming is a highly specialized activity, with a period
of apprenticeship and exclusive membership so that to a greater
extent than in most forms of spoken art, drum literature is a
relatively esoteric and specialized form of expression
understood by many (at least in its simpler forms) but probably
only fully mastered and appreciated by the few.*

RUTH FINNEGAN, *Oral Literature in Africa*

I am Felipe García Villamil, *Balogún* for thirty years; *Olúañá*, of Matanzas,
Cuba, for about forty years; *Omóañá* for almost forty-five years; *Olú Iyesá;
Tata Nganga, Amasa Nkita, Rompe Monte Quinumba Maria Munda,* of the
line *Yo Clava Lo Taca a Rubé; Isunekue* of the *Potencia Efik Kunambere* of
Matanzas; *Ponponte Mio Siro Akanabión;* and my title in Abakuá is:
*Isunekue Bijuraka Mundi, Isunekue Atara Yira Atara Kondó, Isunekue Baibo
Eyene Baibo.*

I am the son of Tomasa Villamil Cárdenas and Benigno García García
(with seven degrees in *Palo*), the grandson of Tomasa Cárdenas (daughter
of Iñoblá Cárdenas) and Juan Villamil, and the grandson of Aniseto (Kongo)
García Gómez and Carlota García.[1]

Background

Felipe García Villamil was the fifth of ten children of Tomasa Villamil
and Benigno García. His parents, like many couples from their socioeconomic background in Matanzas, were united in a common-law mar-
riage. It was not uncommon for people like Felipe's parents to have
successive unions during their lives, and for children to be brought up

by family members other than their biological parents. Households were complex domestic units, where the living space was shared not only by people linked through consanguineous or affinal ties but by people related to one another through ritual ties. Felipe's father had eleven other children, ten from a previous relationship and one daughter born after he separated from Felipe's mother. Every year at Christmastime, Benigno García would gather all his children around the dinner table in the small country town where he was born, Camarioca. Felipe thus knew all his half-brothers and -sisters, whom he regarded as "brothers and sisters taking away the half." Many of them were brought up in Tomasa's house, and they always showed her respect and affection.

The relationship between Felipe's parents remained cordial and supportive after Felipe's father left the house when Felipe was about ten years old. Even after both Tomasa and Benigno had entered into other common-law unions, Benigno would visit frequently and stay in Tomasa's house when he was sick and needed someone to take care of him. Felipe remembers that even when his parents were together, his father was always coming and going. Sometimes the whole family had to follow him in his peregrinations as he searched for work. Felipe recalls how, when the economic situation of the family got rough and they could not afford to live in the city, his father would carry them all—in ragged clothes and without shoes—to the countryside to work in a *batey*—a sugar mill. They would all work—even the smallest child—each according to his or her strength and capabilities. Felipe was very young when he began cutting and loading cane. He also helped his father built a *bohío*—a thatched-roof hut—when there was no house for them in the mills.

Benigno was a well-known and active *palero* (priest of the Palo religion) and trained Felipe as his ritual assistant. Even when he was not living with them anymore, he would frequently call on Felipe to assist him in the ceremonies. Benigno was also an Abakuá, a member of an all-male secret society.[2] Although he could not read or write, Felipe remembers him as someone who had a way with words, who could "communicate well with the intellectuals." He had links with many local politicians, and as Felipe describes it, he "used to do politics for others," which means Benigno would get votes for them. During election time, he would run around with the local politicians. After the elections, the family was usually able to return to the city. According to Felipe, these were the best periods: His father would rent a house and buy clothes and shoes for everybody.

When Felipe was born, the family was living in a big house in Matanzas, in a neighborhood called Pueblo Nuevo. Felipe describes this as a "softer" neighborhood. The family was going through one of the good periods, and the house they were living in was the best Felipe ever knew. This house in Pueblo Nuevo had four bedrooms, a living room, a dining room, a kitchen, and a big patio surrounded by mango and avocado trees. After Felipe's parents separated, although Benigno contributed to the family expenses, the family went through hard periods. Tomasa then had to leave Pueblo Nuevo. The family moved several times until finally Tomasa settled in La Marina, a neighborhood that up to this day is one of the poorest in Matanzas. The streets have no drains, so when it rains heavily they become muddy rivers. Big wooden boards are then thrown from one side of the street to the other so that people may cross. Other members of Tomasa's family later moved to La Marina, and this neighborhood became the "territory" of the Villamil family.

When one visits Felipe's family in Matanzas, addresses and directions are unnecessary. One arrives at La Marina and simply asks to be taken to see the Villamil. Before you come to any of the houses occupied by members of the family, the word has already gotten around; they are already expecting you.

Many houses in La Marina are of the type known in Cuba as *solar*. Although the architectural design of the *solares* varies, in general each consists of a series of rooms that open to a long and narrow patio that runs the length of the building. Each room has a porch that is used as a kitchen. The toilet facilities are shared and are usually found at the end of the patio. The rooms that face the patio are either single or a large space divided into smaller rooms, by curtains or by partitions that do not reach the ceiling. Felipe's sister Beba shares the different rooms of one of these solares with her children and her grandchildren. The furnishings in Beba's house are sparse—a bed, a dining table, a few chairs, a wardrobe, an altar for the *orichas*—the spiritual entities of Santería.

Other houses in La Marina follow the traditional layout of many houses in Latin America: a living room at the entrance and a gallery of bedrooms, each with two doors—a door to connect one room to the next and a door that opens to a central patio located in front of all the bedrooms. Bertina, Felipe's sister, lives in one of these houses, which Felipe built before he left Cuba.

The house where Felipe's mother used to live is located at the intersection of two streets, one of which is a dead-end street flanked by a river. That house has entrances from both of the streets. When I visited Matanzas, Tomasa shared the house with Osvaldo, the ritual expert of the family, and his relatives. The day I visited Osvaldo, I was received through the entrance from the street that faces the river. The day I was taken to see Tomasa, we came in through the other entrance, which seemed to be the main one. The house of Tomasa—the center of the ritual activities of the family and the place of refuge when times were hard—has several rooms in succession alongside the street. A large patio is located opposite the entrance, delimited by the gallery of rooms and the house next door. This is the patio where rituals that involve dancing take place. Here many of the ritual herbs are grown and the animals for the sacrifices are kept.

Felipe left his mother's house when he was very young and eloped with his girlfriend Sofía. Finding a separate place to live as a couple was expected of anyone who eloped, a common practice during Felipe's adolescence, when this was the road many followed to initiate a common-law union. The young man would bring the girl to the house of one of his relatives for several days, after which the fact of their union was considered established. Felipe dropped out of school in the sixth grade and, with the help of his father, built a large room in the solar where his father lived. He moved there with Sofía, and in this solar two of their eight children were born. After Felipe and Sofía separated, he lived with María Salomé, the mother of four of Felipe's daughters. When he left Cuba in 1980, Felipe had been living with the mother of his youngest Cuban son, Yaimel, who was just one year old.

Although Felipe lived in many places after he left his mother's house, he kept returning there when times were rough. Home for Felipe was always Tomasa's house.

· · ·

When Tomasa Villamil, Felipe's mother, was born (around 1903), only seventeen years had elapsed since slavery had been fully abolished in Cuba. In contrast to countries such as the United States, where the slave trade ended in the early nineteenth century, in Cuba slaves were still arriving in the early 1870s. Of the estimated seven hundred thousand to 1 million slaves brought to Cuba, 85 percent were imported in the nineteenth century.[3]

Tomasa's maternal grandfather, Iñoblá, must have arrived in Matanzas with the slaves brought to work on the sugar plantation. Cuba, which had been late in joining other Caribbean countries in the plantation type of economy, by 1840 had become the world's largest producer of sugarcane (Klein 1986: 93). This sugar "revolution" required a large workforce, which the importation of slaves provided.

Most of the slaves brought over the Atlantic during the last decades of the trade ended up working on the sugar plantations. Hence, slavery concentrated increasingly in the major sugar zones. Among them, the provinces of Matanzas and Santa Clara alone held 46 percent of the slave population in 1846; by 1877 it had increased to 57 percent (Scott 1985: 80).

Abolition in Cuba was a slow process that began in the 1860s and was completed only in 1886. Thus, well into the nineteenth century new slaves arrived in Cuba, carrying with them their African cultures and religious practices, thereby revitalizing, replenishing, and influencing the religious knowledge of the existing slave population.

Although the living conditions of the slaves were harsh, the system of slavery was not monolithic; these conditions changed from one period, one region, or one *ingenio* (sugar plantation) to another. In many places there were cracks and fissures in the system, which the slaves took advantage of to piece together their broken lives. In doing so, the slaves had to create "core institutions" that would allow them to deal with the most ordinary yet most important aspects of their lives, that would answer to everyday needs such as cooking, cleaning, giving birth and raising children, burying the dead, establishing friendships and worshiping their deities. These institutions constituted the frameworks by which the material culture they brought from Africa could be partly maintained and transformed innovatively to adapt to the new environment.

In addition to the institutions the slaves created were others that, though created by the masters and given legal sanction, played an important role as places where the cultural material the slaves brought was kept, replenished, mixed, standardized, reinterpreted, and transformed into new traditions. The institution par excellence of this type

as called the *cabildo*. In Cuba, the ethnic groups that repre-
major cultural and linguistic groupings within the slave pop-
referred to as *naciones* (nations). Cabildos, officially recognized by the church and the state, grouped blacks that belonged to
the same "nation" and played the double role of mutual-aid societies
and centers for entertainment. In these societies the slaves were allowed to worship their gods, play their music, and participate as a
group in official governmental and church activities such as proces-
sions, parades, and carnivals. Each cabildo had a house, frequently
owned by the members, that served as its headquarters. Monetary quotas were collected among the members and then used to finance the
activities of the cabildo, to help the members in need, to finance buri-
als, and sometimes to buy members' freedom. The cabildo leaders were
elected and were given names such as king, queen, and captain.

The government began to restrict the activities of these institutions
from 1790 on, with a series of measures. In 1877 their meetings began
to be supervised, and in 1882 it became mandatory for each cabildo to
obtain a license, which had to be renewed every year. The process of
legal intervention in the lives of the cabildos intensified after the abolition of slavery in 1886 and culminated in 1888 with a law that forbade
the formation of any cabildo in the "old style," allowing them to be organized only as common-law associations. Many cabildos disappeared
under these pressures, but many others continued to operate outside
the law or became *casas de santo,* or house-temples.[4]

Felipe's maternal great-grandfather, a slave who bought his freedom, was the head of one of these cabildos. Like many other slaves in
the Spanish colonies, Iñoblá must have obtained his freedom through
a legal process known as manumission, which was based on a Spanish law that gave the right to slaves to obtain their freedom and which
took place during the whole colonial period. One of the most common
systems of manumission was the *coartación,* which involved the payment of a pre-established fee to the master (Castellanos and Castellanos
1988: 77–78).

Iñoblá was a Lucumí, the name given in Cuba to slaves of Yoruba
origin. The slaves were assigned ethnic or tribal names that were usually attached to their personal names and helped identify the region of
Africa they came from. However, these labels were frequently inexact,
contradictory, or erroneous, not only because the records the slave

traders kept were not always accurate but because the criteria used to define the provenance of slaves were not uniform. Thus, some slaves were given the name of the port where they had been embarked instead of that of their place of origin; others were named after towns that later disappeared. Frequently, African names were changed or deformed, and in many cases groups of slaves were falsely classified as belonging to the groups that were priced highest in the market. Yet, in spite of the inconsistencies and errors incurred in ascribing these ethnic and tribal labels, such names were used not only by the slave owners and the government authorities but by the slaves, and they influenced the interactions between both slaves and owners and among the slaves themselves.

The slaves used these names to designate their cabildos, institutions where ethnic provenance was used as a criterion for membership. We find the labels also in government documents about slave rebellions and runaway slaves, in testaments, as well as in the documents kept by the owners of the sugar plantations (*ingenios*). They appear frequently in the recollections of former slaves that Lydia Cabrera has compiled in her many books (see the Bibliography), where it is interesting to note the important role music played in the conceptualization of groups among slaves. Gaytán, one of Cabrera's informants, referring to the group known as Makuá, says: "They made their music with two small drums. One was played with small sticks, the other with the hands. When the Congos from Las Tejas finished their makuta, the Makuá began to play" (Cabrera [1975] 1986b: 71). Nino, another informant, encountered many Lucumís and Congos: "The Lucumí liked me a lot and with them I learned their language . . . but my natural inclination brought me to look for the company of the Congos . . . [b]ecause I liked their songs and dances better" (Cabrera [1975] 1986b: 19).

These ethnic-group names continue to be used to the present day by people like Felipe, whose paternal and maternal ancestors were linked to the three ethnic groups or "nations" that were predominant in the slave population of nineteenth-century Cuba: the Lucumí, the Congo, and the Carabalí.[5]

Thus, Felipe's maternal ancestors belonged to the group of slaves known as Lucumí, who came from the southwestern part of Nigeria and included a heterogeneous group of tribes known today as the Yoruba—tribes such as the Oyo, Egba, Ijebu, Iyesá, and their neighbors.[6] This group dominated among slaves imported during the last years of the trade and were still arriving in Cuba not long before the abolition of slavery. This helps explain the fact that their religious beliefs and their music—which played such an important role in shaping the most widespread Afro-Cuban religion, Santería—prevailed among a large number of slave and free blacks in Cuba. Until late in the nineteenth century, new arrivals were replenishing the religious knowledge of their fellows on the island. Thus, researchers have pointed to a substantial number of Yoruba "continuities" or "survivals" among the Lucumí in Cuba, the most salient ones being the divination practices studied by William Bascom (1952), the worship of the orichas (though major modifications were introduced in the mythology and in the ritual practices), the ritual relationships and the exchange with the deities through sacrifice and possession, and the ritual language. However, what flourished in Cuba was not just a continuation of Yoruba religious and cultural practices but something new, born from the encounter of the diverse Yoruba tribes with one another, with non-Yoruba Africans, and with the Europeans in a new environment and a new social order governed by set of institutions different from those of Africa. Lucumí, which originally referred to the slaves who came from southwestern Nigeria, was the name chosen to describe the creole practices born from this encounter; it was the name given to the religion and to the sacred language used in the rituals. Lucumí was the name used by Felipe's elders to refer to their tradition, their music, and their religion.

Felipe's paternal ancestors belonged to the group called Congo, or Bantú, which were said to come from Angola and southern Congo. Although not by ethnic affiliation, Felipe's father was a member of the Abakuá society, a secret society established by slaves who belonged to the group known as Carabalí in Cuba, which originated in southeast Nigeria (Calabar) and west Cameroon.

Aside from these three "nations," the other important ethnic or tribal groups brought to Cuba prior to the nineteenth century were the Gangá, Arará, Mandinga, and Mina (Castellanos and Castellanos 1988). Of these, only the Arará had an influence in the Afro-Cuban religious world of the nineteenth century. The Arará are said to come from Dahomey (Castellanos and Castellanos1988; Ortíz 1975a); however, some scholars maintain that they really came from Ardra, a kingdom south of Dahomey that the Dahomeans had invaded, and that the Dahomeans sold the Arará as slaves (López Valdés 1985: 62). In Cuba, many Ararás were found in the province of Matanzas, the only province where up to this day their religious practices (in which the cult to the deity Babalú-Ayé is of great importance) and their drumming styles are kept, to some extent, by their descendants.

Entrance into the Afro-Cuban Religious World

Felipe's family in Cuba has been described as a house with two doors: a Lucumí door of Yoruba origin and a Palo door of Congo origin.[7] However, there is another door that escapes the unaware visitor, a secret passage: the Abakuá. These doors open onto the worlds of three of the four Afro-Cuban religious systems that exist nowadays in Cuba.[8]

The first door opens to the world of Lucumí, Regla de Ocha—commonly known as Santería—a religious practice based on the worship of Yoruba deities syncretized with Catholic saints called orichas or *santos*. Worshipers of the orichas are called *santeros*. The second door, the Regla Conga, Palo, or Mayombé, opens to the world of paleros, who worship the spirits, in particular the spirits of the dead; in the sacred world of paleros, the wilderness (*el monte*)—herbs, plants, trees, earth, sticks (*palos*), and animals—plays a central role. The secret passage traversed only by men leads to the world of the Abakuá, an all-male society that evolved from practices brought to Cuba by slaves from the Calabar region in Nigeria. In Cuba, members of this society are called *ñáñigos*.[9]

The section that follows is an overview of Santería, Palo, and Abakuá, addressed to readers unfamiliar with these Afro-Cuban religious systems. Those well acquainted with these religious practices may skip this section and begin to open the doors to Felipe's house.

Overview

The resourceful, flexible, and dynamic ways in which Afro-Cubans like Felipe merged the religious practices of ancestors of diverse ethnic origins are in no way unusual or unique. Back in Africa, the borrowing and incorporation of foreign religious ideas and practices was not uncommon; religious ideas moved with ease through various regions, frequently crossing ethnic and political boundaries (Brenner 1989).

In Cuba, slaves of diverse ethnic backgrounds were forced to live together and confront the cultural practices and religious ideas of varied African ethnic groups, as well as those brought by the European conquistadors. From this forced encounter, through a process of *transculturation* (a word used to describe the encounter of two active cultures that contribute to the formation of a new reality)—in resistance or in respect, in confrontation or in cooperation—a creole culture was formed in Cuba.

Afro-Cuban deities inhabit this creole world, where they have mixed and fused with other deities from Africa on the one hand and with the Catholic saints on the other. In Cuba it is common to find someone like Felipe, who worships the African deity of metals and of war in both its Lucumí (Ogún) and its Congo (Sarabanda) incarnation, celebrating the "feast" of these deities on June 24, the date assigned in the Roman Catholic Church calendar for the feast of Saint John the Baptist, with whom these deities have been syncretized in Matanzas.

In Santería, the spiritual entities that have been syncretized with the Catholic saints are called orichas or santos. Orichas are deities of multifarious nature, disparate origins, and distinct personality traits; these personality traits and attributes (*caminos* or *avatares*) are numerous, complex, and sometimes contradictory. Orichas are identified with specific colors or numbers, show predilections or dislikes for certain foods, and are associated with particular herbs and plants. Furthermore, each oricha possesses a body of chants and a repertoire of drum rhythms and dance movements. There is also a large corpus of myths or sacred narratives about the orichas that recount episodes of their lives and their relationships with one another.[10]

Although paleros do not have a pantheon as complex as the one found in Santería, their religious practice focuses on the worship of the spirits of the dead, the spirits of nature, and a hierarchy of superior spirits, *mpungu,* who have been given a creole identity by identifying them with the orichas and the Catholic saints.

Both paleros and santeros believe in a supreme creator of the world who, after the act of creation, "retires" from it, becoming unreachable; thus, no prayers or sacrifices are offered to this creator. This transcen-

dent creature is known as Olodumare, Olorún, or Olofi in Sant
as Sambia, Nsambi, or Sambi in Palo.

The focus of religious practice in Santería and Palo is cent
the relationship established with the deities and spirits, a complex relationship that involves celebrating their feasts, offering them sacrifices,
consulting their will, following their advice, and sometimes even ma-
nipulating them. Cuban santeros and paleros engage in religious practice looking for the help of these deities and spirits in coping with daily
problems and the obstacles, challenges, and changes of life.

Santeros and paleros approach the world of the sacred through the
practices of divination, sacrifice, and trance. Involvement in these practices requires undergoing a series of initiation rituals that mark different stages in the religious life of the practitioner and create different
roles or ranks within the religious community.

To be initiated, a santero goes through a series of rituals that cul-
minate in a seven-day ceremony called *asiento* or *kariocha* (to place
the oricha over the head). However, religious participation is not limited to those who undergo this initiation. Santeros who have passed
through one or several of the initiation rituals that precede the asiento
may participate actively in the religious activities of the house-temple,
although certain activities are limited to those with special knowledge
or certain levels of initiation.

The initiation process begins when the initiate receives the beaded
necklaces, *ilekes* or *collares,* that serve as dwellings to the spiritual
forces of the orichas and are given for protection. To strengthen this
protection and the bond with a group of orichas called the warriors,
which includes Eleguá, Ogún, and Ochosi, santeros undergo another
ritual to receive a series of sacred objects that are considered the material representation of these orichas. The final stage of the initiation
process is the asiento, seven days of complex ceremonies during which
the novitiate receives the sacred stones of the orichas, the *otanes,* which
are housed in porcelain tureens know as *soperas.* These stones, which
must be ritually attended and cared for, are considered the embodiment
of the orichas, the *fundamento,* or center, of every practitioner's private religious practice. During the course of the year that follows these
ceremonies, the initiate, considered one newly born, or *iyawo,* dresses
in white and follows a series of prescriptions and taboos that vary ac-

cording to the oricha he or she has received. Also within this year, or as part of the kariocha ceremonies, the initiate is presented to the sacred *batá* drums. The ceremony of presentation to the drums authorizes the novitiate to dance in front of the sacred drums in any *toque* or *fiesta de santo* and creates a special link between the initiate and the particular set of drums used in the ceremony. Santeros who are to perform specialized rituals functions receive further initiations.

Aside from initiation, santeros are involved in permanent ritual relationships with their orichas that cover a gamut of ceremonies, from the very simple and personal ones of saluting the orichas daily to the more public ones of celebrating *bembés* (ritual parties) in their honor. Central to the religious activities of santeros are the offerings, called *ebó* or *egbó,* made to propitiate, solicit, placate, or comply with the requests of the orichas. In many cases, these offerings involve the sacrifice of animals, whose blood is used to feed the sacred stones, the otanes.

Rituals accompany santeros all the way to the end of their lives, when, with a ceremony called *itutu,* the soul of the deceased santero is helped in the transit to the world of the spirits. The itutu sets in motion a cycle of rituals that end a year after the santero's death with a ceremony in which a dish is broken to symbolize the departure of the deceased.

All the religious activities of santeros are informed and guided by the will of the orichas, a will consulted and interpreted using several divination systems: the coconuts (*obi*); the shells (*dilogún*); the divining chain (called *ekuelé, opelé,* or *okuelé*); and the table of Ifá. The obi and the dilogún are used by all initiated santeros, while the ekuelé and the Ifá are used and interpreted only by the *babalaos,* the male priests of Orula (the oricha that owns the oracles). In some house-temples, in addition to the role assigned them in the interpretation of the oracles, babalaos exercise important functions in the ritual life of the family. In other houses, although the presence of the babalaos is necessary for certain ceremonies, the religious activities revolve around the figure of a ritual specialist called the *oriaté.* Felipe's family house-temple in Cuba is of the second type.

Communication with the orichas is also accomplished during possession or trance, when an oricha, incarnated in a human being (referred to as the "horse"), gives counsel, warnings, and advice to those present. The state of possession is supported by music. Music and dance are essential elements in virtually every ritual, where most of the liturgical procedures involve chanting, drumming, and dancing. Movement accompanied by drumming becomes a channel of access to the world of the orichas. Thus, the drums used during these ceremonies, the batá drums, are attributed the power to talk to the deities, inviting and enticing them to descend on their children.

· · ·

Paleros are initiated through a series of rituals known as *rayamientos.* This name derives from the marks made during these rituals, with a knife or sharp object, on the body of the neophyte. As in Santería, there are many levels of involvement in the religion; thus, a person may become a member of a house-temple, or *nso nganga,* simply by attending its ceremonies and paying his or her respects to the *prenda* or *nganga* (the spirit of the dead) without undergoing further initiations.

Like santeros, paleros communicate with the spirits or mpungus using trance and divination. The spirits may let their will be known by talking through the initiates who have been ritually prepared to become possessed, called *perros* (dogs) or *criados* (servants) of the nganga. The spirits also answer questions the paleros pose through various types of divination systems. Paleros use two divination systems borrowed from the Lucumí, the coconut (*ndungui*) and the shells (*chamalongos*); and two divination systems of their own: the *fula* (gunpowder) and the *vititi mensu* (small mirror).

To consult the fula, the palero places a certain number of small piles of gunpowder over a board or over the floor, in a ritually separate space. A question is formulated, and the palero sets one of the piles on fire; according to the number of piles that catch fire, the answer to the question is considered positive or negative. The vititi mensu, a small mirror placed in the opening of a horn (*mpaka*) embellished with exquisite beadwork, is said to place the palero in contact with the spirits and to give him a glimpse into the other world. It is read by filling the mirror with smoke soot from a candle and proceeding to interpret the various shapes that are formed.

The fundamento, or center, of the religious practices of paleros is the nganga or prenda, which plays a role equivalent to the one played by the stones in Santería. The word *prenda,* or *nganga,* designates not only a spirit or a supernatural force but also the recipient—an iron pot or cauldron and its contents, such as herbs, sticks, stones, and earth—in which this spirit dwells. This spirit protects the owner of the prenda and is a source of power and support for paleros. Every nganga is always born from another, the *nganga madre* (mother) from which some materials for the new nganga are drawn. At the death of a palero, according to previous consultation with the spirit, the nganga is either buried with its owner or inherited by someone. The spirit in the prendas has a name by which the *mayombero* or palero who owns it is usually known as well. Some of the most famous prendas in Matanzas were known by names such as Paso Largo (Long Steps), Viento Malo (Bad Wind), and Remolino (Whirlwind). Felipe's prendas are called Mariamunda (a name) and Rompe Monte (Forest Breaker).

Music also plays a central role in the rituals of paleros, who celebrate not only initiation and funerary rituals but also rituals to feed the spirits of the dead that may involve the sacrifice of animals. Palo ceremonies are not as elaborate, expensive, and frequent as those of Santería; the mpungus are spirits of nature, worshiped in a more constrained and unostentatious manner. This simplicity is carried over to the music used during the rituals, where there are no special rhythms, chants, and dance gestures for each spirit or deity as is the case in Santería. An indispensable element in the rituals of paleros are a number of magic symbols known as *firmas* (signatures) that represent the spirit that inhabits the nganga. Not only every spirit but also paleros have firmas that identify them. These firmas are traced on the floor, on the walls, on the ritual objects, on the scarves used by paleros, and so forth. Circles, lines, crosses, curves, arrows, the moon, the sun are combined to give these signatures their ritual power.

A salient characteristic of both Santería and Palo, one that has enabled them to adapt flexibly to changing circumstances and environments, is the lack of orthodoxy, the absence of a hierarchical central authority that controls religious practices and beliefs. The head of every casa de santo or nso nganga, guides the practices of his or her own house-temple with total autonomy, without recognizing any outside hierarchy or authority, while respecting the tradition as he or she received it from the elders. Rank is recognized only within the limits of each house-temple, varies from one temple to another, and is based on knowledge and length of membership in the religion (counted from the date of initiation). Differences among the practitioners, not necessarily of a hierarchical nature, also arise from the specialized ritual functions performed by some of the initiates. Such is the case of the *osainista* (who collects and handles the rituals herbs and plants), the *italero* (reader of the dilogún), and the oriaté (the master of ceremonies of all the initiation rituals) in Santería; or the *mayordomo* (assistant of the *padre* [father] *nganga*), the *tikatika nkisi* (the godmother of the nganga), and the criado (who may be possessed or mounted by the spirits) in Palo. Nevertheless, in Santería the male priests of Orula, the babalaos, are considered by many to be of higher rank because of the exclusive nature of their priesthood, as they are the only ones who can interpret the most important divination systems.

· · ·

The same independence that characterizes the running of an *ilé-ocha* and a nso nganga exists among the numerous chapters of the Abakuá secret society, called *juegos, potencias, tierras,* or *partidos.* The Abakuá is an all-male secret society of religious and mutual-aid nature that traces its origins to the Carabalí cabildos in Cuba. Carabalí was the name given in Cuba to the Efik and the Ekpe, or Ejagham (Ekoi in Cuba), from southern Cameroon and Nigeria (Calabar), who in their land of origin organized themselves in all-male secret societies called *ngbe* or *ekpe* (leopard).

The first juego or potencia of the Abakuá society appeared in Cuba in the town Regla in 1836 (Sosa 1982: 118). The society later spread through Havana, Matanzas, and Cárdenas. Members came to be known as ñáñigos, a word used to designate the street dancers of the society (also called *diablitos* or *iremes*) who were well known by the general population in Cuba through their participation in the carnival on the Day of the Three Kings (January 6), when they danced through the streets wearing their ceremonial outfit: a multicolored checkerboard dress, with a conical headpiece topped with tassels. Initially, the Abakuá accepted only blacks as members; however, in the late nineteenth century the admission policies of some juegos or potencias were liberalized to include mulattos and whites. The object of this confraternity was to protect its members spiritually and to help them economically by means of a monthly quota gathered from the members and also used to support the activities of the society.

The society possesses a complex hierarchical organization, where every member, or *obonekue,* has detailed and specific ritual and secular functions. Members treat one another like brothers and are bound by oath to keep absolute secrecy about the society and its hermetic rituals. Each juego has from thirteen to twenty-five dignitaries, or *plazas,* who govern the society and celebrate the rites, as well as an unlimited number of initiates. The four main plazas are occupied by members who are given the names Iyamba, Mokongo, Isué, and Isunekue (the post occupied by Felipe in his juego). These names are taken from the complex origin myth of the society, which plays a pervasive role in the rituals and in the hierarchical organization of the Abakuá potencias.

Aside from its activities as a mutual-aid society, the Abakuá performs elaborate rituals and ceremonies (*plantes*) full of theatricality and drama, particularly those where the myth of origin is re-enacted. Ceremonies such as initiations and funerals, the naming of dignitaries, the founding of new groups, or the annual homage to Ekué are secret and take place in the sacred room of the temple, called the *fambá, irongo,* or *fambayín.* This room is prepared for the ritual using mystical signs, called *anaforuana* or firmas, that are drawn on the ritual space and objects. This pictographic writing system is also used by the Abakuá to convey information.

As with other Afro-Cuban *reglas,* music is central to the rituals activities of the Abakuá, who have two types of drum ensemble. One ensemble is used for public celebrations, and the other, a set of ritual, symbolic drums, is used for the esoteric ceremonies.

The first type of ensemble is made up of four open, slightly conical drums, each built from a single wood log. This ensemble is completed with other percussion instruments: two rattles, called *erikundí,* and a bell (*ekón*) made with two triangular pieces of iron to which a handle is attached. The largest drum in the ensemble is sometimes built from staves. The skin (goat) is mounted on a hoop, which is kept in place by a series of cords and wedges (usually four) called *itón* or *bekumá.* These drums lack any type of ornament or decorative painting. As sacred drums, they undergo a series of ceremonies to be consecrated and require special ritual care. They are "fed" with the blood of the sacrifices and their skin has to be marked with the Abakuá ideographs, the anaforuana.

The largest drum in this ensemble (approximately one meter tall and twenty-three centimeters in diameter) is called the *bonkó enchemiyá.* It is placed slightly tilted on the floor, with the end not touching the floor on a stone or a similar object. One drummer (*monibonkó*) sits on top of the body of the drum and plays it with his hands, while another (*monitón*) crouches close to the lower end of the drum and hits the body with two sticks called itón. Sometimes the drum is placed flat on the floor and the drummer stands while performing (Ortíz 1952: vol. 4, 35). The other three drums are given the generic name of *enkomó*.[11] Their sizes range between nine and ten inches in height and eight and ten inches in diameter. Even though they do not differ considerably in size, they are tuned to produce three types of sound: the highest drum is the *binkomé,* the middle one is the *kuchí yeremá,* and the lowest is called the *obiapá* or *salidor* (in Spanish). Each is played by placing the drum under one arm and striking it with the other. The playing technique is similar to the one used to play *bongo,* where finger strokes instead of strokes with the whole hand are involved. Traditionally, the funeral liturgy is performed using these three drums; however, some juegos use the full ensemble (Ortíz 1952: vol. 4, 42).[12]

The ensemble of "symbolic" drums is also comprised of four drums—the *enkríkamo,* the *ekueñón,* the *empegó,* and the *eribó* or *seseribó*—which, except for the eribó, are similar in morphology to the drums described above. Aside from these four drums, however, is another symbolic drum, the *ekue,* a secret drum that is kept hidden behind a curtain in the sacred chamber, the fambá. The four visible symbolic drums differ from those of the other ensemble in the way in which they are decorated: a staff with feathers, similar to the staff (*muñon*) used by the dignitary in charge of each drum, is located on the end of the drum, where the skin is placed. Each drum has one feathered staff, while the eribó has four. In addition to this ornament, each symbolic drum is sometimes decorated with a "skirt" placed close to the skin, made of shreds of fiber called *belemé* or *belefé.*

The empegó, the drum used by the dignitary of the same name, is used for special ritual invocations and to identify the participants in a *plante* as members or nonmembers of the society. It is also called *tambor de orden* (drum of order) because it is used to impose discipline within the temple. It is also the drum that opens and closes all the rituals. The ekueñón is the drum used by the dignitary who "bestows justice." This personage is assigned the task of ritual sacrifices, which have to be witnessed by the drum that personifies him. The enkríkamo is the drum used to convene the iremes, or "little devils," that represent the spirits of the deceased or supernatural beings. The eribó is built somewhat differently from the other three drums: the skin is glued or sewn to a hoop made of a flexible material. The sacrificial offerings are placed over this drum, which represents the dignitary called Isué (said to be the "bishop"). This drum is highly revered by the Abakuá (Ortíz 1952, vol. 4, 61–67).

The secret drum, or *ekue*, is a single-headed wooden friction drum, with a tensioning system based on wedges. At the base it has three openings that form a stand with the shape of three small legs. It is played by "rubbing" a stick over the skin of the drum. It is always hidden in the sacred room (*fambá*). The sound of the ekue symbolizes the magic voice of Tanze the fish, which according to the origin myth of the Abakuá was found by a woman named Sikán.

The origin myth of the Abakuá has numerous versions, some of them contradictory. It revolves around the tale of how the god Abisi delivered a source of power in the form of a fish, Tanze, to two rival tribes (known in Cuba with the names Efor and Efik). A woman, Sikán, first found the fish in the river, and different versions of the myth explain the reason for her sacrifice and for the exclusion of women from the society. Some say Sikán, who belonged to the Efor tribe, indiscreetly revealed the secret to the Efik; others say she betrayed her people by marrying a member of the rival tribe. In other versions of the myth, Sikán, the original owner of the secret, is killed by men to seize the power from her, and they ban women from participation in the ceremonies so that the power will never return to women's hands.

In one version of the myth (Cabrera 1970), two tribes from Calabar, the Efor and the Efik, hostile to each other, lived separated by a sacred river, the Oddán, where, according to the tradition, Abisi (God) was to deliver the secret to the chosen ones (the Efor). It was in this river that fishermen first heard the thundering voice of the Sacred, a supernatural force that, following the prophecies, had assumed the form of a fish and promised honor, wealth, and prosperity to the tribe that could secure its possession.

Sikán, the daughter of a prestigious elder—Mokuire or Mokongo—from the Efor tribe, went to the river to fetch water, as she did every day. Not long after she had placed the calabash full of water on her head, she heard a ghostly roaring sound that filled her with fear. Mokuire, having been advised that the fish was in the hands of a mortal, followed the path to the river and encountered his daughter. He admonished her to keep the secret of what she had experienced, fearing the reaction of Nasakó, the sorcerer of the tribe, who had told him that whoever found the secret should die.

Nevertheless, Mokuire brought Sikán to the cave of Nasakó, who took the calabash with the fish and hid it. The most important members of the tribe were notified and spent many days consulting the oracles, discussing, inquiring, trying to decide whether or not Sikán had indeed seen the sacred fish Tanze. In the meantime Tanze became weaker and finally died. A drum, the ekue, was built with palm wood and covered with the skin of Tanze, but the sacred voice refused to talk. Something had to be done to recover it. Nasakó believed that only the blood of Sikán, who discovered the secret, might bring it back to life. Sikán was sacrificed, but the drum remained silent. Finally, Nasakó performed a series of ritual ceremonies, which included the sacrifice of a rooster and a goat, and the fundamento, or power, of the drum was guaranteed, its voice was recovered.

The Efor, under pressure from their rivals the Efik, agreed to share the secret with them. Therefore, seven members of each tribe met to sign an agreement, but Nasakó did not sign. From this stems the tradition of having thirteen major plazas or posts within the society, recalling the thirteen original members who signed the pact (Castellanos and Castellanos 1992).

This summary of the myths, structure, and rituals of the Abakuá society helps us understand the letter Felipe wrote, which I used to begin the narration about his life at the beginning of this part. When he lists his titles and the branch of the Abakuá society he belongs to, he says: "Isunekue de la Potencia Efik Kunambere de Matanzas, Ponponte Mio Siro Akanabión, and my title in Abakuá is: Isunekue Bijuraka Mundi, Isunekue Atara Yira Atara Kondó, Isunekue Baibo Eyene Baibo."

Isunekue is one of the four most important posts or plazas within the Abakuá society. The Isunekue is the custodian of the irongo or fambayín—the concealed chamber in the temple where the sacred drum, the ekue, is kept. He is the guardian of the Voice and represents Sikán. In one of the versions of the origin myth, Isún or Isunekue was the husband of Sikán. This must be the version kept in Felipe's juego, because when I asked him about the meaning of Isunekue, he told me it was the name of "the husband of the woman who found the secret, the keeper of the secret."

Efik Kunambere is the name of the juego to which Felipe belongs. This potencia is from the Efik line and was born from a juego called Kerewá. According to one of Cabrera's informants: "Ekerewá bordered the land of Efó. In Ekerewá there were three hills, in each hill lived the three families of Ekenerón, Kerewá Momi and Kerewá Kunambere. As neighbors of the place of the event, Nasakó made them keepers, and when the society was formed they participated in the sharing of the relics" (Cabrera 1970: 82). Felipe's father belonged to a juego named Kerewá, from which Kunambere was born.

Akanabión is the name of a place ruled by King Awaná, the brother of Isún Bengué, mother of the famous Sikán (Cabrera 1970: 83).

In the Abakuá society, the dignitaries are given titles according to the ritual acts they perform (Cabrera 1970: 176). Felipe's titles in the society were as follows:

- When taking an oath, the Isunekue is called *Isunekue Bijuráka Mundi*. Felipe defines it as the oath taken by the husband of Sikán, who promised to keep the secret in order to avoid being killed.
- *Atara Yira Atara Kondó* is defined by Felipe as the king born in a golden cradle.
- *Baibo Eyene Baibo,* according to Felipe, is the "name of the husband of the woman who found the secret."

• • •

In prerevolutionary Cuba, rivalry among different Abakuá juegos led frequently to violent confrontations that conferred a dubious reputation upon these societies. They were viewed by the establishment as linked to a culture of poverty and marginalization. In addition, the alleged criminal connections of some of the Abakuá society's members (sometimes accurate), racism, sensationalist press reports, and utter ignorance incited coercion and persecution.

At the end of the nineteenth century and several decades into the twentieth, to be an Abakuá was considered a crime (Sosa 1982: 328). However, during the republic the Abakuá became an electoral force that could not be ignored. Many politicians sought their support and even printed some of their electoral materials in Efik (Sosa 1982: 330).

In postrevolutionary Cuba, the Abakuá continued to be the most repressed and misunderstood Afro-Cuban religious practice. In the 1960s, indiscriminate arrests of known Abakuás were carried out, and repressive measures against them continued into the 1970s (Moore 1988: 306).

Thus, pre- and postrevolutionary governments have viewed the Abakuá juegos as potential "centers for resistance." The threat these societies were perceived to pose to the "establishment" may explain in part the prejudice, persecutions, and misrepresentation these societies have suffered.

Entering Felipe's House

Santería: The Lucumí Door

The Lucumí ancestors belong to Felipe's maternal side. His mother, Tomasa Villamil Cárdenas, was the daughter of Tomasa Cárdenas, the only female child born in the house of an African slave who had bought his freedom, Iñoblá Cárdenas.[13]

Iñoblá Cárdenas's home in Pueblo Nuevo, on a street called Buen Viaje, was the headquarters of a well-known cabildo in Matanzas. Felipe speaks always with pride about his great-grandfather:

Iñoblá Cárdenas, my great-grandfather from my mother's side of the family, was a king; he came from his land as a king. He had his own house and he had land because he bought his freedom. In his house you couldn't speak the way we are speaking right now. There, you could only talk Lucumí.

Because what did the Spanish and slave traders do? They didn't allow the slaves to have a lot of knowledge concentrated in one place. But they made a mistake with Matanzas. Because in Matanzas they [the slaves] rooted the religion firmly. So much so that in many families, like our family, that originate from Africans, and in many casas de santos, they speak Lucumí. Because there in Cuba we call it Lucumí even though here in the U.S., it's said that Lucumí doesn't exist and it's called Yoruba.

I met a man that belonged to the branch of our house. His name was Benerando Alfonso. He was one of the wise men in the religion. You couldn't speak Spanish in his house. You had to go in that house and greet everyone saying *ago* and they would answer *agoya*. You couldn't say

orning" or "good afternoon" or anything, because nobody would
There you could only speak in African. Everything was African,
ɔod, everything.

Because those who came from Africa had another way of thinking, as
well as another way of talking. They could not bring anything from Africa
and they went through a lot of hardships . . . because they were made prisoners in those ships where they could not move. Crowded in those ships
. . . it was not easy for them. And the trip was long, three, four, five, six
months, and they could not see the sun. They would sleep there, eat
there, defecate there, like animals. Then there in Cuba you can see how
they tried to lay the foundations for their religion in spite of all the changes:
the change in climate, the change in plants, in everything. So they had to
begin to figure out how to do their things because Africa was different
from Cuba.

So when we arrived at the religion, our ancestors took a long time
to begin to teach us a little bit. Some of them refused to teach to us
criollos, because they were afraid we would take over or misuse the
knowledge.

When Felipe talks about his house in Cuba, he frequently uses the
word *house* in the way in which many santeros use it, to refer to the
ilé-ocha (*ilé-oricha* or casa de santo), or house-temple, of his extended
ritual family. In Santería, a person who initiates others into the religion
forms a ritual family whose center of worship becomes the house of
the founding santero. This house-temple, the fundamental unit of worship in Santería, is simultaneously a place of dwelling, a place of worship, a community, and a family.

Three spaces of worship are kept within the house: the *igbodu*, or
inner sanctum, commonly known as the *cuarto*, where the more esoteric rites are carried out; the *eyá aránla* or *sala*, often the living room
of the house, used for semiprivate rituals and, in houses without a patio, also for public ceremonies; the *iban balo* or patio, where the public ceremonies are held. Traditionally used for drum dances and com-
munal meals, the patio is also the place to cultivate plants and herbs
and to keep the sacrificial animals.

Furthermore, santeros consider the orichas members of their family. After initiation into the religion, through a complex series of rituals
the initiate establishes a special relationship with an oricha, who is said

to be seated or placed over the person's head and from there guides the initiate's life.

Thus, when Felipe talks about his mother, he may be referring to either Tomasa Villamil, one of Matanzas's best known and respected older santeras, or Oyá, the oricha that governs her head. Tomasa's house, located in the neighborhood in Matanzas called La Marina, is the seat of the famous cabildo of Saint Teresa (the Catholic saint syncretized with Oyá in Matanzas); here, during the month of October, weeklong festivities are held in honor of Oyá.

In our house we celebrated ceremonies from the ninth to the fifteenth of October. Because my mother became initiated on the twelfth, and we celebrated also the feast of Saint Teresa on the fifteenth. So during the week before the fifteenth people started arriving from everywhere: Havana, Colón, Canasí, and during this period a lot of ceremonies took place. We played bembé all day long, *rumba* all day long, and *güiro*.[14] There was a constant coming and going in the house, it never stopped—and the batá drums were played on the fifteenth.

In Santería, religious ceremonies (the bembé, *tambor,* or *fiesta*)[15] where music plays a central role are special occasions for initiates to communicate with the orichas. It is during these ceremonies that devotees may become possessed by an oricha, who sometimes uses the occasion to give advice to those present. Santeros use expressions such as being "mounted" or "getting" an oricha to describe this state of trance.

My mother "gets an Oyá" that is phenomenal. Oyá is phenomenal when she dances! Oyá is a warrior and a fighter. My mother's Oyá sings whenever she arrives. I remember a chant she used to sing a lot that says: "Look, *chico,* don't you bother me, 'cause I am a woman that walks around with nine dead spirits. The wind takes me wherever I want. I am a woman that can play santo, as well as *brujo,* as well as *muerto.* Don't fool around with me because I kill with the wind, I don't need weapons to kill."

It is not true that Oyá lives in the cemetery. She is the owner of the cemetery but she lives in the perimeter of the world. Because Oyá is three things: she is fire, she is wind, and she is the owner of the cemetery.

Listen to me, at a ceremony she would stand and tell you: "Tomorrow you're going to break your legs," and sure enough you'll break them. You always had to address her with *usted* [you—formal] never with *tú* [you—informal]. Once at a ceremony a man dared to use the tú and Oyá took a gourd full of water, gave it to the man, and said: "Now he is going to break the bathroom." Do you know what was called the bathroom? It was outside in the patio, a latrine. He went out there and broke the door of the latrine and stuck his head in there. He had to run to the beach to wash himself up. Oyá said, "I am Oyá," and listen, the wind began to blow. . . .

But I didn't fear her because Oyá brought me up. Oyá is very good, very good to me. We were children of Oyá, we were her children. I was impetuous; I was crazy about Oyá. I was and I am. But there, in Cuba, I was crazy about Oyá. I would build the thrones, I would look for food and look for everything for my mother's saint. Well, yes, that saint brought us up. And when I would get sick she would take care of me and say to me: "He who knows doesn't die." She had us all prepared.

In contrast, when Felipe talks about his father, it is Ogún to whom he is referring most of the time, because Felipe is a son of Ogún.

I learned to play *iyesá* drums at the cabildo Iyesá, because that was the cabildo of my father Ogún. Ogún's cabildo in Matanzas is located in Salamanca and Campostela in the house of the García family. That is the Iyesá cabildo where I used to go.

The cabildo Iyesá modu San Juan Bautista, where Felipe became familiar with the Iyesá music traditions, was officially founded on June 24, 1845, and sponsored by the Lucumí cabildo of Santa Teresa, which served as its godfather. The members of this cabildo worship all the Lucumí orichas but have a special devotion for Ogún (whom they equate with Saint John the Baptist) and Ochún (the deity of rivers and streams, syncretized in Cuba as the Virgin of La Caridad del Cobre), whom they consider "native" Iyesá orichas. Nowadays, this cabildo owns the only set of sacred *iyesá* drums left in Cuba.[16]

Ogún is not only the oricha that "owns" Felipe's head but also an oricha that has played a significant role in the life of Felipe's family in Cuba. Ogún was the santo of Felipe's maternal grandfather, Juan.

My mother used to tell me stories about my grandfather, like: "Where is father? Where is father?" Because you would be talking to my grandfather and—suddenly you didn't know whom you were talking to; it was with Ogún. That saint Ogún would lie down to look for food for his children; at very bad times when there was nothing to look for, when Machado was in Cuba. My mother says that one time they didn't have money even for food, and my grandfather was thinking and thinking—sitting on an armless chair. Finally he got up and said to everyone: "Today you are going to eat, you are going to eat"; he went down a road over there and he lay in the mud, he lay in the mud. He lived in the countryside, that is also where my uncle Jorge used to live, it was called Sumidero. A Moor[17] was coming with a drove of mules with food: roasts, rice, everything; he had a string of about fifteen or sixteen horses, carrying his merchandise down that road. Then the Moor saw my grandfather. The Moor spoke a bit of Spanish, in the way they used to talk, and he picked him up from the mud: "*Ay señor,* what are you doing here?" So my grandfather told him: "I am here because I have my children back there in the house and they have nothing to eat." Then the man said: "But how can that be? And you, what are you going to do here? You are going to die in the mud. "I am not going to die, I am going to get food." Do you know what the Moor did? He untied one of the horses, and he gave him the horse packed with food—the mule, mule included—he gave it to him, so that they could go and eat; and the family had food for about two months.

Ogún not only provided food for the family but also protected them from the police at the time when santeros in Matanzas were not allowed to perform their ceremonies for their orichas. Afro-Cuban religions suffered from the general discrimination practiced against the black population during the early decades of the twentieth century. Prejudice and ignorance, fueled by sensationalist press reports that linked Afro-Cuban religions to criminal activities, unleashed a persecution of religious practices of African origin. During those days, it was common for the police to raid the centers of worship, arrest the practitioners, and confiscate the ritual objects. Many of these objects, which nowadays are kept in museums in Cuba, bear inscriptions that testify to the use of these pieces as evidence in judicial cases. However, Afro-Cubans devised ways to respond to these repressive measures: Houses were used as temples; closets were used as altars; Catholic saints stood as the public face for the orichas.

At the time of José Claro, the policeman that I talked to you about, you could not play the drums in Matanzas. He was always looking for places where there was drumming, and if he grabbed the "saints" he would take them away. The police would arrive and they would take the saints to the station. And in Matanzas everyone knew about it, eh? Celebrations at my grandfather's house would begin today and end next week. Because they would play music—they played guitar and bass and bongos and everything—all day long and then at night was the bembé. One day when these people were celebrating the police came: "We hear that you're playing a drum." "But there's no drum here," said Ogún standing at the door, "there's no drum here; come in, come in!" When the police came in everything there, all the food and all the things Ogún had in front of him in his altar, were turned into drinks by Ogún. "OK, if this is a family reunion, let the family reunion continue," said the cop.

Two stories about Ogún figured prominently in Felipe's narrative repertoire when he spoke about this oricha.[18] Felipe used them whenever he had arguments on religious issues with babalaos in New York. They are related to the divination system in Santería known as the ekuelé.

So how can it be possible for a babalao to say to me that he doesn't recognize the power of Ogún if Ogún was the first *awó?* You know what *awó* means? It means diviner. Because if it was not for Ogún that divining chain, the ekuelé, would never have been put together again. Because originally the ekuelé was not the way it is now; before it was made with coconut shells and the skin of deer. But one day Obatalá, in a fury with the things of life—with people—when he saw so much ingratitude and so many bad things, took the ekuelé and said: "Ah, now I am not going to cure anyone and I am not going to do anything"; and he took the ekuelé and flung it. He flung it and it landed on top of a roof and it stayed there for many years. But then in a town a lot of people began to get sick, and there was no doctor, nothing. Nobody could say: "Take this plant to cure this sickness or that . . . ,"—nothing could be said. So everybody made an offering to Obatalá, pleading to him to do something. Obatalá said: "Fine, I'm going to pick up the ekuelé, but it isn't going to be good for anything, because it has been lying out there picking up humidity and water." So there is an Eleguá that lives up in the roof, and this Eleguá said: "I am going to go up to the roof and bring the ekuelé down." He brought it down, but every time they threw it, it would break, because it was rotten, and nothing could be done about it. Then Eleguá said: "I know the only man that can fix that thing there," and he went to look for Ogún. When Ogún came he told everyone: "Fine, I will fix the ekuelé, but I want to know what share I'm going to get in it." The others stared at each other and finally said: "Well, you decide on what share you want to have." And Ogún put himself to work and began to make chains and to tie the ekuelé with chains. Then he said: "While the world is a world, those seeds will speak, tied by me." So that is the participation he has in the ekuelé, the chains. Then if a babalao doesn't get along well with Ogún, he is nobody, because he doesn't respect Ogún, who is the one that feeds him.

Well, let us continue with Ogún. There is a picture that is called the Great Supper [the Last Supper] where you see someone standing close to Jesus Christ; that one is Ogún. Because what happened was that this great meeting took place and they didn't call Ogún. So he went up to the heavens and wanted to go into the kingdom, but the guardians stopped him. "No, no, you cannot come in because Olofi is having a meeting there with some people." "Who says I cannot go in if I am Olofi's great ambassador?" "There is an order not to let anyone in." "So who are those people in there, dressed in white?" "Some babalaos . . . " "Ah! Babalaos . . . fine." And he left and went to the periphery of the world and made an ekuelé, but one made with iron, and he threw that ekuelé and the earth began to tremble. So Olofi asked: "Why is everything trembling?" "Well, Ogún is out there throwing an ekuelé." And he had Ogún called in, and when Ogún arrived at the table there were twelve guests; and he arrived but he didn't take a seat. He remained standing, telling Olofi what had happened. That is the reason why, for santeros, thirteen people are not supposed to sit at a table.

Whoever painted that picture did a good job, that picture of the Great Supper. Because the one that is standing there, that is Ogún who refused to sit, and he is standing there telling Olofi what happened. For us that is the tradition; the reading of that picture is that way for us.

Thus, Santería has been a powerful presence in Felipe's life since his youth and was an integral part of the everyday life of his family. He frequently and passionately emphasized it in our talks as the foundation and the source of his ritual knowledge, especially when he complained about the way in which some of the religious ceremonies were carried out in New York, compared to the way in which they were conducted in Cuba.

I know because since I was little, I've seen this, I've been seeing this since I was a kid. I've seen how these things are done in my house. What we have believed, that is what we do. The years go by. My mother is a hundred years old. And I have a family, very big but very old—my family has a lot of old people.

When Felipe talks about his old family, he is referring to the elders—those who knew everything about the rituals, the carriers of religious knowledge, the bearers of tradition. The notion of the elder as the source of religious knowledge has its origins in Cuba in the plantations, where elders were spared work in the fields and had time and space for their religious activities, serving as guides and teachers of other slaves in religious matters. Most of the elders Felipe learned from are now dead. It is Felipe's generation that has become the source of knowledge for the younger members of the family.

Palo Monte: The Congo Door

Even though his mother's side of the family was heavily involved in Santería, Felipe was not initiated into this religion until early adulthood. He first became a palero, practicing the religion of his father, Benigno. Benigno's family, the García, came from a town in the province of Matanzas called Cárdenas, where Palo traditions are very strong.

I was first a palero before becoming a santero. My father, this one here in the picture, had seven degrees in Palo [seven levels of initiation]. I have such stories to tell about him. Well, my father was called Benigno García y García, son of Aniceto García Gómez and of Carlota García.
    . . . My father was incredulous. He didn't believe in Santería, he only believed in the "pot"[19] and nothing else. And I made santo quite late because of him. The problem was that he used to say that while he was alive none of us would "make saint." But those were other times.
    I was *rayado* [name given to the initiation process in Palo] when I was born; I have been rayado since the day I was born from my mother's belly. Look, in my house, when someone was born, the one that went to pick the newborn up from the hospital was the old man—my father. It was from the hospital to the house, so that nobody would have the opportunity to touch him or nothing. In the house, the first place where he took him was to the

prenda; and at night he would perform a ceremony and then the newborn had to be taken to my grandfather's house, and they would perform another ceremony. Thank God we never got sick. Just like everybody, a small headache or something like that, but never a bad sickness. We were brought up in the worst *patios* of Cuba—because that Marina was bad. I was really born in Pueblo Nuevo, in Buen Viaje 17; but during the worst time we had, we had to leave the house. Then we moved to La Marina in a small house where we paid less, but it was in bad condition. In La Marina, filth would run all over the streets and cover them, because there were no drains. We would walk in that dirty water catching fish with a little net.

Felipe's father taught him what he thought Felipe was prepared to learn. What parents taught their children was selective and did not include all their ritual knowledge. Furthermore, not all the children were deemed eligible or qualified to learn the "secrets" of the ancestors. The reluctance Felipe's father showed in revealing the secrets of his religious practice was very common among the descendants of Congos in Cuba. Congos never liked to communicate their knowledge and were keen on secrecy. This secrecy and the role the cult of the dead plays in their religion favored frequent misrepresentations of their religious practices; viewed with suspicion, it was not uncommon for Congo practices to be defined or characterized by many as *brujería* (witchcraft).[20]

They used to call us criollos, but we didn't stop being their children. Criollos yes, because we were born there in Cuba, we were not born in their lands. "My son is a criollo." Then you know that when they say a criollo, it is the son of a Congo or a Lucumí or an African born in Cuba. . . .

They didn't want to teach us, their own children, because we were criollos. "No," they said, "we are not going to teach these people, because if we teach them we are going to be cheated. Because they are from here and we are from there"—you see? They didn't take into account that we were their own children, that that was not going to happen. If the human race brought them to Cuba as slaves they thought: "At least we are alive, and if these people grab this knowledge and learn it, they are going to take it for themselves and they are going to kill us with this very same thing. We are not going to teach them."

My father used to tell me that there were a lot of things that he wouldn't teach me, because I didn't belong to his generation, and at the time he learned, he had to work hard. And he would tell us the same thing his ancestors used to tell him: "You'll end humanity if I teach you." See? And he took much knowledge with him to the grave. Because my father was one that would make these little figures he had in his prenda walk. You see? So that was one tradition he didn't want us to have and he took it with him and that was the end of that tradition.

I was my father's mayordomo [ritual assistant]. I went with him everywhere. He often traveled from Matanzas to Havana—and I always had to go there. When he had anything big going on, he would send for me. The thirty-first of December I had to be there; if I was not there he would come and look for me: "Come, I came to look for you because you have to be present in the ceremonies."

When they had ceremonies, well, then I had to sit there close to the prenda. He would put a bench there for me, and I would be sitting there taking care of everything. Because when Mariamunda came [when the spirit possessed Felipe's father], I attended to everything she demanded. And my father would say: "Give me this, and a bit of that; this is used for this and this is used for that, and—give me this other thing and I will not tell you what it is used for"—and so on. Just like that, he would tell me one thing but not the other. Gradually I was learning; but Nino my brother, they would call him many times and he would sit beside me, but he didn't have much interest, Nino was just not into it, you see?

Mariamunda was the name of Felipe's father's prenda . Prendas are more than a source of power and support for paleros. They represent the knowledge paleros have acquired from those who initiated them into the religion. Felipe explains that the word *prenda* derives from the fact that his ancestors had no wealth, land, or property to leave to their children. The only possession they had was their culture—the knowledge of their rituals, the use of herbs, the divination systems, and so forth—which was symbolized by the prenda. This was what they left to their children as inheritance.[21]

For me prenda is something you learn gradually, by steps. It means medicine, it means good; it is a source of power. My father used to tell us: "I have no house, I have no money; so this is your only inheritance. You have to learn this, because it is the only thing I am leaving to you, so you will be protected from the evil things in life." In that sense we took the nganga as a prenda, because it was the most precious prenda we could have.

Felipe inherited Mariamunda from his father and another prenda, Sarabanda Rompe Monte, from his grandfather. Although Felipe never met his paternal grandfather, he inherited his grandfather's prenda because in the family he was considered to have a special link with his grandfather's spirit. These prendas are now housed in Felipe's home in New York. When I first met Felipe in 1992, he had transformed a closet in his house into an altar where these prendas were placed.

While on his mother's side of the family Ogún was the source of protection, Felipe's father relied on the power of Mariamunda for guidance and refuge.

Because my father is from a little town called Camarioca. And . . . all his family were well known in Cárdenas—in a *colonia* called La Festé. It is located close to Cárdenas. Well, they had their prenda named Mariamunda. Because all of my father's relatives were veterans in the religion. Fabián, my uncle, Fabián García, who was a veteran also, played *yuka* drums. But there was a period when things were not good for religious matters. During this period they went one time to take the prenda in a carriage to the cemetery.[22] My uncle whose name was Cundo looked for the cemetery. Well, my father went and took the prenda with Cundo, Catalino and Fabián. So they went to the cemetery and buried the prenda and did what they had to do there. Well, a coachman had accompanied them, because in Cárdenas there were only carriages and nothing else. At that time there were no more than four cars in town. So that same coachman went and reported them to the police. He said that they went to the cemetery and the place where he took them and everything. The police went and took everything that was in the cemetery. Then they went to look for them, because the coachman told them those things belonged to them. He gave them the address where he had picked each one of them up; so they were sent to prison. Well, my father had kept a pouch that night; it was a small triangular pouch. He was there with that pouch in the precinct; they had not taken it away from him. He was sent to the prison in Cárdenas. Then in the prison yard he looked for a stone, and he placed the pouch under the stone and he did his ceremonies there. Their photograph came out; they were photographed with all of what they found in the cemetery, and the picture appeared in the newspaper. At that time in Cuba there was a newspaper called *El Mundo,* yes, *El Mundo.* I used to keep the clip of that newspaper, I had it; it was already yellow. Apparently they were hit in the face, because their cheeks appeared swollen. There they were, the four of them: Catalino, Cundo, Fabián, and my father, prisoners. He in the middle with the prenda and the dolls and everything. It was a scandal in Matanzas, in the whole of Cuba, because it came out in the papers. Because the things of the paleros were considered bad at that time, really bad.[23]

You know that the judge in Cárdenas who had to examine the case, well, he couldn't sleep. He went to see my father: "Who is Benigno García in here?" "Me." He had him taken out. My father said: "Well, if you're going to take me out you have to take out the others too." And the judge said: "The only thing I want from you is for you to sincerely tell me what the hell is—I'm going to release everyone, everybody is going to go out, but I want you to tell me something. Of these things here, what belongs to you?" My father pointed to his things. "That's what belongs to you?" The judge said to a policeman: "Bring two cops. Start packing that," and called my father aside: "Who is called Mariamunda?" My father was panicky. "Who is called Mariamunda? "Mariamunda is what you have taken there from me." And the judge: "It's been driving me crazy, I haven't been able to sleep." Well, after that incident he became such a good friend of my father that they became *compadres,* because he baptized my brother. It's not a lie, my brother Nino was baptized by him. This judge paid for his studies, he paid for anything Nino wanted.

It was, then, through his father that the door to the world of paleros opened up for Felipe. By following and creatively mixing these religious practices with the ones he learned from his mother's family, Felipe did what was not uncommon among Afro-Cubans in Matanzas of a background similar to his: He worshiped the orichas and at the same time took care of a nganga, a practice known as *cruzar palo con ocha* (to cross Palo with Ocha).[24]

The Abakuá Society: A Secret Passage from Calabar

It was also through his father that Felipe became a ñáñigo, the name given in Cuba to the members of the Abakuá society.

I was thirteen when I became an Abakuá. My father got us both, Nino my brother and I, in. The old man belonged to the juego where Nino became a member, to Kerewá. Kerewá was or is the name of that juego.

A juego is a potencia, a group that is called *juego de ñáñigos* or *juego de Abakuá*. The same as in Palo, where we call it *plante de Palo*, this one is the juego de Abakuá. Well, then, in a meeting they had in Kerewá there was a misunderstanding. Being brothers in the religion they couldn't have a fist-fight, only words; they could offend someone, get mad, but never use their hands. Well, after this incident my father and Pipe decided to form another group. They explained to the Abakuá group that if they were allowed to, they had enough men to "make a new land" [found a new group]. The main man of Kerewá, the Iyamba of Kerewá, called for a toast and said: "You can do it whenever you want to."[25] They wrote the minutes and signed them and placed their conditions. The four people that were going to establish the new land came out: my father Benigno García, Pipe—who was a palero like my father—Manuel, who they called Manuel Tortoise, and the mulatto Abreu. They told the members of the old group: "We know we have an obligation, so each one of the four of us is going to bring a person of our own blood to swear him into this juego so that they stay here. Then each one of us will bring a person of our own blood to swear him into the new juego." So my father brought my brother Nino to swear into the old juego, into the first juego of my father, which continued to be Kerewá. I was sworn into the new one, the same day that the new "land" came out I was sworn in. The four plazas [dignitaries or members] that had founded the new juego took an oath saying that when they died, the person they had brought to the new land would inherit their post. So I inherited my father's post. I became the Isunekue, and my cousin inherited the post of Manuel "Tortoise." . . . This new potencia was called Efik Kunambere.

• • •

It was in the nucleus of this family—assisting his father in his ritual obligations, learning from him about the use of plants and herbs and about the way to sing to Centella and Sarabanda, listening to the chants for the orichas that his mother and aunts sang daily, hiding under the kitchen stove with two sticks picked up in the street and imitating the sounds of the batá drums his uncles played during the Santería ceremonies, taking part in the meetings and rituals of his Abakuá potencia—that Felipe spent his childhood and his adolescence. It was there he learned and developed his knowledge of the music of these traditions, in the heart of a family prominent in Matanzas not only as performers of sacred Afro-Cuban music but also as secular musicians, well versed in the popular genre that has made this region famous: the *rumba*.

Early Musical Experiences

Born in 1931 in Matanzas, Cuba, Felipe began playing the drums when he was only four or five years old. He hid under the kitchen stove to play on cans, sticks, small drums, whatever percussive object he could get hold of.

I was not taught by anybody. I just play. I began at the *comparsas* [carnival street bands]. I would arrive at a comparsa and the guys would tell me: "No, no, play this like this and play that." I didn't want to be one of the bell players; I wanted to play the drums. So I had to grab a drum.

To put it in few words, God gave me a resource and it was that, drumming. I began to play drums when I was just a kid. They used to hit me for playing cans under the hearth. I would snuggle under the stove, as they call it here; but in Cuba it is made of cement and the fire doesn't reach underneath. I used to snuggle there to play. My father always said playing with cans was a bad thing, and he really gave it to me, he hit me. My father didn't want me to be a drummer, because he said that drums were for blacks that didn't work. It meant for him an *aguardiente* drinker, with the shirt knotted, standing at the corner wearing peasant shoes like the *gallegos*.[26] Drumming didn't give anything. He wanted a trade for me. He wanted me to learn a trade: shoemaker, mechanic, some other trade but drumming. He thought I was wasting my time drumming and that I would never learn anything. But he didn't go out to look for a place for me to learn a trade. I was left on my own, and I did what I liked to do, drumming. When my father first saw me playing the batá drum, he had to come into the room to listen. He usually never came in because he didn't like Santería ceremonies, he was a palero. When he came in and finally saw me playing the batá drum, he had to congratulate me. When he was able to see . . .

Even though Felipe learned many trades and held all kinds of jobs during his adult life, drumming was his trade, the one he mastered and identified with. He became a musician who had to earn his living as an electrician, a plumber, a dockworker, a bricklayer, to name a few of his occupations.

Listen, let me tell you something, there's a word that we use in Cuba to describe what I did, we call these people "amphibious." There is also that expression: musician, poet, drunk, and crazy. In Cuba I was both an amphibious and a musician. I never said no to anything. I worked as an electrician, a carpenter, a mason. Then I also got into the sugar, and working there in the sugar was good for me.

But the drum, well, I began playing the drums since I was in my mother's belly.

Felipe began earning money as a drummer at the age of fourteen, playing congas in a big band conducted by Rafael Somavilla in Matanzas. Somavilla was among a group of brilliant orchestrators and composers that included, among others, Armando Romeau, Bebo Valdéz, Arturo O'Farill, and Dámaso Pérez Prado, who built successful careers in the jazz bands that began to appear in Cuba during the 1930s. These jazz bands slowly underwent a process of "Cubanization," including in their repertoire Cuban dance genres such as the rumba and the *danzón* (Acosta 1983: 22–23).

Well, around the year 1945 or '46—I was very young, I was like fifteen years old—I played with a band in Cuba, one of the best bands in Matanzas. I played with a professor called Rafael Somavilla. Everyone in his family is a musician. He had a lot of power, a lot of connections with the Casino Español, with people from above in high positions. He gave lessons at an orphanage that was called the Casal Asylum. He "made" a lot of kids from the streets. It was an orphanage that was paid for by the masons and he was the music director there. It was for kids with problems, but not all of them were street kids. Some belonged to the families of masons, and had talent, so they were sent there.

I had a great friendship with Somavilla. Somavilla had a lot of affection for me, and he wanted me to learn to play an instrument. But I didn't want to study an instrument; I lost that opportunity by chasing the drums in the streets. Also, in my house my mother would have fiestas de santo, and I was always hanging around at those fiestas.

Somavilla saw Felipe at a bembé and was very impressed with his playing. He contacted him through one of Felipe's neighbors.

Somavilla first saw me at a bembé. I used to go to the bembé behind my father's back, you know? One time Somavilla was walking by a bembé and came in. He's a Catholic and all of that, but he is a musician and he went in to see. I was playing congas at that bembé. He stayed there for a while looking at all of those who were playing and he fell in love with my personality. Then he said to Elisa my neighbor: "I saw a *morenito* there who played the drums and I would like to know if he plays *tumbadoras* [congas] at least a little, to see if when I organize the band I can include him, because I like that black kid; you can see that that black kid . . . "

Elisa had been watching for me for four days so one day that I passed by she came out to the door and said: "Boy, I've been looking for you for the past four days and I have a errand for you. Look, take these *pesetas* for the bus and go to this address because they are looking for you to join a band." Oh! I went wild.

Felipe joined Somavilla's orchestra, where he began to earn his first wages as a musician and acquired experience performing popular Cuban music.

I thought it was an *orquesta típica,* a small band. But no, it was a big jazz orchestra, a jazz band—well, five saxophones, four trumpets, three trombones, drum set here, bongos, tumbadoras. Then—I started working in the band.

They placed two congas in front of me. I was really scared because everybody there was white. I was the only black—a fly inside the coffee—that was me. So during the rehearsal I knew the rhythm went this way: [He plays the ostinato rhythm used in *salsa* on the table]. At that time this rhythm was played somewhat laid back. Then the *boleros—tintintintin pata pati—*"Fine, it's fine." The first tryout went very well. I joined the band and I really matured there because Somavilla's son would then have a rehearsal with each section. And that mulatto would take a bell, and would take the piano, and he would do **tinkitin,** and so on and so forth, to us. We would take a "number" and rip it off in no time. They were practically the ones who taught me.

We would play at all the matinees at the officers' club, we would play all the music of the officers' club, we would play in the best places in Varadero, we would play with the Chavales de España, almost always we would join those gallegos [Spanish] there—so I would earn my money.

Then he talked to me about the municipal band, I went there to his house and he told me about the band: "If you behave well I will make you a part of the band." Because I was not of age to become a member of the municipal band, in the orchestra he could get me in, but in the band he could not get me in, the band was a government thing. So: "If you behave well when you are a little bit older—" Then he would ask: "What instrument do you want to play, what instrument would you like to learn? Learn something. You have an ear, you have an ear boy; you could be a teacher." I would say to him: "Yes"; but I was never interested in doing so. I never wanted to study anything, because with the tumbadora alone I was doing well.

Learning to Play Batá

Music is central to the rituals of all the Afro-Cuban religious systems, where it is used as a channel to communicate with the sacred world. In Santería rituals that include drumming—those that are open to the uninitiated—a specific set of drums rhythms (*toques*), chants, and dance movements addresses each oricha, and it is through the medium of music that the orichas descend during rituals to possess or "mount" their "horses."

Several types of instrumental ensembles are used in these Santería rituals. In one ensemble, three beaded gourds of different sizes, known as *chekerés* or *güiros,* are played. Another ensemble uses drums (usually congas), chekerés, and a *guataca* (a hoe blade played with a metal rod). The ensemble make up depends on the number of musicians and instruments available. In Cuba, where they are still available, a set of drums known as bembé drums replace the congas in this second ensemble. The third type of ensemble, the batá, is used for the most involved ceremonies and is considered one of the most powerful channels of communication with the orichas. This is an ensemble of three double-membrane bipercussive drums of different sizes: the *iyá* or *caja,* the *itótele* or *segundo,* and the *okónkolo* or *omelé,* shaped in the form of an irregular hourglass.

The six heads of the batá, and the diverse playing techniques the drummers use—open tones, slaps, closed tones (*tapados*), hitting the drum at the edge with only two fingers—create a complex melodic effect, a conversation that calls the orichas, to which they respond by descending on the initiates. It is said that the batá "speak tongue," meaning that they imitate the ritual language used to address the deities—Lucumí or *anagó,* a language that has origins in several Yoruba dialects. Yoruba is a tonal language in which intonation has semantic value—intonation that can be imitated with the drums. It is said that older Cuban drummers could understand the language the drums speak, but this ability has been lost by the younger generations, who play in a style oriented more toward dancing. Miguel Somodevilla, one of the best known older batá players in Havana, complained in the 1950s that "nowadays you have to please more the dancers" and play batá with the style of a rumba (Ortíz 1952: vol. 4, 280).

However, drummers still consider playing batá as conducting a conversation between and among three drums, and they use metaphors based on the dialogue that takes place among the drums to guide their performances and evaluate them. Each toque is made up of a set of specific rhythmic patterns or structures that support a series of variations—what batá drummers call conversations. These conversations result from the way in which the different rhythms the drums play interlock to create a phrase. The change from one rhythmic pattern to another is referred to as *virar* (to turn), and the different patterns within each toque are called *viros* or *vueltas* (turns). The number of vueltas in each toque varies. The toques for some orichas (e.g., Ochosi) present a complex interplay of many viros and conversations, while the toques for other orichas (e.g., Korikoto) are quite simple.[27]

At the end of the 1940s, Felipe began playing in the batá ensemble that his great-grandfather Iñoblá Cárdenas had founded. To this point Felipe had expressed his passion for the sacred drums by splitting the rail of his wooden bed while practicing the rhythms he heard coming from the drums at the religious ceremonies he frequently attended, or by playing güiro or congas in the many religious festivities he attended.

I am telling you, I broke my wooden bed by hitting it at the rail, I broke it because that is how I learned to play the drum. I would go and listen to a tambor and when I returned, the toque [rhythmic pattern] I didn't know I would have here inside my mind, and I would practice it on my bed.

I began around 1945, '46, around those years, it was a fifteenth of October. I remember the exact date because it was the day of my mother's fiesta [Oyá or Saint Teresa]. This is a day I never forget because what happens is that in my house there are nine consecutive days of celebration; during all those days drums are played in my house: bembé, güiro, and then on the fifteenth the batá drums are played.

. . . It happened at the time I was playing in the band of Rafael Somavilla. One day I arrived, I did not have to work so I arrived—all dressed up, with my half-ironed hair[28] and my tie—like a personality, like a different personality, no? I wanted to stay in the house of the old lady watching the drums. There they were playing, my uncle Jorge Villamil, another guy, who was *ligado,* he was a mixture of African and Spanish, and other guys. When they took a break they began to talk about toques and who knows what. I said: "You are all talking a lot of rubbish because I can play those drums with my eyes closed." My uncle replies: "You are crazy, kid. Stop talking nonsense." "Yes, yes, yes I can play. You think you are important because you play batá and that's nothing. I play in a band that . . . so how is it possible that I can't play this rubbish?" "What?" shouted Jorge, and he sat me down at the drum and told me: "Now you have to play. There, sit down. Play! You say that you play? Show it!" It was just a joke, I was joking and they took me seriously. Because you know how I respected my uncles, and I respected the elder, and Jorge even more. Jorge was a very serious person. I have to be grateful for the encouragement he gave me and for what he taught me. Because aside from the fact that he knew how to play, he understood what was said in the chants. He was brought up in that because he was the drummer of the "house" of Iñoblá.

So I humbled myself a little, you know? I told him: "No, uncle, I was just—" He went on: "No, because you think that by just playing in a band with all the white guys you are going to come here and—" So they marked the toque of Eleguá for me, and I didn't know what I was supposed to play so I said: "No, but you have to explain to me how it goes." And Jorge: "But you say that you play it, you don't need explanations because you are a born player, you are a player by birth; so if you were born playing you have to play." It was Candito who helped me and told me: "Now, move the hand like this here and there and you will see that the toque will come out." So I began like *kimpá, kimpá, kimpá* [29] and I liked that first toque. It was the only one that I played that day.

. . . Then I went and I told my uncle: "Well, I see you need a lad here so I am going to start learning with you guys." I began to play with them. Many times I would skip the jobs I had, to be able to go to the toques. But

I had to wait until they asked me to play with them. In those days in Cuba, there was a lot of respect for the religion, and unless you found someone that would call you: "Come I want you to do this and to learn that"; you would not do it, even if you wanted to.

Felipe was attracted to the batá drums not simply because of a passion for drumming in general but because he considered it his fate, something he had been predestined to by his mother's oricha, Oyá.

It had been predicted, it was part of my destiny that I would play batá. Because my mother's Oyá said that I was her official drummer; that in the earth there would be no one that would play the drum for her as I did. Because if she would just move a nail, I would mark the *golpe* [hit the drum]. It was really that way; every time my mother's Oyá moved this way, or that way, I would immediately answer with the drum. Oyá told me she would make of me a drummer of "conditions" and that I would "program" the drums a lot; that I would be on the streets with the drums, up and down the streets. So it appears to be that it was something that had to be done, you see?

As an apprentice, Felipe was expected to participate in as many ritual ceremonies as possible, in order to familiarize himself with the numerous toques used to praise, entice, and accompany the dance of the orichas and with the extensive body of chants and ritual dances that are part of the Lucumí liturgy.

Apprentices usually began their training by playing during that part of the music ritual known as *oro seco* (dry oro), because it involves only drumming, not singing. It is also called the *oro de igbodu,* alluding to the space in the house-temple where this ceremonial music is performed. This oro involves a series of toques to salute and invite the orichas to the ceremony and to transform the secular, domestic space into the sacred place of the ritual. The oro seco is always performed at the beginning of the ceremony, in front of the altar set up for the ritual. The composition and arrangement of the altars or thrones varies depending on the nature of the ritual, the financial situation of the celebrants, and personal preferences and tastes of the santero who is celebrating the ritual. The emblems of the orichas and the soperas may be set against a simple piece of colored cloth, or they may form part of a dazzling installation that includes beaded ritual objects, colorful cloth, plants, flowers, fruits, and prepared food.

The initial salute to the orichas in front of the altar is usually performed just as the guests arrive. Only the presence of the person offering the ritual is mandatory. Therefore, although ritually important, this section of the ceremony is not heavily attended, and drummers take advantage of it to give their apprentices a chance to play. Because the order of the toques is fixed, and no dancing or possession takes place during this part of the ceremony, the oro seco offers a good opportunity for apprentices to gain experience they need before they are allowed to play in the more challenging part of the ceremony: the *oro del eyá aránla*. The oro seco is, then, basic to the repertoire of every ritual drummer and the skill each has to master first. Apprentices are then taught the toques, not according to their technical difficulty but following the order they have in this liturgy. In any ceremony Eleguá, the oricha of the crossroads who opens the way, has to be saluted first; therefore, this is the first toque an apprentice learns.[30]

The oro del eyá aránla is performed in the part of the temple where the uninitiated are admitted. In house-temples without separate spaces, it is performed in the same room as the oro seco, but the musicians turn their backs to the altar and face the audience. Also known as *oro cantado* (sung oro), this oro is assigned to the more experienced drummers, who are able to follow the complexities of drumming when singing and dance are incorporated into the ritual. This part of the ceremony is less standardized and, musically, more context-dependent. As the energy level rises and the orichas mount their horses, the drummers have to be able to follow not only the constant calls and changes of the lead singer but the requests of the dancers as they exalt, salute, lure, or call the orichas or, when possessed, convey the presence of a particular oricha through their gestures.

The drums, considered the voices that talk to the orichas, play an essential role during this part of the ritual. They build up the atmosphere and contribute in the creation of an emotional climate that incites the orichas to mount their horses. Once possession occurs, the "horse" is taken to a separate room, dressed with the ritual outfit that belongs to his or her oricha, and then brought back to the ritual area. Here the deity participates in the ritual, answering questions, giving advice, dancing, and enticing others to dance.

Music is thus central to possession. The orichas descend only in response to their specific musical themes (drum rhythms and chants), and once present, they express their identity through stereotyped dance movements (modeled on the personality of the oricha) that carry symbolic meaning—meaning that is culturally constructed and learned.[31] It is through music and dance that the presence of the oricha is conveyed to the group.

The drummers who play during this part of the ritual must therefore be thoroughly acquainted with the repertoire of chants, the dance movements, the behavior of the initiates when they are about to be possessed by their orichas, and the behavior through which the presence of a particular oricha is manifested. Rivalry among drummers is not uncommon and surfaces even while they are playing in a ceremony. Thus a good drummer not only has to master his drum but needs to know what to expect from the other two drummers in terms of the rhythmic conversations that take place between the drums and to be able to demand it authoritatively from them.

Jorge, Felipe's uncle, made sure his nephew sat at each of the drums to prepare him to face the challenge.

In Cuba it's not like here [in the United States]. There, there were no drum lessons, it was just play and play. It was also not as closed as it is here, where they take the drum away from you if you don't know how to play something. In Cuba they made you play to the saint. Sitting in the oro, and nothing else; at least in my town, I am not talking about Havana. That is how I gradually studied all those rhythms.

You go early and you do an oro, you learn by playing the oro. One comes in early. Because you have to be there early and carry the drums and all of that. If you don't do it, they won't let you sit and play. I was always early because I was interested in learning.

They explain the rhythms to you as they play. The drummer that usually plays the drum you are playing sits by your side. Then when you are lost he gets up and says: "Look, this way," and you follow him. Because at that time there is no one in the house yet, only the owners of the house. And the guests are just arriving and they are aware that you are learning.

An apprentice in those days would begin by learning the patterns of the smaller drum (okónkolo), then gradually move to the medium drum (itótele). and then learn to play the iyá. This progression reflected the complexity of the rhythms played by each drum. However, many drummers would never master all three drums. Batá players with a complete knowledge of all ritual songs, dances, and toques of the three drums, and with the ability to teach and to guide an ensemble, were a minority.

Apprentices usually begin with the okónkolo—the timekeeper of the ensemble—because it plays fixed, simple ostinato patterns. Although the itótele (or segundo) also plays many fixed patterns, it has the role of answering the calls of the principal drum and conversing with it and therefore gets to play many complex and changing patterns. This drum also has a repertoire of calls that the drummer, when he is a knowledgeable itótele player, can use to call the principal drum. This happens when the lead drummer (who plays the iyá or caja) "forgets" to perform the calls himself or when the itótele player wants to challenge the iyá player's ability. According to Felipe, the itótele is the drum that sings, so if the singer changes the chant the itótele player has to follow the change and warn the other drummers through a rhythmic cue. The iyá, as the head drum of the ensemble, calls or cues the switch from one toque to another, introduces the viros within a toque, improvises within the framework established by each pattern, and leads the conversations with the itótele.

To go from the okónkolo to the itótele it took me like one odd year. The drum I used to play was the okónkolo. I started like that until Tano [one of the drummers who taught Felipe] died. Then we made an agreement that during the oro seco I would play caja, and during the oro cantado I would play some segundo. Because my uncle Jorge didn't want me to play caja without playing segundo. Jorge was a drummer that played all the drums, but he liked to play as a *segundero*. He used to say that if you are not well prepared, then the segunderos come and play badly for you. They play badly so that they can shine and you are left below them. That is what Julito [another drummer] used to do to me. He wanted me to play with "flavor," but then he wanted to play his drum as he felt like it. Julito had this thing that if he asked you for a toque you had to give it to him, otherwise he would be annoyed. But when you "called" him with your drum he would not answer back.

. . . Then in my house I would practice. I would hear a toque played by the old guys; I would go home and I would be in bed playing. I would walk the streets *[he paces and hits his body like a drum]* and people would say: "Man, you are crazy." "No, I'm not, I'm going to be a *cajero*, you see?" And so I got myself in there, in there, in there.

In addition to his uncle Jorge, an older drummer called Tano guided Felipe in mastering the intricacies of batá drumming. He had met Felipe's great-grandfather and had numerous anecdotes to tell Felipe about the way in which his African great-grandfather used to teach batá to the members of his *casa de ocha* (casa de santo or house-temple).

Tano taught me a lot. If I have anybody to be grateful to, I have to be grateful to Tano. To that old man who everyone said was a black brujo [sorcerer], to that one. I have to be grateful to him because he taught me all about the drums. He was one of those people who are painted, you know what I mean? He was black but he had white spots all over. He lived in the same neighborhood where I used to live, close to my house. I would buy a pack of coffee, a three-cent cigar, and two cents of sugar. When I bought the sugar they would give it to me wrapped in a big paper. In total I would spend ten cents every time. I would go there to Tano's house and I would sit down with him. "Hey! You came." "Yes, I brought you some coffee here." Then he would start telling me stories about my great-grandfather. That was what I was interested in. I didn't speak about the drum or nothing. Then he would say: "You know, I like you coming here, because you always come alone. You don't bring anybody and it can be seen that you are a serious person." Then all of a sudden he would say: "Bring down that drum that I am going to teach you something. This is done this way, and this that way, that goes through here and that other thing through there." Then I began growing, growing, growing in the toque, you know? I made a lot of progress because when I grew in the toque I began to take the things to my house. . . .

Tano was one of those who used to keep an earthen cooking pan close to the door, full of "that" water—with herbs and those kinds of things. A smell! You know. You had to wash your hands there, come in and wet your hands, in case you came, as they said, dirty. Then he would start talking, and he would start telling me stories about my great-grandfather Iñoblá Cárdenas; on how Iñoblá used to teach people to drum. I am telling you what Tano told me, because he was always in Iñoblá's house. Look, my great-grandfather gave classes, but they were classes where you would get beaten like a madman. Iñoblá would never tell you how to play, he would just play with his feet what you where supposed to play with your hands and you had to follow. When you made a mistake he would hit you with a *cuarta* [large whip], he would hit your hands. Ah! And that cuarta of Iñoblá Cárdenas! I saw it once at Unión de Reyes. It didn't matter if you were young or old, he would hit you with the cuarta; so whoever came out of there came out as a real drummer. And everyone in my family is a drummer, everyone is a drummer.

Becoming a batá player in Cuba before the revolution was a challenging activity that required many years of apprenticeship. Aspiring drummers were accepted as *yambokis* (apprentices) by experienced drummers who had already complied with the ritual and musical requirements to become an *olúañá* (he who knows the secrets of Añá). Under their supervision, the apprentices became the servants of the drums.

As an apprentice, Felipe was expected to arrive at the house of Tano Bleque, the *olúbatá* owner of the set of drums that Felipe was learning to play, a few hours before leaving for the place where the ceremony was going to be celebrated, in order to help prepare the drums for the ritual. He learned how to clean, tune, and "feed" the drums ritually[32] and was responsible for packing and carrying the drums. He was also expected to learn about and participate in the maintenance of the drums: repairing the drums, fixing or making the liturgical ornaments called *bandeles*—beaded garments that are wrapped around the drums during certain ceremonies—and learning how to make *fardela,* a resinous paste placed in the head of the iyá and the itótele for tuning. It was Tano who taught Felipe that the "sound" of the drums had to be found in a corner of the house; corners were then the ideal places for tuning the drums.

I saw how the old men there would tune the drums and I learned to tune them. I learned with Tano. I was learning with him, and what he did, I did. I didn't ask him questions. I would work with him and when we finished he would say: "Take the drum over there and give it this; you have to put more fardela or remove some fardela" or "The sound of the drum, you have to look for it at the corners of the house, because there is where you can hear it better, there is where you can find it." But I never asked questions. I thought: "Why is he doing this? Well, he would tell me some day, when he feels like telling me."

Then, when I started doing it myself, I would do something and he would tell me: "It's fine" or "No! It's wrong, you have to put a little bit more fardela," et cetera, and I began to adapt to that, I began to adapt.

Then I started taking all the things to my house, because Tano was very old and he didn't care. And there I was, fixing them, looking for a case to carry them, stretching the skin. . . .

Even though all the aspiring batá players in Cuba were expected as apprentices to learn about and help with the basic maintenance of the drums, not all of them learned how to build the drums, nor were they all initiated into the secrets of Añá, the spirit that inhabits the drums, the source of their sacred power and efficacy.

Añá comes to inhabit the drums after a series of elaborate rituals, which transform unconsecrated or "unbaptized" drums (also known as *judíos*—Jews—or *aberikulá*) into sacred drums. The consecrated drums, also known as fundamento drums, are considered the only ones that can be used to call the orichas. For Felipe, Añá is not an oricha, yet it is a manifestation of the same vital force, *aché,* the power or the strength of all things, that the orichas express and personify. Aché for santeros is the principle of life that animates everything. In his study of Santería, where he examines the central role aché plays in the religious life of santeros, Joseph Murphy conveys insightfully the link between the spirit that inhabits the drums (Añá), a spirit closely related to movement, and the "current" or "flow" that is aché. Murphy views Santería as a "danced religion because dancing expresses the fundamental dynamism of aché," a force or flow that santeros reach through movement (Murphy [1988] 1993: 130–31).

Felipe gained his reputation as a serious apprentice with Tano, who initiated him into the secrets of Añá. But it was a man named Amado Díaz who taught Felipe how to make batá drums and completed his training as a "priest" of Añá.

Amado is a pioneer of that, a pioneer; because any instrument, any object made of wood, wears out; it can be attacked by moths, termites, or something and it has to be "renovated." What is inside no, because what is inside is the secret. Making drums and fixing them was what Amado did; but Amado also knew all the secrets of Añá. Amado is the nephew of Carlos Alfonso [famous olúbatá from Matanzas] because he is the son of Inés Alfonso.[33]

He died not long ago. Amado was the one who taught me how to make drums. He was a carpenter, an excellent carpenter. He taught me because he had a drum in his house that nobody played, and it was me who started handling those drums for him. He used to give names to his drums; he had like four or five drums and he would give them names. There was one that was called "The Atomic," because of the stories about the atomic bomb. There was another one that was called "Quintín Bandera,"[34] and then there was one that was called "Nobody Can Beat Me"—nobody can beat me because truly enough, the drums he made! They really had a good sound. He did not play the drums a lot because he was "antirhythmic," but he made some drums, and he tuned them—because he knew a lot, he really knew.

Introduced into batá drumming by his uncle Jorge, and with the guidance of people like Tano and Amado Díaz, Felipe not only gained knowledge and experience as a sacred drummer but followed the steps and went through the necessary initiations to become an olúbatá. The three main steps in the process are described by Felipe as follows:

So there are three stages: [first,] washing the hands to be able to *ochiché añá,* to work with añá, and it gives the power to sit and play the drums. The hands are washed with an *omiero* [sacred herbal mix]. Then comes the step of making an oath to the drums, when you take that oath you become an *omóañá,* because you take an oath with the secret that drums have. A small cross is made in your wrist; you become then a son of Añá. If then you want to continue and you have the intelligence, you go and you hang in there, you know? The way I did. So time passes and you become an olúbatá, he who knows everything about the batá; *olú* means wise, because he knows how to manage everything concerning the batá.

The hierarchy that existed among batá players was independent from the priestly hierarchy. One did not have to be initiated as a santero to become an omóañá or olúañá; it sufficed to be accepted by the others drummers and undergo the apprenticeship. As was the case with Felipe's teacher Amado Díaz, the owner of a set of sacred drums—the

vho also was given the name *aláña*—did not have to be a
himself. He was the keeper of the drums and took care of
_.tenance.

History of the Drums

Batá drums are cultural artifacts, objects that "speak and should be
heard as significant statements of personal and cultural reflexivity"
(Babcock 1986: 317). Following the history of a set of drums (who built
them, for whom, who could own them, etc.) helps us understand the
social relationships that determine the significance of batá drums as cultural artifacts (Johnson 1997).

For santeros, batá drums are not just musical instruments; they are
a spiritual entity (Añá) in and of themselves. Drums are considered to
have a will of their own, which can oppose the drummer's will. Batá
drums, not batá drummers, are sacred; they are the ones saluted and
paid tribute to during the rituals. It is with the set of drums that an initiate, after a special ritual, establishes a special relationship that will last
during his or her lifetime. Drums talk to the orichas or speak with the
voices of the orichas; they are the actors. Drummers are vehicles to
make this "voice" heard; they are the instruments. The history of sacred
batá drumming and drummers is, then, intimately intertwined with the
history of sacred batá drums.

In Cuba, sacred batá drums have to be "born" from a previously
consecrated set of drums, which transmits to them the "voice," that is,
the power to talk to the orichas. The older set of drums becomes the
"godfather" of the newly consecrated set; in this way, lineages (or families) of drums arise that have great significance for sacred batá drummers, who rely on them for the religious credentials of their drums.
Drums that are not given the voice by an already consecrated (fundamento) set of drums cannot be used for ritual purposes. Therefore, lineages are important not only to drummers but to santeros, who, when
offering a tambor or bembé to their oricha, worry about every detail of
the ceremony's ritual propriety.

Most of what is known at present about the history of batá drums
and their lineages comes from the writings of Fernando Ortíz, who
worked mainly with drummers from Havana and offers little informa-

tion on the lineages of drums in Matanzas.[35] An emic chronicle on the history of the sacred batá drums in Matanzas, such as the one Felipe gives us, is one of the few sources available to those interested in reconstructing their history.[36]

• • •

The second part of the letter that opened Felipe's story follows here:

My drums are called Añábí Oyó [Añábí, the son of Añá]. They were born from Iñoblá Cárdenas and they came to my hands like this:

The founders of the drums were four black men *de nación* [born in Africa] born in the land nowadays called "Nigeria":

- Iñoblá Cárdenas, grandfather of Tomasa Villamil from her mother's side of the family[37]
- Mauricio Piloto, grandfather of Tomasa Villamil from her father's side of the family
- Oba Enkolé
- Abiawo Ochabiowo

The house of Iñoblá Cárdenas was in Calle Buen Viaje #96 of Pueblo Nuevo, in the city of Matanzas, Cuba. These four people taught others how to play the batá drums. The following are the omóañás initiated by Iñoblá Cárdenas. Some of them also came to be olúañás—that is to say, a person that keeps the drums, feeds them, fixes them, etc.

- Juan Villamil, my grandfather, who didn't play, because every time he played he was possessed by Ogún
- Pedro José Cárdenas, son of Iñoblá, who sang
- Bonifacio Martínez Cárdenas "Patato"
- Tano Bleque
- Jorge Villamil Cárdenas, grandson of Iñoblá Cárdenas and my own uncle
- Ernesto Chambelona Torriente—he played caja, he left for Havana
- Candelario Fernández—he played okónkolo and segundo, he was not family
- Juan "the mailman" (Little Juan)—omelé player, he was not family
- Dionisio "Pipe" Ulloa—caja player, he was family

Together with Añábí Oyó, Iñoblá Cárdenas made another set of fundamento drums that was called Ilú Añá. The set Añábí Oyó was used only in
the cabildo of Iñoblá Cárdenas; the Ilú Añá set was played in ceremonies in
other houses of ocha.[38]

From the hands of Iñoblá the two Añá sets went to the hands of
"Patato" Bonifacio Martínez Cárdenas (Alangayú) [his religious name], my
uncle, who was a luggage carrier in the railroad. That Bonifacio was the best
. . . his drum couldn't be played by anybody because he was a huge man
with large arms—and so his caja was of the size of a sofa. Patato had a talent among santeros, it seems to be that he had an influence from the ancestors, who taught him everything. When he said: "This is going to happen," it happened. When he had the drums, those drums used to play
everywhere, even in Havana and in the cabildo of Regla. . . .

From Patato the drums went to Dionisio "Pipe" Ulloa, another uncle of
mine. They called him Escopeta [shotgun] because he was always drawing
out his revolver, even though he never did anything wrong because he was
an intelligent black man, and was also very good looking. Pipe was a well-
respected man, who was also an Abakuá. He was the iyamba of my juego.[39]

Pipe, in turn, gave the drums to Tano Bleque. And it was Tano Bleque
who taught me how to work with Añá. He was the osainista of the house
of Iñoblá, because he was the one who looked for the herbs and prepared
the omiero.

For Felipe, as a religious drummer who learned his trade in the "old
days" in Cuba, the lineages of the sacred batá drums are of great importance. When he left Cuba for the United States, he found himself
facing a practice of Santería in which the written word was given a significance it never had in Cuba. Thus, Felipe felt the need to register the
history of his set of drums in a book. Back in Matanzas, for drummers
like Felipe this type of written record was not only unnecessary but unknown. Among santeros it was common knowledge who owned a set
of sacred batá drums. The drums of Iñoblá and the drummers who
played them were known by all of the santeros.

There are some things that, if not kept properly, a lot of tradition is lost.
When my drum arrived in the U.S. I had to make a book, a notebook: how
did I play, with whom did I play—even though many people here know me
from Cuba, know that I have been a drummer since I was born. They know

I played with Amado, they know I played with all those drummers in Matanzas that I used to play with. They know that I was an official drummer, who
played in all the places in Cuba, in Havana, here and there. What I mean is
that I have to make an account because this drum is going to live here. If I
don't have some documents—how the manual work was done, who
brought them, who played with me in Cuba, who the dead drummers that
I know from Cuba were—without that I have nothing. Right now, you ask
any of these people that have drums: "Who played with you in Cuba?" and
they don't have a thing stamped on a paper that can say: "Look, this is what
it is." In Cuba it was different, because in Cuba you didn't need this type
of organization.

    According to Ortíz, the first set of batá drums made in Havana was
built in 1830 by Juan el Cojo (Añabí) and Filomeno García (Atandá)—
drums that were later inherited by one of Cuba's most famous batá players, Andrés Roche (Ortíz 1952: vol. 4, 315–16).

    There are no records about the time when the first batá sets were
built in Matanzas, and Felipe does not know the date when the sacred
batá drums of Iñoblá were made. It is conceivable that a process of reconstruction of the tradition of drum building similar to that which took
place in Havana occurred in Matanzas, considering the large Lucumí
population present in this province, who led an active religious life in
the many cabildos operating during the first decades of the nineteenth
century.

The first drum there was in Matanzas, it was the drum of Iñoblá Cárdenas;
those were the drums . . . everybody learned on. Because, yes, there was
the set of Carlos [Carlos Alfonso], but Carlos didn't apply himself to that,
Carlos didn't play. . . .[40]

    The drums of Iñoblá were born in his house. Because he was a king.
He was a king in his land. In Cuba, after he bought his freedom, he had his
own house and he had his line of drums. There were two sets of drums in
the house of Iñoblá Cárdenas, because there was a set of drums to play for
the "house" only. At my great-grandfather Iñoblá Cárdenas's house they
held celebrations for La Mercedes and San Lázaro. The other set was used
to play in other houses.

    I think those drums were made sometime in the 1800s, because my
mother was born like in 1903 and the drums were already there. They must

be from the past century, because I was born in the thirties and didn't get to know my grandfather, and these were the drums of my great-grandfather.

During one of the frequent periods in which Afro-Cuban religious practices were repressed and drums and rituals objects were confiscated by the police, the fundamento or Añá—what makes the drum sacred—of Iñoblá's drums was taken out and saved, while the bodies of the drums were disposed of.

In Matanzas, around the thirties, there was a persecution—according to my ancestors. They told me about a police inspector called José Claro. At the time of José Claro, playing drums in Matanzas was not allowed. They had to take the fundamento out of the drums, which at that time used to be in Matanzas. They were in the house of my great-grandfather Iñoblá Cárdenas, where two sets of batá drums used to "rule." I was very small but I still remember, in a neighborhood that is called La Calle; they used to call it La Cuadrita, and we had a house there in La Cuadrita. Back then they couldn't play the drums, they couldn't do anything. They had to take the fundamento out and throw the drums inside a "blind" well until the persecution disappeared. But the activities were not stopped because of this.[41]

They kept on playing because they had the fundamentos out; they would put the fundamentos in a bag inside their pockets, and they played and presented with güiro. They would play with güiro because the güiros are not so loud. At that time the toque with güiro didn't require drums. Now with us drums are used, we were the ones that introduced the use of drums into the güiro.

After a santero has undergone the initiation process known as asiento, a series of complex rituals that last seven days, he or she is ready to be "presented" to the drums. Through this ritual, which authorizes the initiate to dance in front of the sacred drums, santeros establish a special relationship to the set of sacred drums to which they are presented. In Matanzas, at Felipe's house, this ceremony was performed immediately after the asiento.

The drum represents a commitment that here in the States people don't respect. Because once you are presented to a set of drums it is like a birth certificate. It means that after you "put your head" to a drum, you establish a direct pact with that drum, because it is the drum that has recognized you. You have to be aware that when you die, that is the drum that is going to take you to—that has to say goodbye to you. It is also the only drum that can play for your birthday in santo. For other ceremonies you can choose other drums, but for your birthday, no.

The set of drums in Felipe's family was well known in Matanzas and respected by the older generation of santeros, many of whom had been presented to these drums at their initiation into the religion. Having been presented to these drums, they continued to use them in many rituals, even though some of them had relatives who owned other sets of drums. This was how it was with Adela Alfonso, the mother of the well-known olúbatá Carlos Alfonso.

Our drums were very well respected, because the majority of the older santeros were presented with that drum, you see? Most of the *alaguas* who are now dead and the older people that are now dead. In the house of Felipita Calderón, there, no other drum could come in, because she recognized only that drum. . . . For Adela Alfonso, for all of them, no other drum could be played if it wasn't that one; because that was the drum that they knew, the drum of Iñoblá Cárdenas.

However, during Tano's time the drums began to lose their reputation, because Tano was old and did not give the drums the appropriate care.

Later the drums lost prestige. Of course, Tano didn't tighten the skins or anything. The old man didn't take care of stretching them or anything. He wasn't up to it anymore. When we were going to play the drums, he would put them in the sun; and yes, they would play well for a while, but then of course they would go off and drop! Because they were stretched by the sun. They were stretched by the sun and the sun in Cuba is strong. At that time people used to call our drums *la lata* [the can], because they sounded like cans. "Who's playing today?" "Well, la lata." So the reputation of the drums went down. It is true that they sounded like cans, because what the sun does to the skins is "toast" them and make them sound like cans. So when Carlos Alfonso brought his drums from the countryside everyone went to him. At that time the drums became divided by neighborhoods.

They were the drums from Simpson and we were the drums from Pueblo Nuevo. So when they were playing ten toques we would be playing only two, you see?

When Felipe learned enough about handling the drums he began working with them, trying to tune them properly and improve their sound in order to regain the reputation once enjoyed by these sets of batá drums.

When I began playing, the people that were there were old and didn't busy themselves with anything. Then, I was there fixing things. So one day, there, running my hands through the drums I said: "I know what I have to do," and said to Tano: "Old man, I can stretch that drum because I have the skill." "You think so? Take it, let me see." And when he saw that I could tighten it he gave it to me, and then the "thing" started rising again.

There were additional difficulties with one set of batá drums. The iyá that used to belong to Patato, an imposing monumental man with huge arms, had been built according to measurements that made it easy for him to play, but which created problems for drummers with shorter arms; so it was decided that they would make a new iyá for the set.

We spoke with this guy, who also died, who is called Amado Díaz, so that he would make us a shorter caja. Then I got myself into Amado's house; it was there where I learned. When the caja was made the drum changed, you see? We called Benerando Alfonso, and Benerando Alfonso was the one that washed it, he washed the wood so that we could make the drum. Then the drum started sounding different, it regained strength.

When Tano died, the set of drums that was not dismantled was inherited by his stepson Ricardo Suárez "Fantómas." The Añá of the set that was disassembled was kept by Felipe's mother at her house, and she sent it to the United States when Felipe emigrated to this country.

One week before Tano died, we went to play, and he wanted me to take the drums. He told me: "I have two sets of drums, one that's dismantled and the other that's there; take one." I told him: "I don't want to take the drums with me." "You're going to regret not taking the drums with you because I'm go-

ing to die soon." Tano gave the dismantled set to my mother and t
"This is a secret that's for Felipe for when I die, don't tell anybody."

. . . One day we went to a toque and when we came back he ir
again: "I'm telling you kid, take the drum with you." "No, you aren't going
to die." I went home, and at five in the morning they came to look for me:
"Listen, old Tano died."

Tano Bleque's stepson was called Ricardo Fantómas, the son of Tano's
wife Sixta Puey. At the time of Tano's death, Ricardo Fantómas kept the
set of drums called Ilú Añá. But before dying, Tano had taken out the fundamento from the set called Añábí Oyó and had wrapped it in a packet. At
the time of his death he had given instructions to send me the package,
and that was what happened.

I left Cuba in 1980, but before leaving I left the package with my mother,
Tomasa Villamil, and she saved it. When a santera from New York made a
trip to Cuba, she visited my mother. My mother gave her the package so
that she would bring it to the United States.

When "Fantómas" became the olúañá of the set of drums known as
Ilú Añá, he worked closely with Felipe in regaining the sound that had
given these drums their reputation. Another iyá was made, and new
drummers joined the group.

Our drum was really discredited. When Ricardo Fantómas took it, then our
drum began to surge. That man started from the bottom. The one who knew
how to fix the drums there was me. So I began to stretch the drums, with
the little we had seen. One day Fantómas sat with me there and he said: "I'm
going to learn." And it's true, what an apprentice! He started taking care of
them. There is more—he invited me and so we went and cut a log and we
held the ceremony for the log and we made a drum, another drum. In the solar, where my sister still lives, she's the owner of the whole solar, there we
did that. Well, then when the drums were made, new guys started coming—
Minini [leader of Afro-Cuba] came, Francisco Zamora, Reynaldo Gobel; a
nephew of mine that was called Joseíto came. Young faces came, and Julito,
Daniel Alfonso, and I complemented the younger ones. There were also my
uncle Jorge, Ernesto Chambrona . . . so the group grew strong.

Years later, when the revolution arrived, Fantómas had built a reputation as one of the "most serious and respected olúbatás in Cuba"

and as one knowledgeable in the art of building drums with all the necessary ritual steps. His ensemble of batá drums was included in the well-known anthology of Afro-Cuban music compiled by Cuban musicologist María Teresa Linares.[42]

Other Batá Lineages in Matanzas

When one inquires into the history of batá drums in Matanzas, two lineages are always mentioned as being the oldest sacred drums in the city: the lineage of the drums in Felipe's family and of the drums of a man named Carlos Alfonso (Carlos Alfonso Díaz). According to Ortíz, Carlos Alfonso's drums were built by Atandá, one of the drum makers who built the first set of drums in Havana (Ortíz 1952: vol. 4, 315–18). Carlos Alfonso's drums are now in the hands of Chachá—Estéban Vega Bacayao—considered by many the best olúbatá in present-day Cuba.

Alfonso's drums used to be in Cidra, in the province of Matanzas. When the drums were brought to the city of Matanzas, Chachá was called to fix them and become a member of this ensemble. Like all sacred drummers, Chachá learned by playing with many older drummers; however, he recalls in particular a drummer whom he considers his "teacher," Miguel Alcina. Drummers well known in Matanzas, such as Isaac Calderón, Felipe Calderón, and Ernesto Torrigente, used to play in the group with Alcina. This was also the group in which Francisco Aguabella learned.[43] Aguabella later left for Havana and, in 1954, came to the United States as a member of the Katherine Dunham Dance Troupe. He remained in this country and has been instrumental in establishing batá drumming on the West Coast, where he remains active as a percussionist.

The drums of Alfonso were in the countryside, and were not played, because he wasn't into toques or into anything. He had made Changó but he was into women, politics, and the like; always with his suit, his tie, and all of that. Then Alfonso went there to Cidra—there were two sets of drums in Cidra—and picked one set of drums and brought them to Matanzas. They began "playing politics" [competing] with Pipe and began to get hired for most of the ceremonies.

. . . So the line of drummers who played those drums of Alfonso were: Chachá, Isaac Calderón, Felipito Calderón, and a kid, "Baton," he was known as Baton; he died very young. Ah! And Miguel Alcina, who was the number-one player in Matanzas. Matanzas? No, the whole of Cuba. He left the drum because he had problems with Chachá, after that he played no more. But he sang and played like it was the end of the world! That man made the drum talk, the drums really talked when he played. It was a gift God gave to Miguel Alcina, and Alcina was the biggest thing Matanzas gave to the drums. After Alcina came Jorge Villamil, then Chachá, called Bacayao, Estéban Bacayao.

Ortíz (1952: vol. 4, 317) mentions two other sets of drums in Matanzas. One was built by Atandá for Manuel Guantica. Ortíz does not provide any information about him, but a Manuel Guantica is a nephew of Carlos Alfonso. His full name, according to Felipe, is Amado Manuel Díaz Guantica (the Amado who taught Felipe to build drums). The other set of drums belonged to Eduardo Salakó, the father of the drummer Ernesto Torrigente. No lineages came from this set of drums, and after the death of Salakó, they were not played anymore.

Unless a drummer owned a set of batá drums, it was not unusual for him to play with different ensembles or to change the ensemble with whom he played regularly. Numerous reasons contributed to this mobility, the most frequent being misunderstandings or conflicts among drummers.

It was not unusual also for drummers who played one set to be "presented" to another set of drums when they were initiated into the religion. This happened especially if the set they were being presented to was that traditionally played for the house into which they were being initiated. Thus, many drummers were presented to the set that belonged to Felipe's house, as it was one of the oldest in Matanzas. This was the case for the son of one of the most famous older santeras from Matanzas, Felipita Calderón.

Felipita Calderón had a mystery, that woman had a mystery, and the ones who played for her house were us, and nobody else. The children of Felipita played with Carlos, but when Calderón made Eleguá, we were the ones that presented him. He was not presented to the drums he played, because he made saint in the house of his mother, Felipita Calderón. In that house no drum could go in because she only recognized one drum, that of Iñoblá.

Although each batá set has a sacred name, the name given to Añá, nowadays batá drums both in Cuba and in the United States are commonly known by the name of the owner of the set.

From the older sets of batá drums prominent in Matanzas new sets were born. Felipe himself contributed to establishing some of the new sets of drums. Before Felipe left Cuba, three sets of new batá drums had been recognized: one belonging to a man named Pucho, whose name in santo was Echudina; another belonging to a man who had Calvo as his last name; and the third one the set of Miguel Alcina, who died before he ever got a chance to play his own set of drums. Chachá, too, was instrumental in building new sets of drums, born from the ones he had inherited from Carlos Alfonso; but all the sets he made were for drummers outside the city of Matanzas. Two of these sets were made for drummers in the United States.[44]

Other Drumming Traditions in Matanzas

Felipe knew many batá drummers in Matanzas who not only used to play with several batá sets but also were proficient drummers of other traditions, such as the Iyesá, Olókun, and Arará. Although Felipe never played as a ritual drummer in these ensembles, from childhood he lived closely with people who retained these traditions and participated in their rituals. By contact and close observation Felipe gained knowledge that was to be useful to him as a leader of a folkloric ensemble after the revolution.

The Iyesá (a subgroup of the Lucumí in Cuba), notwithstanding the many similarities and the syncretism of their practices with those of the Lucumí santeros, kept some of their own liturgical practices, their ensemble of drums, and a repertoire of chants. Earlier in the twentieth century, Iyesá cabildos could be found in the provinces of Matanzas, Havana, and Las Villas. At present there is only one Iyesá cabildo left in Cuba, the one mentioned by Felipe, which is located in the city of Matanzas. Felipe's casa de ocha had strong ties with this cabildo, and many members of Felipe's extended family drummed there.

The iyesá ensemble is made up of four wooden drums (*ilú*), two iron bells, and a rattle (*agbe*).[45] The drums are cylindrical and have two membranes, but only one is used in playing. The skin is attached on hoops and laced to the drum by a band of ropes woven into different types of patterns (N- or V-shaped.). The largest drum is played with the hands, while the others are played with sticks. Like the batá drums, the iyesá drums are sacred and are therefore the objects of special rites in their construction and their care. The drums are usually painted with the colors of the two orichas to which the ensemble belongs, yellow and green for Ochún and Ogún.[46]

Another, less well known Lucumí drumming tradition is that of the *olókun* drums, used to worship Olókun, the Lucumí deity of the bottomless sea. The ensemble has four single-membrane cylindrical drums with wedges. The largest (olókun) is played with the hand; of two other drums (*yeguá*), one is played with one hand and a stick and the other with two bare hands; and the smallest drum (*oddúa*) is played with two sticks (Ortíz 1952: vol.3, 413–14).

In Matanzas at the time of Felipe's adolescence, there was a set of olókun drums at the house of a famous santera, Ferminita Gómez.

Ernesto Torrigente played iyesá, played *arará,* and played olókun, the olókun from Fermina's house. But he only liked to play batá; he liked the batá better. All the young kids that are now into the Iyesá are also batá drummers, so it could be seen that the traditions were being lost. I am talking about the younger drummers, the new ones, because the old ones are too old now, and are dying or died. Loreto died, all the old people died: Loreto García, who lasted one hundred–odd years;[47] his son, called Jorge, who was affectionately called "Luz Brillante" [literally, "bright light"] because it seems that he was always drunk; a compadre of mine that went blind; and a lad that was a bell player. My nephew, the one you know, who is here in the States, played in the Iyesá also.[48]

In my case I didn't like the Iyesá, because I used to listen to the Iyesá and I would say: "No! No! I'm leaving." I used to watch their ceremonies and go to the cabildo and salute, but nothing else; then I would leave. Because there was something in that music, that if I was coming from afar that toque made me dizzy, it made me dizzy. That's why I didn't like to play iyesá—but I knew how to play it. Look, in my house, the house of Tomasa Villamil, they play iyesá all the twenty-third or twenty-fourth or twenty-fifth of June. That's something that never failed, so I used to listen and watched them play. First the bell. How does it go? I watched how this guy played, and how this other guy played: *tinguiling, tangalang,* and I practiced it by myself. I was studying by myself, I played with nobody, just by myself practicing what I heard. I would take the first bell: *kinkin kaka kinkin kaka.* I would take the second bell: *tantan titin tantan titin,* and alone I would begin "annexing" them in my mind. Later on that knowledge came in handy. I knew very well the oldest man from the Iyesá, who was a hundred-odd years, old Loreto. He used to play *clave: tintin tintin tintin tintin.* Then my compadre would be going: *keeen keken keeen keken.* . . . The way I do here in the States when I teach, that's the way I used to do it back then. I studied all the rhythms and combined them later. That is how I learned how to play iyesá, because nobody taught me how. When playing iyesá the rhythms that give more trouble are the bass and the caja. I used to practice them the same way I teach them to Jessy now . . . I tell him *tukutun,* with this call I'm telling him when to come in. Then I teach him how to answer when the caja calls him.

The Arará traditions of Dahomean origin also became closely related to the Lucumí in Cuba. Their deities, called *vodú* or *foddún,* are identified with the orichas and also communicate with the practitioners through divination and possession. As in the case of the Lucumí, music comprises a fundamental part of their rituals. Nowadays, the Arará Regla has followers only in the provinces of Matanzas, Las Villas, and Oriente, Matanzas being the most important center for these traditions. Here the worship of Babalú-Ayé has become central to the religious practices of this religious group (Vinueza 1988).

The Arará had their own branch, the Arará were not together with us, with the santeros, with the Lucumís; they were alone. Therefore, in Matanzas the Arará couldn't go to the celebrations of the Lucumí. Because they did things differently from us. They did their saints and their things separately. We couldn't go into their ceremonies but they didn't go into ours either. So there was an Arará, the deceased Mayito, who had a lot of understanding and who also understood a lot about santo. Although he was an Arará he had studied a lot of santo, and he knew a lot. He said one day: "Here we have to unify, because our thing and yours is the same thing, gentlemen. The only difference is that our ancestor came from another land, but it is the same thing with different characteristics; in the end the food, rice and beans, is the same." So the Arará started inviting us to begin to promote the union. "We are going to send five or six of our people to work with you and you send five or six of yours to work here." The unification began like that. Thereafter we began to go to them to cleanse ourselves, to sing, and to help in their ceremonies.

The Arará in Cuba recognized three subgroups among themselves, based on origin and ethnicity: Arará Magino (Mahino or Majino), Arará Savalú (Sabalú), and Arará Dajomé (Dahomé) (Vinueza 1988).

They don't have Arará in Havana, only in Matanzas and in the provinces: in Perico and Jovellanos and Cárdenas, which have the same system but it is Magino, of the land of San Lázaro, but the toque is similar.

Present-day *arará* music ensembles use from two to four drums, an iron bell (*ogán*), and a metal rattle; older ensembles had four to five drums. The arará drums are unipercussive, single-headed wooden drums, with the skin attached to the drums by pegs or mounted on a hoop held through a system of pegs and laces. They are footed and slightly conical. Older sets of arará drums were heavily decorated with carvings and paintings; present-day drums are only painted. As with other sets of religious drums, the arará drums become sacred after undergoing a series of religious ceremonies. They are played directly with the hands or by using a stick with one end slightly hooked. The names given to the drums have changed with time, and in present-day ensembles they are commonly called *caja, mula,* and *cachimbo* (Vinueza 1988: 71). However, when Felipe refers to the largest drum of the ensemble, he uses the old name, *yonofó.*

The good arará players in Matanzas were: Mayito; Chiquitico [Little One], one who was called Chiquitico, who had made Changó; and Juan de Dios. All those people played arará. After the revolution the young guys began to play arará. Even some batá players—Francisco Zamora Minini, who plays with Afro-Cuba, were playing arará. But for a while, when the old ones died, the Arará went through some hard times and all their things were left unattended.

After the revolution, with the attention given to these traditions by the government, younger people started to play other drums in addition to the batá. When the drums are not available to them, they learn the rhythmic patterns and substitute the missing drums with others, such as congas. María Elena Vinueza, a musicologist who researched the Arará traditions in the 1980s, considers Francisco Zamora Minini, the drummer Felipe mentioned, who is closely linked to Felipe's family and drummed with him in the batá ensemble, as one of the three most outstanding arará players in Matanzas (Vinueza 1988: 86).

I never participated in the rituals of the Arará as a drummer. I learned to play arará by myself. When I went to their rituals and would listen, I would watch them play and then I practiced. I would go to their cabildo for a while when I had some time. Back then I had a *comadre* [godmother of one's children] who baptized my daughter Mercedes. Every time she had a fiesta she would invite me. She is an Arará, and what they played in her house was arará. There, by listening, I learned.

Being also a palero and an Abakuá, Felipe was familiar with the music of both these traditions and participated actively in their ceremonies, not only as a drummer but also as a ritual expert. His father had taught him the use of the various herbs and plants and had also trained him in the ritual slaughter of animals. At his father's side, Felipe also learned a large repertoire of *mambos,* the Palo chants that are sung antiphonally by a leader (*gallo* or *insusu*) and a chorus during rituals.[49]

Aside from the music used in the rituals of paleros, some secular musical traditions of Congo origin frequently were performed after the religious celebrations had taken place, such as the dances known as *yuka, makuta,* and *maní.* What characterizes the dances of Congo origin is a movement known as *vacunao* (also used in dancing the rumba), a pelvic thrust used to mimic a game of seduction between a male and a female dancer.[50]

The dance known as maní (peanut) is a pugilistic dance similar to the Brazilian *capoeria;* but in contrast to the latter, the dancers of the maní try to strike the "opponents" not with their feet but with their hands as they dance. According to the rules of the game, blows are allowed on the upper part of the body only: on the stomach, the chest, and the head.

Me, nobody had to teach me a lot of things. Because if I heard yuka being performed, I could play yuka, and if I heard maní, I could play maní.

In my family the place where they had the Palo drums, the yuka was in the house of my father's brothers, Cundo and Fabián, that is located in Cárdenas. Those drums were there, tied up, and they had them covered. Those drums are linked to Palo, and in Cárdenas they played a lot of yuka and maní. It is like a dance, like a long party. One day we would give a fiesta de Palo [ritual ceremony] and the next day they would say: "Let's play maní" or "Let's play yuka," which are Congo rhythms. They are dances to have fun with, that belong to the Congos. In those celebrations they would play yuka, makuta, and maní. They played in the *verbenas,* which is to say like a popular dance, a party but outside of Palo, outside of the rituals. However, they would use Palo for strength because maní is a game of blows.

Then in the dance of the yuka they would place some sugarcane and someone would come with a machete and . . . dancing to cut the cane, like this: **shshshsh.** It had things of danger, you see? It had a lot of things that nowadays people don't talk about. . . . In the makuta they used the vacunao of the rumba. It's like a sensual dance, a dance of provocation with the woman mimicking a chicken and the man mimicking the rooster, and those things.

All those dances were not Palo. But they used Palo to have the strength to dance them, they looked for power in Palo. So frequently there were people dancing those dances while they were possessed by Palo spirits, in order to have more strength than the others.

The makuta drum ensemble consists of two drums; two *maracas* (rattles), which are tied around the wrist of the main drummer; a copper bell called *ngunga;* and a circular rattle with a handle (maraca). The single-headed, barrel- or cylinder-shaped drums are played with the performer standing and directly struck with the hands. However, a third musician uses a stick to strike the base of the second drum. These drums, like the batá, are said to have a secret power inside them. They are considered "persons" and are ritually fed. Drummers also have to undergo a series of ceremonies to be able to play them. This ensemble began to be used to accompany secular dances and by 1952 mainly were played to accompany such dances. Around the same period, the sacred rhythms (toques) played on these drums, which varied according to the deity or spirit being praised, invoked, or saluted were disappearing in Cuba.

The yuka drum ensemble resembles the bembé ensemble of the Lucumís in that it is used for secular occasions. The drums are not fed, nor do they have a "secret" inside them, and drummers do not have to undergo special initiations to play them.[51] It is an ensemble of three drums of different sizes; two wrist rattles (maracas); two wooden sticks, used to play the lower body of the largest drum; a *guagua,* which is a type of wooden slit drum; and a metal idiophone, the *muela* (a pick used for plowing). The drums are wooden, single-headed, nailed, and shaped as elongated cylinders. The largest drum, called caja, is performed with one hand and a large stick. Sometimes the drum is placed over a support, and the drummer "mounts it" when playing it; another musician plays the lower part of the frame of the drum with two wooden sticks. Sometimes this part of the drum is covered with cans to generate a special sound. The second drum is called mula, is slightly smaller, and is played using a stick and one hand. The smallest is performed in the same fashion and is called the cachimbo.

Although Felipe's maternal uncles owned a set of yuka and makuta drums, these drums were kept in the countryside. When Felipe was young, this type of drum ensemble had become uncommon in the city, where they were replaced by three congas and the muela. The lead drummer played his conga using a stick and his hand, while the two other drummers used only their hands.

• • •

When the revolution arrives, we find Felipe heavily involved in the trade he had chosen, among many others that he had to learn to be able to support himself and his family. He is a drummer; not only a drummer but a *completo* (complete), a name given in Cuba to drummers who not only can perform the secular styles, such as rumba—*guaguancó, yambú, columbia*—but are familiar with the different Afro-Cuban religious styles of drumming. It is a trade learned, as Felipe says:

Watching and listening and watching and listening, and teaching also. In a word: God gave me a resource and it was that one.

PART TWO

Life as a Musician during the Revolution

Making Ends Meet

When the revolution arrived—Fidel Castro took power in January 1959—Felipe continued his struggle to earn a living, working all sorts of jobs alongside his main trade: music.

While Felipe was working in road construction, many of the laborers in the sugar industry found themselves unemployed because of difficulties in the sugar trade as a consequence of the American embargo and the antimonocrop ideology of the revolutionary government. The years 1960 and 1962 were characterized by a strong antisugar bias on the part of the government, with emphasis placed on diversification and industrialization. Schools were opened to train former sugar workers for jobs in other industries.

Felipe had worked in the sugar industry before the revolution, and his name was included in the list given to the government of people entitled to join the training program. He was contacted and decided to join the school because he was paid to attend.

When Fidel arrived we were left "exceeding" [laid off] from the sugar. At that time I had like three or four jobs, I was never idle. If I was not doing some music, because things were not going well, I was doing something else. So when Fidel came I was sent to a school. But I couldn't stand that school, because I didn't have the background for that. They spoke about neutrons, protons, machinery, energy, and what not. I kept going to school to let time go by; but they were driving me nuts. Then they opened a sugar plant and I fought and fought until I went there. Do you know how much money I was earning at that sugar plant? I did three or four shifts; sometimes I didn't even go home to sleep. This was a time when there was no control; later they began regulating it.

However, work in the sugar industry in the early stages of the revolution was not secure, and soon Felipe found himself unemployed. He was then sent to the Escambray Mountains, located in the province of Las Villas, which were the center of counterrevolutionary activities in the early 1960s.

When I was left without work in the sugar, they took me to the Cambray [Escambray] Sierra. While I was there I decided to cook for the people that were there with me, because nobody knew how to cook. I didn't want to eat raw food so I named myself the official cook. There I met a *blanco* [white man] who was called—well, Del Pino was his last name. Del Pino became a captain, or rather lieutenant, lieutenant of the rebel army.[1] When things were normal again at the Cambray, I went home and back to the sugar.

One day this Del Pino came to look for me at my house and took me to see the head of the state security forces in Matanzas. This captain, or whatever he was, looked at me from top to bottom and asked me: "Is it true that you are a good cook?" "Not that I know. I don't consider myself a good cook. The work is all done by the fire. I put the food there and the fire cooks it, so the good cook is the fire not me." "That's a good one," he said; and they gave me the keys and all the things to manage the dining facilities of the security forces. That man Del Pino was taking a big responsibility, because there I was cooking for these big shots, and what if I decided to poison them? But Del Pino really trusted me, and I worked there until he left for Havana. Then I returned again to the sugar.

So I'm into the sugar and into music at the same time. I could do this because music was done in the evenings; I could go to work, work the regular hours, and then do my music. Sometimes I would be falling asleep at work because of the hours I spent with the music. During carnival we would play every day from five in the afternoon to three o'clock in the morning, and on weekends in the afternoon from three to seven. But we also played in a music stand that was open twenty-four hours.

Because when the revolution came—not the first year, because that first year there were no carnivals or anything—it was really "burning the tennis shoes" [dancing]. They were giving people a ball.

Carnival, since the time it was reinstated by the revolution, takes place in every town in Cuba after the *zafra* (sugar season), that is, at the sugar harvest. The type of music Felipe performed during carnival (*comparsa* or *conga, pachanga,* and *mozambique*) belongs to a category known as *bailable* (music for dancing), and it is specifically, though not exclusively, performed during carnival. The names used to describe these music genres refer to both the dance and the type of ensemble that accompanies them.

We had several types of groups organized for the music during carnival. To march in the carnivals we had the comparsa. We went to the parade, then when our comparsa finished marching we left and went to play for those comparsas that didn't have musicians. It was wild the way we used to drag people along with our music! People from other comparsas used to run over to us and say: "Listen to these guys, they are really burning." Our comparsa was a blast. That comparsa was put together for the whole municipality of Matanzas. We had work for three or four months because when the carnivals ended in Matanzas, we went to Varadero, when they ended in Varadero, we went to Colón, and so forth throughout the whole province.

Then to play in the *trochas,* those drink and food stands that were set on the streets, we played rumba and we played pachanga. Then at nine o'clock in the evening, when the dancing began, we played with a group of mozambique.

Becoming a "Cultural Worker"

The revolutionary government considered all manifestations of culture important tools to achieve the ideological goals of the revolution (LICA 1982: 9).[2] Thus, the state monopolized all cultural initiatives and became the sole sponsor, promoter, manager, and deployer of cultural policies, emphasizing and encouraging certain aspects and values of traditional culture while reforming those that were considered to undermine the revolutionary goals. Artists were expected to work in and for the revolution, if need be sacrificing artistic freedom to achieve more pressing revolutionary goals.

In implementing the cultural policies, considerable freedom of expression was granted to an elite of artists and intellectuals placed in the higher echelons of the revolutionary cultural and educational agencies (Marshall 1987: 210) who, in turn, "guided," coordinated, and endorsed the work of the rest of the artistic and intellectual community, in particular of the "folkloric" artists. Moreover, freedom of expression, like all matters pertaining to cultural policies, was caught up in the dynamics of other political and economical factors, national and international. Hence, cultural policies went through several periods during the forty years of revolutionary government: from the initial "carnival stage of the revolution," when freedom, enthusiasm, and renewal predominated (Marshall 1987: 99), through what some scholars have described as the "cultural terrorism" (Stubbs 1989: 77) of the late 1960s and early 1970s,[3] to a less dogmatic period that began after the creation of the Ministry of Culture in 1976, headed by Armando Hart Dávalos (Levinson 1989: 490; Stubbs 1989: 77).

Irrespective of how we view the cultural monopoly exercised by the state, it cannot be denied that the revolution played a positive role in many aspects of the artistic and cultural life of Cuba. During the 1960s, the revolution took significant steps to expand the cultural resources at the national and local levels, making them accessible to all segments of the population.

In this framework of strong support for artistic enterprises, music in particular was heavily subsidized and strongly promoted. The government organized numerous music schools and performing venues, and the Centro de Investigación y Desarrollo de la Música Cubana (CIDMUC) was organized to coordinate all institutions connected with music.

Likewise during these years, many music activities, in particular those related to *música bailable* (dance music), were organized through a system of autonomous *empresas* (enterprises). These enterprises—which managed their own budgets, enjoyed some independence in hiring and dismissing labor, and implemented their own plans—were established in the early 1960s under the supervision of regional planning boards called Juntas Unificadas de Coordinación Económica (JUCEI).[4] Other genres of music (e.g., classical music) were handled through centralized, state-subsidized cultural institutions.

In the early 1960s, Felipe worked for a música bailable group that initially was privately owned and managed and later became one of the empresas under the supervision of the JUCEI of Matanzas. This placed Felipe in the group of professional musicians who were paid for their work, as opposed to amateur musicians who were not.

While working for the empresa, Felipe enjoyed the two working statuses that exist in Cuba among professional musicians: he first worked by contract, and later he became a *plantilla* musician. Musicians who work by contracts (which can be definite or indefinite) are paid less and have less stability; those who have definite contracts are not even entitled to vacation and retirement benefits. Those with definite contracts are evaluated every three months, whereas those with indefinite contracts are evaluated every three years and may work for any enterprise.[5]

We had one music group that worked for three things: the pachanga, the mozambique, and the comparsa. It was all done through the JULCEI [sic], that was a government agency. In that period the groups were still the property of the people. We played based on a contract.

At that time Cultura [governmental cultural agencies][6] had not opened in Matanzas. So they created an office to deal with all the cultural affairs. They were the ones who looked for funds for the comparsa, they gave the funds for the drums, and everything. The office was called the JULCEI of Matanzas. Later on the JULCEI was given a hard time because the leaders were messing around, so they formed the ORI [Organizaciones Revolucionarias Integradas]. But we really worked well with the JULCEI, they were really organized. When you went there to look for something, bang! There it was, real fast.[7]

In 1962 the Music Directorate of the Cultural Council began to implement a plan for evaluating and hiring musicians on a permanent basis as what we would call cultural workers or "artists of the people." This program, which initially included only classical performers, by 1968 was broadened to include popular musicians and aimed at the professionalization of "all the country's musicians . . . putting an end to the instability and insecurity which characterized their avocation when they were often forced to do jobs quite unrelated to their art to ensure their subsistence" (Otero 1972: 26–27).

When this process began to include popular musicians, Felipe's group had to go through an audition to be evaluated. The evaluation was carried out by councils controlled by the Ministry of Culture and the Bodies of People's Power. These governmental agencies had local directorates in the provinces in charge of electing the members of the Artistic Councils, who were in turn the ones responsible for rating musicians at the local level. The members of the Artistic Councils were chosen among musicians reputed to be knowledgeable and distinguished. This system, however, has been criticized because although the councils were composed of musicians, their members were not necessarily familiar with the genres of music they had to evaluate.[8] In addition, musicians felt that decisions were at times based more on personal or political reasons than on musical skills.

Initially, members of the folkloric ensembles were ranked as "C" while classical dancers were classified as "A." The founding members of the folkloric ensembles fought successfully to get categories defined on quality and not on style or genre.

There were two forms of evaluation: the one Felipe went through, which consisted of an audition, and another usually undergone by music students, done through a graduation exam. After the evaluation, Felipe became a plantilla musician, which brought better pay and a guaranteed minimum income. He also enjoyed job stability and was entitled to vacation and retirement benefits.

Then I got into Cultura and I used to work well. But, what happened was that then I had two jobs: I worked in sugar and I worked in the mozambique, you see? But when the evaluation came around '66 or '68 they told me: "Here or there, sugar or music." So I thought about keeping the work in the sugar but people told me: "Don't be a fool, you have a week to answer, and look—in the music you are going to have clothes, you won't have to pay for transportation to go from here to there, and you won't have to work a lot." Because work in the sugar was hard, and with the little food we were seeing those days . . . So I thought for a while and then I decided to join Cultura.

For the evaluation they made like an audition. The government made a committee, a jury. There were singers and percussionists, trumpet players, trombone players, musicians of different genres, and they put together a jury. Then it went like this. They would give you a piece of paper with the points that were evaluated: presentation, wardrobe—that our group had none—appreciation, manners, et cetera. Because in Cuba it's not like here in the U.S., that any artist, if they feel like it, can come up on stage wearing short pants, or with their shirts opened up. There in Cuba you can't do that. With those people you had to be on top of everything. So we fulfilled all the requirements because we gave a party to make some money. Then we bought ourselves something nice to wear, so we would have something to go up on stage with everybody looking the same. Everyone got a haircut, everyone with shoes really clean, watching carefully what we said, and so on.

After the evaluation I began collecting three hundred pesos a month, my clothes, and my shoes, sometimes by just sitting at home. Then our group broke up and I was left without a job. In our group there used to be many people from outside, from Havana, from here and from there; so they began to say that the group was not profitable. There was also the problem that those who were not from Matanzas wanted to try to make it closer to home, and they left the group. So they dissolved the group: One musician was sent to perform with a *punto guajiro,* another one left for the municipal band, and so on.

Nowadays it is very difficult to acquire plantilla status, which leaves many young musicians, who frequently complain about the "fossilization" of the system of employment, without access to the more prestigious and well paid musical positions (Robbins 1991: 243).

Performing Afro-Cuban Religious Music in Secular Public Contexts

When Felipe's work with the música bailable group ended, he was able to continue working as a musician by performing in secular public contexts the music of the religious traditions that were part of his heritage. After the revolution, these traditions became part of the "pool of ancestors" that were evaluated and selected for inclusion in the definition of the national culture of the new society. The process of selection of the "cultural roots of the nation" and of definition of the national culture was led by the state, which through its cultural institutes and agencies decided what ancestors were to be chosen, what cultural practices were to be studied, conserved, or rescued. Within this framework, Afro-Cuban culture was reinterpreted to integrate it into the official nationalist narrative.

In 1959 the National Theater (Teatro Nacional), headed by Argeliers León, organized a Department of Folklore that undertook the task of developing folklore as an academic field.[9] In 1961 the research activities of the department were separated from the representational ones; thus the Institute of Ethnology and Folklore, associated to the Academy of Science of Cuba, and the Conjunto Folklórico Nacional were created. The Conjunto Folklórico assumed the task of representing, as stage productions, manifestations of Cuban popular culture "through the artistic stylization of the folkloric event," based on research and information on these traditions that was "systematically compiled" (CCS 1982: 188; PPCC 1986: 70).

Following the same philosophy as the Conjunto Folklórico Nacional, other folkloric groups developed around the country and were joined by local cultural organizations, such as the Casas de la Cultura and the Movimiento de Aficionados, in researching and staging the folkloric traditions. Workshops were organized and contests, annual festivals, and competitions were instituted. Moreover, the most prestigious of these groups toured many foreign countries.

Within this framework, the musical traditions of the Afro-Cuban religions were included as part of the folkloric heritage of the country,[10] and together with other folkloric manifestations, they received strong support from the state. Through the activities of groups like the Conjunto Folklórico Nacional (who also toured extensively outside of Cuba), these musical traditions got national and international stage exposure of a magnitude they had never enjoyed before. Many government officials, artists, and scholars believed this was a positive step toward overcoming the ignorance that had generated contempt for and neglect of Afro-Cuban traditions before the revolution. However, while the Afro-Cuban musical traditions were integrated into the cultural heritage of the nation and made part of the new socialist culture, the religious beliefs and the rituals tightly linked to them were ignored, discouraged, or at best tolerated. It was assumed that they would eventually disappear as a result of education and the improvement of the living conditions of the general population.[11]

Amateur Groups

In the arts, the most important cultural tool at the local level was the Movimiento de Aficionados (Amateur Artists Movement), which began by opening schools for instructors, who in turn organized amateur artist groups at the local level.[12] The musical groups that belonged to this movement participated in intensive concert activity at both the national and the international level. Amateur activities were controlled by two institutions: Casas de la Cultura (Houses of Culture) and Consejos Populares de Cultura. Amateur activities were also sponsored by mass organizations such as the CTC (Confederation of Cuban Workers) and the CDR (Committees for the Defense of the Revolution). Felipe participated in an amateur group organized by the CTC.

When the revolution arrived they began to take the religious music to the theater. They began to organize the Conjunto Folklórico, but oriented by them. They began to do so because they had something in mind. They knew there was a richness in there. You know, the communists were very smart. Everything they did, they did it with pencil and paper. They knew there was a cultural richness in those traditions that they were not exploiting, and that it had to be exploited, you see? Slowly they began to look for the roots of these traditions in order to teach them; even though Fidel had the religions closed at the time. They first created the amateur groups. That was around—'61 or '62. and around that time the Conjunto Folklórico Nacional also came out. They took the best theaters they had in Havana to present the Conjunto Folklórico there. The strong guy in the Conjunto Folklórico was a guy who was called Furé, who is from Matanzas.[13]

To carry on the work of research, selection and "theatralization" of the Afro-Cuban musical traditions, a modus operandi was designed that consisted of identifying a group of carriers of a particular tradition (e.g., Arará, Lucumí), establishing with its members the necessary rapport, and engaging one or more of them as informants after "overcoming their misgivings and their sense of the secrecy of the tradition" (Guerra 1989: 30–37). At the local level, many of these informants were employed in organizing and training amateur groups that not only performed in local festivities but also participated in nationwide encounters of folkloric groups. Many researchers and musicologists viewed the recruitment of religious practitioners into these amateur groups as a way to incorporate the "real carriers" of these traditions into the "massive diffusion" of these practices to all the population, "despoiled from their ancient religious function" (Vinueza 1988: 56–57).

I worked in one of those amateur groups staging the Santería dances. A guy named Jesús Fernández, who worked as an instructor of folkloric music, came from Havana to Matanzas. He saw us playing and decided to organize a group with us. Because in Matanzas it was very easy to find people who knew the dances, the chants, and who could play. There, you could find everything easily. You had no problem in getting people to do something. They would be dying for an opportunity to dance and play. The group was first called CTC and then the Commerce Group. There were about fifteen people, youngsters most of them. They were people that had a good "notation" and all of that—people from the school and some people from work.

The rest of the group was made up of five percussionists like Felipe, who were familiar with the music of Santería because they either were santeros themselves or came from families where Santería was practiced. They were the ones who taught the other members of the group the dances to the different orichas, contributed to the choreography, and provided the musical accompaniment.

We went to Havana and staged—Eleguá, Ogún, Yemayá, Changó, Obatalá—different dances. We went to present it at that theater that is facing the Capitol. Moreover, there we met, well, I already had met Benny Moré, but there I was able to embrace him.[14]

Organizing a Professional Folkloric Ensemble

Notwithstanding the problems that arose from centralized cultural policies and state-controlled cultural institutions, the socialist state created in Cuba a stable cultural infrastructure, which allowed musicians like Felipe to earn a living exclusively from music and entitled them to benefits hitherto unavailable. When the empresa Felipe worked for was dissolved, he was able to organize his own group and get it approved by the local cultural authorities in Matanzas, although he had refused an offer to become a party member and was known by everyone in Matanzas as a practicing palero and santero. Moreover, he became the leader (therefore entitled to better pay) of his group even though he did not comply with the literacy requirements that many considered important to advancement in the music field, especially in the case of the conductor or director of an ensemble. Literacy requirements, although considered an ideal to strive for, were not imposed on popular and folkloric musicians like Felipe (Robbins 1991: 243).

This group, Emikeké, was active until Felipe left Cuba for the United States in 1980, and it became in the 1970s one of the most prestigious folkloric ensembles in Matanzas.[15] When Felipe left, the group dissolved, and many of its members joined other folkloric groups in Cuba, such as the famous Muñequitos de Matanzas, the Conjunto Folklórico Nacional, and Afro-Cuba.[16]

I began to organize Emikeké because I didn't belong to any group but was getting paid as a plantilla musician. One month I would sign the payroll of one group, the next month of another. I knew this situation would not last. So I got together with my friend Cheo, who worked in the union and had the same problem, and we decided to organize a group ourselves. We got the percussionists, Amado, Cundo, Reinaldo . . . and looked for two women dancers. We put together the project, wrote a letter, and had someone type it and send everything to Cultura. They liked the idea because there were other groups in Matanzas that performed rumba and that type of music, but they didn't have a group that would perform all the religious traditions. The group was approved and they gave us some instruments, and some wood to build others. At the beginning, while we got all the instruments, outfits, and everything else ready, we performed popular songs. Then we were able to do the first presentation of the religious music, organized by a man who worked in Cultura named Moline.

That was around 1970. So when I made the group we needed a name. I told the people in Cultura: "The group is going to be called Emikeké." They asked me: "So what does that mean?" I replied: "Man, it means small group, 'cause there are not a lot of people." Before I talked to Cultura I already knew the meaning of the name because Osvaldo, my cousin,[17] had explained it to me: "That name has two meanings. You can say *omi keké* because it is a small water spring; and you can say *emi keké,* which is saying: 'I little', you see?"

Negotiating the Limits of Secrecy

As the leader of Emikeké, Felipe faced problems that arose from the decontextualization of musical traditions that had been, until then, part of religious rituals. A practitioner himself, he had to confront other practitioners (santeros, paleros, and in particular Abakuás) as they defined and sometimes "negotiated" the limits of secrecy, which is at the heart of these religious practices.

According to Felipe, when the cultural institutions of the revolutionary government began to present dances and music of the Afro-Cuban religious rituals in public, the santeros in Matanzas were divided: Older santeros did not approve of these "theatralized" performances, while younger santeros were generally open to the idea.[18] There was also a difference in attitude between the santeros in Havana and the santeros in Matanzas. In Matanzas, santeros tended to be less open and held more strongly to the practice of secrecy.

Because of the nonhierarchical character of Afro-Cuban religious practices, the lack of a codified orthodoxy, and the way in which worship is organized (no central authority but rather individualized and subject to reinterpretation), many groups and individual practitioners found no problem in "opening up" to researchers and participating in the folkloric ensembles. Others, however, kept their doors closed.

Even before the revolution came, the older santeros in Matanzas were against those public performances. There were even two radio stations, Radio Suarito and La Mil Diez, where the owners apparently were believers. So for the feast of La Mercedes, La Caridad, San Lázaro, and Santa Barbara, they would bring drums to the station and give toques for those santos, and you could hear them on the radio. The older santeros were always bothered by that. They didn't like it.

Then the revolution came and they took our things to the theater. Initially santeros didn't look at it favorably, you see? Because they thought that it was like doing profane things. The older santeros were really bothered. Within that group there wasn't a . . . culture, a "consensus," to admit something like that or not. So in those days, these older santeros showed themselves as rebels against opening up. They said: "No! No! How are they going to do that?" Then other people began to develop a consciousness. They realized that with these presentations they were making these traditions international, that their culture was gaining recognition. So they loosened up a little. It was only then that you began to see people with drums hanging from their necks, going up and down the streets, and nobody ran away from them. Before, when something like this happened, people would come out of their houses shouting: "No! No!, No! That's the devil."

. . . At the Folklórico Nacional, many of those people there were santeros. But santeros from Havana, which is different. Look, they never went to the interior searching for santeros, because maybe Furé explained to them the situation in Matanzas. The situation in Matanzas was different from that in Havana. People in Havana are used to being—it's a city and they are easier to convince than the people from the countryside. It's not that in the countryside people are less cultured. In Matanzas there were a lot of good santeros at that time that came out of the university and things like that. But they "carried" their Santería strongly. Because it seems that in each region people are brought up differently. In Matanzas it was never easy to present the religious things in public. But slowly things changed, people began to change their mind. People also had to change because they had to look for a way to survive, and those concerts for people were a job, they were work.

When Felipe decided to organize his group Emikeké, he had to present and defend his position in front of the older santeros.

I told them: "This is not done as Santería, this is done as a didactic thing, to teach our roots. Now I give an example; in a fiesta de santo, not everyone sees what is done inside the room,[19] but everybody can be part of the fiesta, whether they have santo or not. We are all children of santo even if we are not santeros. What we play in a fiesta is music with which we are sending a message to Olofi, to a supreme being in whom we believe, to God, OK? Everybody has the right to participate in that according to the rules of Santería.

"Because what we present in the concerts is dance, and dance can be seen by anyone. You go to a fiesta de santo and you see everybody dancing; you see the drums, you see everything. Now, if you hold a ceremony at the theater—with plants, with animals, with the people, with the required things that are used in the room—then you are profaning. But we are not going to do that. We are only showing or teaching what can be seen."

Many of the older generation of santeros never came to terms with these public performances. However, Felipe's mother gave him her support.

When I started in Cultura it was a job, like many of the other jobs I had. My mother never told me not to do such things. She said to me: "What you should not present are the ceremonies, but the rest—it's your job." And she supported me in that, but not everyone is the same.

Even though there was opposition among paleros and santeros with regard to the performance of their ritual music and dances in public, they were more open than the members of the different Abakúa plantes that were active in Matanzas, because of the more secretive character of these all-male societies. Felipe included some Abakuá music and dances in the first important concert of his group Emikeké. The Conjunto Folklórico Nacional had staged the first public presentation of Abakuá traditions in 1964, organized by Argeliers León. This presentation generated a lot of discontent in the Abakuá juegos—discontent that was manifested by some of the Abakuás after the performance.

When I began to prepare for the Abakuá concert in Matanzas, many of the Abakuá were fuming. People were telling me: "Hey, look, be careful 'cause they are going to kill you." I said: "But to kill me they would have had to kill the people of the Folklórico Nacional first."

The Abakúa went around telling others: "We are going to see what is it that he does, what is he going to say, how and what is he going to present in the theater."

I knew the Abakuá were going to come to see what I was going to present; to check if there was a ceremony, or something that shouldn't be shown. But I was not planning to "do" ceremonies, I was not going to do anything that was secret. It was a—what do you call that?—a concert, a separate concert, not religious and not of a profane character.

Felipe first had to gain the support of the Abakuá group to which he belonged, because he knew they could then help him face any opposition from members of other juegos.

If my juego, as we call it, somehow repressed me, everybody was going to shut me out. But if I had the support of my juego I was not going to have a lot of problems. I had some power in my Abakuá juego. So if the members of other juegos tried to block me, I would block them in my own juego.

My juego supported me when I said what I said. But I had to be careful with the way I said things to them. Because you see, I was the one that sewed and made all the ritual outfits for my juego. I didn't want them to think that I was trying to get away with something in exchange for the work I did for them. I began with a story that what the whole thing is all about is playing, singing, saying a prayer, and that's that. Singing and playing and saying a prayer there in the plante is seen by women and is seen by everyone. Because when you do a plante, everyone comes in because it's a public celebration. You can't tell anybody not to come in. If you feel like coming in, you can come in. You even see tourists nowadays there taking shots. But no one can come into the room where we have the secrets. So I was not going to do anything of what is done inside the room, I was going to present only what is done outside.[20]

"You all have to decide and tell me if it's right or wrong. Anyway, I have to tell you that I think this is right. That if you are going to repress me somehow, I want you to know that I do it because it's my job. Performing music is how I look for the everyday bread for my children; not only the food for my children but the support of the things of my religion. If I don't earn money, how would I pay here the quotas in the Abakuá society? How would I give a religious fiesta? I am going to do it, and I'm making it clear here that I'm not going to profane it. I'm not going to do any of the profound Abakuá or Santería ceremonies in public or anything." And my Abakuá group understood.

Another of the arguments Felipe used to support his position was that of using these performances as a means of educating the public, which in its way served to defend the Abakuá from the widespread prejudices against ñáñigos in Cuba that prevailed both before and after the revolution. During the whole history of these societies in Cuba, they have been discriminated against and persecuted more than other Afro-Cuban religious practices. This continued to be the case during the first decades of the revolution, when these societies were considered the site of criminal and antirevolutionary activity.

People used to say that the Abakuás were drunkards, and murderers, and *criminals*. Things were also tough for the Abakuá because the Abakuá have the reputation that they never talk, they protect each other. So after the revolution, when they stopped people in the street or took them to prison, they would immediately begin asking: "Are you an Abakuá? Because we know you guys don't talk, but here you are going to talk." Thank God I was never stopped, because there was a black guard in the prison in Matanzas, whom they used to call "the asthmatic," that was something else. He used to hit people with chains.

So I explained to my Abakuá juego that what I would do with the concerts was to teach people who we really were. The culture of the Abakuá, the culture of our religion, is what I would teach. I would not show in a public performance how we are sworn into the society, nor how we initiate a new member or give a rank to someone. I would teach just dance and music. I would use only the accessories and objects that come out to the living room [the public room]. What is seen by anybody that goes to the public fiesta. The three canes: the one that has the figure of a goat on top, and the others with the moon and the sun. So people can be told and learn what they represent. They represent justice. One is the district attorney, the other the judge and the other the lawyer. The defense attorney is the moon. The goat, that is the district attorney, and the sun is the judge. And the big crown with the feathers represents the church, and the priests, you see?

And there is a drum for calling to order—when that drum passes in front of where the men are, if they are wearing a hat they have to take it off. Because it's an instrument of order. They can be very upset, so much so that they want to kill each other, but if they are Abakuá and they are fighting and that instrument arrives and they play it and say: "This is finished now!" Then, not a word is said. Even the bullies, the bullies do it, they shut up; because they took an oath on that drum. That drum is the empegó, that's how they call it, it's a drum that represents order, it's a "work of order." The fiesta begins with it and the fiesta ends with it. And so, if you don't say that to the public, the public thinks that the canes are there for when a "tragedy" forms, to take those sticks and hit someone on the head and kill him, you see? And that's not like that.

So it was done that way. It got really good, because it was in a hall of the society of physicians that was called the Sala White, Fidel named it that way. In that hall it's not like you can just present anything, because it's a luxurious hall and concerts by great pianists and big shows were presented there. When we finished the presentation and I went out everybody was very happy: "That was right because you were letting people know. They say that we ñáñigos, that we eat people, that we take the children away, and you were telling people that it was not like that."

· · ·

One wonders if the "reinterpretation" of their religious practices and the negotiation and debates on the limits of secrecy that practitioners like Felipe undertook would have taken place if the pressure to make a living and the opportunity to resolve this matter by becoming a cultural worker in the folkloric ensembles that staged the musical traditions of his religion had not existed. However, santeros have always been flexible and ready to adapt their traditions to the ever-changing circumstances of their environment, a strategy that has allowed them to survive, as a subcultural group, the numerous struggles with the hegemonic forces that have controlled the country in which they lived—first the Spanish, then the powerful white creoles who declared independence and organized the republic, then the occupying forces of the United States, and finally the revolutionary forces that established the socialist state.

Performing Other Afro-Cuban Secular and Sacred Drumming Styles

Emikeké, like other folkloric groups in Cuba, gave demonstrations and performed many of the sacred and secular Afro-Cuban styles of drumming, dances, songs, and chants. Secular genres such as the rumba were a must. However, other, less well known secular genres of Congo origin linked to the religious group known in Cuba as paleros—makuta, yuka, and maní—were also included in the repertoire. The group also performed religious genres that Felipe was familiar with before the revolution: Arará and Iyesá.

Although Felipe had never played arará and iyesá in a religious context, he was familiar with these styles of drumming and with the religious practices that were at their basis. The cabildo of Felipe's family had strong links with the only surviving Iyesá cabildo in Matanzas. Felipe had also participated in numerous Arará ceremonies after the Arará from the city of Matanzas opened the doors to the Lucumí. However, though this was the case with most of the members of Emikeké, the same did not apply to many of the folkloric ensembles organized after the revolution. Many of these ensembles included people who had no link to the Afro-Cuban religious practices or who had connections with only one of them yet had to perform the music and dances of all the other reglas. Many of these performers were trained in professional schools, outside the traditional system of apprenticeship that is tightly linked to the context of religious ceremonies and rituals. In these schools, the musical aspects of the traditions were taught without any reference to the system of religious beliefs that was at their basis.

I'm a *batalero,* and before the revolution I didn't play arará or iyesá for rituals. Even though I knew how to play arará and iyesá, I did not play in their rituals because I was not part of those cabildos. There were other drummers who played with them, but not me. Still, I could play arará and iyesá for a concert of Cultura.[21] If I had to play with any arará, they would let me play because I knew what I was doing. I was aware of what I was about to play. In my group we played iyesá and we also played arará. I knew those rhythms from having heard them so many times, so I used my ear. Because I have a special ear, and I played. Because you see I'm a musician—a musicologist, ha! ha! ha!

And they used to bring me "special" people, so that I would give demonstrations of batá, and demonstrations of arará and rumba. And we had to do the cycles you see? The iyesá, the arará, the batá cycles. They brought people from Africa who also went to Havana, and they compared what they heard in Havana with what was played in Matanzas. They used to say that the "stuff" in Matanzas was stronger, that it looked more original.

Like many other revolutionary policies, strategies, and processes, the process of selecting and presenting on stage the musical traditions of the Afro-Cuban religions, or reglas, has undergone many changes during the lifetime of the revolution. In the initial period, the musical groups had many members who either were practitioners of or had close links to the Afro-Cuban religious practices. During this period a separate group of performers was used to stage the music of each regla: one for Santería, another for the Arará, and so forth. In time, many of the members of these folkloric groups were coming from the performing schools that had been opened after the revolution and had no personal links to the religious practices. The groups became less specialized and were expected to perform all the Afro-Cuban musical traditions, sometimes within the same concert.

Argeliers León, credited for the institutionalization of these staged versions of the Afro-Cuban religious rituals, considered the early performances of the 1960s "authentic presentations" of the traditions; performers were believers deeply involved in the religions. In contrast, he viewed the presentations of later decades primarily as entertainment and spectacle (Hagedorn 1995: 234–36).

With stage exposure inevitably comes aestheticization. Afro-Cuban religious practices become material for artistic (re)creation and (re)interpretation. Dissociated from their ritual and religious contexts, these traditions are decontextualized, secularized, and simplified to meet the demands of the theater. Secrecy and mystery are lost to glamor and technical perfection. The music and dance of these traditions now are learned in performing schools with hardly any reference to the religious world they belong to.

Performing Afro-Cuban Religious Music in Private Ritual Contexts

The position of the Cuban government on religion in general (be it Afro-Cuban, Catholic, Protestant, or Jewish) has evolved through a series of stages characterized by attitudes and approaches that range from hostility to accommodation and acceptance, a mixture of tolerance with "selective repression and control" (Eckstein 1994: 25).

With the triumph of the revolution, numerous performances of Afro-Cuban music (including religious music) were featured throughout the country in festivals that were organized to "pay homage to the revolutionary army." Performances such as the one organized at the plaza of Havana's cathedral, under the title "The Voice That Was Not Silenced," and a concert organized at the National Theater by Argeliers León are just two examples of the numerous performances of Afro-Cuban music that followed the revolution (CCS 1982:164–65). Felipe participated in one such festival organized by Lázaro Peña, who had been an important leader of the labor movement in Cuba before the revolution and was the founder of the CTC. Peña, who was a member of the Communist Party before 1959, was one of the few blacks to occupy a high position of leadership during the early years of the revolution. He was also an initiated santero and belonged to the house of Arcadio, a well-known santero from Guanabacoa.

Like a year after Batista fell, a great *egbó* was held, authorized by the government. Lázaro Peña was the one who authorized it. That big fiesta that was celebrated in Guanabacoa's stadium. The stadium was one of the headquarters, but the main headquarters was the cemetery. The government gave horses to march through the streets, they gave everything. It was to celebrate a mass for all of those who had died in the revolution and it was called the Great Egbó. There were sheep, goats, and such walking through the street in costume, with their *manteles* [decorated aprons], and those white horses. . . . The drummers from my house went to play in the Great Egbó. We were there with all the cabildos that played. We also played in the house of Arcadio, that was called the house of the brujo of Guanabacoa, that was the society of Saint Anthony.[22]

After the initial enthusiasm, a period of consolidation of the revolution followed in which, as occurred in the cultural field, the government took the position that any activity considered to be opposed to the revolution would be banned—or persecuted. The government's relations with the various religious communities during this period were tense, and in some cases hostile. Afro-Cuban religious practices were discouraged, when not explicitly forbidden. Many Afro-Cuban house-temples and the Abakuá secret societies were accused of being the focus of antirevolutionary activities. Consequently, the meetings of these types of groups initially were banned and later were subjected to approval of the local authorities (Barnet 1988: 5–7).

When the revolution arrived everything closed. Afterward they formed a bureau, at least in Matanzas, but before the bureau everything was closed. You know we couldn't play, santos couldn't be made, Abakuá was not planted, nothing. We did some Santería and Palo, but in hiding, you understand? Because we even had children do santo secretly.

It was worse with the Abakuá. When Fidel arrived, all our things, all the "furnishings" that we had, got ruined; we couldn't function for about four years. We had everything locked in a room.

Later, the party had to call people. They would give you a small paper summoning you to the Ministry of the Interior: "Present yourself at the Ministry of the Interior," without excuse or pretext. When you went to the Ministry of the Interior they would talk to you: "We know that you are a santero." "Yes." "And why don't you have any fiestas?" "Because you don't give the permits." "Well, you know you can't 'make' [initiate] children, you can't make this and that. We are going to make a bureau." Then they began to ask for pictures, and everybody began bringing the pictures and they began giving the permits, you see?[23]

You had to get your permit thirty days in advance and tell them what things you were going to do and what santo you were going to make—and, and bring a picture of the person who was making *santo*. You had to tell them how many chickens you were going to kill, how many roosters you were going to kill, how many people were coming to the house. The problem was that they didn't want any meetings in the houses. So they asked a lot of questions. They would interrogate the person I was going to initiate in front of me. They would ask: "Is he intimidating you or what? How much is he charging you for this? Why are you going to make santo?" and so on. Then they would continue: "Look, think it over well because if you make santo right now then you won't be able to belong to any of the institutions of the revolution." Even when people insisted: "I am not interested in belonging to any revolutionary institution. I want to do santo because it's my tradition," they would continue asking them garbage.

During this period, members of any religious group were barred from the Communist Party. Religious affiliation could also hinder occupational advancement and jeopardize admission to university programs and selective high schools (Rabkin 1991: 189). Therefore, it was not infrequent that santeros would hold ceremonies and initiate youngsters without authorization.

We made one or two santos with permission and two or three without permission, those were the youngsters; because you couldn't initiate youngsters. They had to be adults, because they said that if a youngster then wanted to join the party tomorrow, he wouldn't be able to do so.

According to Felipe, in some house-temples, because of their connections to members of the party, unauthorized ceremonies were more the rule than the exception.

At that stage, there was place where they played without permission, it was in the house of Arcadio.[24] That happened while Lázaro Peña was alive. Lázaro Peña was a compadre of Arcadio and he had made Obatalá—and that's why he didn't tighten a lot the business of the Santería in Havana. Because Lázaro belonged to the house of Arcadio. A big picture of him was placed there at the entrance. Lázaro Peña was black, you know? He was the one who made all those [labor] laws that Fidel has. There were also other people that were with Fidel in the *sierra,* that people say they were *brujeros.* There was one called el Gran Ple, that guy walked around the sierra without shoes or nothing, and he was one of the ones who helped Fidel.

When Felipe organized Emikeké, he was also doing volunteer work administering a dining facility for the party in Matanzas. He was then asked to become a member of the party.

To me they [the party]—three, four, six times—they called me. At that time I was working in Cultura and I also attended a diner that belonged to them. I did that voluntarily, outside of my regular job. I worked so many hours, and my behavior with people was good. So they called me. It was as though they wanted to promote me, you know? They didn't ask me anything about the religion, I was the one who was supposed to tell them. Because after the interview follows an investigation. The first time I just answered: "No, no, I can't belong."

Another time they called me and told me: "Well, we are going to have a meeting and you are going to explain to us the reason why you don't want to belong." It was then I finally had to say: "Look, I don't want to deceive you because I do work here, but me, I don't like politics." I said I didn't like politics so I wouldn't have to say I didn't like communism. Then I went on: "I know you are going to tell me it doesn't matter that I am religious, because you think I don't go to the rituals anymore, that I have renounced that already." It is true that at that time I had so much work that they could very well think I had no time to go to rituals; but I always found the time. I always went to my house when they were playing, I would go to an Abakuá plante, I would go to a rumba; I went wherever I wanted.

Finally I had to tell them: "I'm not going to change what I've known all my life for something I don't know. I'm not going to leave my religion now, because tomorrow you are going to reproach me for that yourselves. You see, the revolution arrived in '59 and I was born in '31, under that thing that now you say doesn't exist of Santería, of brujería [witchcraft], of Abakuá, and all of that. That is what I was born seeing and this [communism] is new for me. My religion is old for me and your thing is new. Put yourself in my position. It is as if you were now to renounce your thing to go into mine, which you don't know anything about. It's a new thing for you, no? So I don't understand why I have to renounce. My feelings tell me not to do it, because tomorrow, in the same way that I'm betraying my religion, I'm going to betray you, and I don't want to be a traitor either to my religion or to you; for that reason I can't join the party."

They didn't want religious people in the party. But there were many people who were religious, so they would lie: "No, no, no I threw everything away." Because for them to be able to be accepted as members of the party they had to take all the religious things and throw them away. So what many santeros did was to pick up stones anywhere and throw those away, pretending they were the sacred stones from the soperas.

To the religious individual, the interest or support the government showed toward the artistic manifestations of the Afro-Cuban religions meant little: Many party members still viewed the religious beliefs themselves as subcultures that belonged to a legacy of ignorance and underdevelopment that would be overcome with socialism. Prohibition (in subtle and not so subtle disguises), exclusion (from employment, from membership in the party, etc.), and prejudice forced many santeros to clandestine practice, yet the number of initiates continued to grow.

I would see people from the party making santo in hiding, they were making santo. I *saaaaw* it! Because we were into that and we used to play for the ceremonies. When I played, I played all over the place. If I had an important tambor, I would go to the doctor and have him give me a certificate saying I was sick. Then I would drop work and go to the toque. In one of those toques, in a place that is called the Nave de Marianao, all the people that were presented to the drums had the "red card" [party ID card]. They all made santo and then they were all in that room, like thirty or forty people. When we began to play the oro the madrina [godmother] told us: "Play just one chant gentlemen, only one chant that this people are in a hurry." Then the big cars arriving and all of them getting in and leaving.

They had to hide the fact that they were initiated so they didn't use the beads.[25] Also when they made santo—instead of shaving all their hair, they would do a crown. Others came up with the story that "I got lice, so I had to shave my hair." They had to wait and take their leaves from work for seven days in order to make the santo, but they did it.

In the 1970s a more conciliatory tone characterized the pronouncements of the government on religion, as when the Cuban Educational and Cultural Congress declared religion to be a private matter, outside the purview of the state. In 1976 the constitution guaranteed the freedom to profess any religious belief. During this decade, the oppositional attitude of the government toward Afro-Cuban religion relaxed, and these practices became officially tolerated. Other, parallel and connected actions make this the "African decade": During this period Cuba intensified military and economic involvement with liberation movements in Africa, and cultural exchange between Africa and Cuba— which Castro now defined as an Afro-Latin nation—followed suit.

Developments such as a renewed interest in all things African that the troops returning from Africa brought home,[26] increased numbers of African students educated in Cuba's educational institutions, and numerous cultural and political exchanges between Cuba and the nations of Africa definitively contributed to the process of "Africanization," or "re-Africanization," of the cultural and religious traditions of Cuba's black population and helped integrate Cuba culturally into the "global" Pan-Africanist discourse of the diaspora. A logical offshoot of this was the growing discourse on return to the "roots," Africa as a motherland, and reinterpretation of the Afro-Cuban religious heritage, a discourse that has been gaining strength since the 1980s.[27]

After Felipe left Cuba in 1980, a radical change took place in the relations between the government and the Catholic and Protestant churches, paralleled by a similar rapprochement with practitioners of the Afro-Cuban religions. An Office of Religious Affairs, attached to the Central Committee of the Communist Party, was established in 1984, and an Afro-Cuban scholar, Jose Carneado Rodriguez, was called to head it. Wide exposure was given to Afro-Cuban religious practices in the media, and Carneado not only organized meetings with several babalaos but officially invited to Cuba the Yoruba leader the Ooni of the Ifé, Alaiyeluwa Oba Okunade Sijuwade Olubuse II, who visited the country in 1986 and met with top-ranking government officials.[28] Also during the 1980s, the first institutionalized group of Afro-Cuban priests came into existence when several babalaos created a cultural religious group called Ifá Yesterday, Ifá Today, Ifá Tomorrow (*Granma International,* February 28, 1988).

These days in Cuba the lads are making Abakuá, are becoming paleros and are making—everything. Because now they accept it; now . . . it doesn't matter if I'm a palero, or if I'm whatever. This is now with the new constitution that Fidel made. A barefaced that Fidel, ha! ha! ha! It is because he knows that santeros have a power, that there are many of them, so he decided to let them in.

The process of rapprochement between the socialist state and the various religious groups in Cuba was institutionalized in 1991, when the Fourth Party Congress of the Cuban Communist Party approved the motion that religious membership of any kind should be no bar to party membership. In 1992 the Cuban Constitution was reformed, declaring the country a secular rather than an atheist state (Bunck 1994: 60, 86). An important event in the 1990s that signaled the state's decreasing opposition to religion was Pope John Paul II's visit to Cuba in January 1998, more than a decade after the visit of the Yoruba Ooni of the Ifé.

The 1990s have also been an important and active decade for the official and public status of the Afro-Cuban religions. In 1992 the Fourth International Congress of Orisha Tradition and Culture took place in Havana, organized by the Yoruba Cultural Association of Cuba. Delegates from the United States, Puerto Rico, Benin, and Nigeria joined Cuban "believers, religious leaders, dignitaries, practitioners, ethnologists and socio-religious researchers, most of them from the Academy of Sciences of Cuba," in discussions and conferences. Guided visits to the museums of Regla, Guanabacoa, and the Africa House and a drum ceremony dedicated to Changó were part of the event (García 1992). The 1990s also saw the publication in Cuba of scholarly works on Afro-Cuban religions and culture and new editions of the works of Ortíz. A series of books on the orichas, divination systems, and Afro-Cuban cuisine were written by Natalia Bolívar, an active member in the cultural institutions of the revolution since the 1960s, who provided in these books answers to many questions that were frequently posed to playwrights and cultural workers when they featured these traditions on stage or in their work (Colina 1991).

In the "transformed" official atmosphere, it is interesting to note the contrast between the noninstitutionalized way in which ritual families like Felipe's continue to practice their religion and the more "literate," written, intellectualized, and institutionalized practices of people who have links to the government or to cultural and educational institutions. One begins to witness developments such as officially recognized organizations of babalaos (a concept foreign to Santería in Cuba until recently, and one that introduces the idea of hierarchy and, to some extent, orthodoxy) that the government chooses for meetings with spiritual leaders from Nigeria, and meetings of practitioners, scholars, and researchers to debate religious issues in public forums. One such meeting, the Yoruba conference of 1992, was labeled by the official newspaper of the party in Cuba to be a "milestone in the relationship between scientists and believers." According to Aníbal Argüelles, a specialist in religion at the Academy of Science of Cuba, believers "need researchers in order to discover their roots" (García 1992). While Felipe and his family have never considered themselves anything but santeros and continue to refer to the deities they worship using Lucumí names and names of Catholic saints alternately, without any uneasiness or qualms about issues such as syncretism and purity, the major cause of disagreement at the Yoruba conference was the refusal of many believers to accept terms like *Santería* and *syncretism* to refer to the "Yoruba religion" ("Lucumí is a term of the past") (García 1992).[29]

Searching for Alternatives: Becoming a Craftsman of Religious Objects

After four years of inactivity, the ritual objects of the Abakuá group Felipe belonged to had deteriorated, some to the point of being unusable. When the group started meeting again in the late 1960s, Felipe decided to reconstitute all the ritual paraphernalia of his juego. In the process, he gained experience and a reputation among other Abakuá groups, who began to call him to do similar artisan work for them.

Earlier in his life, Felipe had developed his artisan skills by crafting ritual objects for his casa de ocha and had been taught by his father how to craft many of the ritual objects used by paleros. Felipe had kept this activity private and free of charge. During the revolution, however, he started earning money by manufacturing ritual objects for people outside his ritual family circle, an activity that would become extremely important as a source of income when he emigrated to the United States.

I earned more in my house than what I earned in "culture," you see? I began making crafts—and so I lived better. They were things I did with my own hands, they are artisan's things.

At the beginning I didn't sell them. I used to do them for my house, for the drums. I kept the drums beautiful—I began to work during the revolution objects for Abakuá: clothes, muñones [staff decorated with feathers]; covering *eribós,* hats; decorating things for people. Fixing the outfits of the dignitaries. I would have to take a piece from an old one—because no more material could be found; inventing, making another from little pieces of fabric, patches that I found—I charged, but not a lot. I didn't do many other things because there were no beads available during those days; there was nothing.

It all began when the Abakuá began to move again, giving meetings, and all the rest. I went and collected all the things of our juego that were ruined and began to do them all over again. I hadn't done that before, never had I done it—not the objects with feathers or the like. I began working—I would pick up one of the objects and I would loosen it all. After I had loosened it, I: "How do I fix this? Ha! Ha! Ha!" Me inside of myself: "How do I fix this?" And I went over there to the house. At that time we had bought some fabric, and I took a piece and I began. I went to the house of my old lady and I closed myself in a room there: *tin tin tin tin tin.* The following week we gave a meeting and I took one of the pieces. Then I began taking all the outfits with me. I began cutting, and throwing a piece there, and I made all new outfits and things.

I would invent. From small pieces of fabric I began sewing, I began sewing and I made sixteen outfits. We had set a quota of fifty *pesos.* So when I laid down my fifty pesos they told me: "No, you don't have to lay down anything because you are working for us." I replied: "No, this—fixing the outfits, et cetera—I'm doing for free. Because I want the spirit of my father and my uncle to see their things again as they used to be." And it really became a reality. We gave a big fiesta, a big fiesta with food and everything. We gave away beer and fine sweets for the kids. Then everyone began to look for me to fix their ritual objects, so I did the same for all the other juegos; but this time I charged them.

There was a guy called Mario, who was the only one that did Abakuá things. He began calling me to go out with him to work Abakuá around, because he said that I was a very spiritual person for the Abakuá, that I had—that I knew how to work. You see, I'm an Abakuá, and for me any other juego is like my own. If they have money I can do the things for them; but if they don't I do them all the same.

I would never finish telling you about the Abakuá outfits that I made for the presentation of our group. I couldn't sell them or give them away. The tourists, when they arrived in Varadero, wanted to buy them anyway. They snatched them—"Take it off! Give it to me! How much do you want? Take it off that I'll buy it. Whatever you want, dollars, whatever you want there. How much is it?" But I couldn't give it to them because, how was I supposed to turn back without the outfits to give another presentation? Also at that time I didn't have the mentality that I have now. Now I would have made outfits for the pleasure of it, and I would have them there just in case. I wasn't thinking—you always have it in your mind to try and live a little bit better but, I wasn't thinking. And also I felt repressed by what could happen, you see? That they could send me to prison—or something like that.

In the foregoing narrative, one sees the beginning of a process of commodification. Although at this time Felipe could not sell his creations without running into trouble, later many stores in Cuba began to sell these type of "crafts" to tourists. Commodification of Afro-Cuban culture was not strong while Felipe still lived in Matanzas; it developed later, when the country began to rely on tourism as one of the main sources of hard currency. Culture in general—in which music, musical instruments, literature, cinema, and visual arts were included—began to be viewed as a source not only of internal revenues but of foreign revenues (PPCC 1986: 60).[30]

Although Felipe's group Emikeké went to resorts such as Varadero to perform during the tourist season and gave percussion and dance lessons to tourists, it was only after Felipe left Cuba that government-sponsored workshops were organized to offer foreigners courses in religious and secular Afro-Cuban music.[31]

Crafting a Bembé Drum: "Manufacturing" Material Culture to Obey the Orichas

Drums have been part of Felipe's life since he was just a child; they have connected him to ancestral powers and given him a sense of identity, a trade, and a way of life. Drums have shaped Felipe's experiences in many ways, and in this process they have also become the expression of Felipe's personal and cultural practices. Drums have contributed to shape Felipe's sense of identity and have played an important role in his reconstruction or re-creation of this identity. As the world changes around him, Felipe's strategy to give a meaning to his life has always been channeled through the drums—building them, playing them, fixing them, summoning his deities and spirits with them, teaching others to play them. As Felipe himself tells us, drums have not only given him life but have been "life itself."

In his building of drums since the revolution, Felipe has obeyed two imperatives: On the one hand, he has built drums as part of his job as a "cultural worker," drums that are to be played in secular contexts and that, although physically similar to those used in ritual contexts, do not have the power to talk to the spirits; on the other hand, he has obeyed the commands of the orichas (his mother's Oyá), who during this period asked him to build a bembé drum. Building this drum also created the opportunity to reconstruct the cabildo of Saint Teresa at the house of Tomasa; when the drums were finished, rules were drawn up, fees for playing the drums were fixed, and membership was regulated in a way that resembled the practices of the old cabildos.

Bembé drums belong to one of the music ensembles the Lucumís originally used. In Cuba the ensemble is made up of three drums, an *acheré* (rattle), and a guataca (metal hoe blade).[32] The morphology of the drums has changed with time: older drums were cylindrical, while more recent ones tend to be slightly barrel-shaped. According to the wood available to the instrument maker, they may be hollowed from a single log or built using staves. The skin of each of these single-headed drums is either nailed to the drum or attached through a series of cords, which are tensioned through the use of wedges. The drums are played by striking with wooden sticks or using a stick and the bare hand (*a mano limpia*). The largest drum (lowest in pitch) is called *caja* or *llamador,* the second (medium pitch) *segundo,* and the smallest (high pitch) *salidor.* These drums are not sacred and do not require special rituals in their construction. They are freely decorated, and when used for performance they also bear a *maribó* or *mariwó,* a skirt made of coconut palm or raffia that is placed around the upper rim of the drum. The occasions in which they are used, even though not strictly sacred, are linked to the religious practices of Santería, mainly fiestas organized to entertain the orichas and for the amusement of the group.

Felipe considers the bembé drums "free" instruments, which means they can be used for many types of celebrations and may be dedicated to any oricha. Therefore, when a non-initiated person decides to offer a tribute to the orichas, he or she may hire a bembé ensemble for the occasion. Bembé ensembles are also hired for cleansing rituals.

My mother's santo asked me to make a big drum. I didn't have wood, but the wood just appeared one day that I went with one of my cousins to the monte to look for plants to make his throne. Anyway the monte was almost there, two or three blocks away. There I found the wood. Well, it was a lot of work, because I had no saw or nothing. I had to look for a piece of saw there, to cut it. It was a big log! Then I knew this blanco [white man], who used to take me to the toques in his car; so I spoke to him to take me to pick up the wood.

We used to have bembé drums in our house. But like everything else, life kept evolving. People left, one left to work here and the other there, leaving the drums behind. The drums began to "take water," the skin broke, the wood rotted, they came apart. Drums that the ancestors had left. God knows who made them. I saw them there—like three or four drums—I saw them. But I made a bigger one, I made it a little bit bigger. Because I had already seen the bembés that were playing around in Matanzas, the one of Pucho and others. I decided: "I'm going to make a drum that is more modern." Of the drums I saw, one was too wide and it sounded funny. I used to say it was a barrel of lard. So I made a thinner structure and then I used five "keys" [tuning pegs]. But you can't see them because the skin is on the outside and covers them. That drum has its maribó and its bells. After the drum was made, I painted it the way I liked it and then we began forming a society with the drum. We did the ceremony for the drums, and whatnot.

Then I made some sacks, some covers to keep the drum always clean.

And there I got the idea, I started and I had about nine metal *marugas* [rattles], with their ribbons. And so I made a flag of patches, a flag for Ochosi, a flag for Eleguá, a flag for Ogún, and—I made nine flags of different colors, plus the flag of patches that is the one of Oyá, because the drum was being offered to Oyá, who was the one who asked me to make it. So I had a figure of Saint Teresa made, and I had a Saint Teresa painted on a banner.

We organized then a society—a cabildo. We began to do the things we believed should be done. We thought that drum had to be played first for all the *ahijados* [godchildren] of the house, before being played for people outside. We made bylaws. For example: You were going to have a fiesta and you didn't have money. We took money we had made with the drums and we had the sweets and all the other things that were needed, made for you. This was done, if you belonged to the cabildo. You didn't have to pay any fees, only support the cabildo. When the thing began, none of the drummers charged nothing for themselves, so the money made playing remained there. We fixed a fee of fifty-nine pesos, to charge for playing in other houses. We agreed on that; then we named a director, an administrator, a secretary. We made a big deal, as if it was a political party or something like that. That was good, because the organization worked out well; respect was not missing and a lot of attention was paid to the drum and everything.

So Cultura had a newspaper, and I had worked on that newspaper. Some people from the newspaper—a sculptor—went to see a toque at my house, the house of my mother. That man went and was really enthusiastic about what he saw. Then he went and spoke to another one called Moliné,[33] that Moliné is a folklore researcher. Moliné wanted me to give him a chance to see what it was all about. I said: "Well, but there's no fiesta right now." And he said: "No, no, we'll have the fiesta. I'm going to give Saint Teresa two hundred pesos in flowers." They made a decoration with flowers, they brought in flowerpots; a lot, a lot of flowers. So I said: "We are going to play to her." And we played there like nobody else plays! And so it came out in the newspaper of Cultura that at present the best group—that what else and whatnot. . . .

Those drums really had a reputation, they were called the *rebullones* [a type of bird]. At that time they were showing a soap opera from South America on the TV. And there was a woman who was a witch and used these birds when she wanted to do her things. So people began to call our drums the rebullones, like the birds in the soap opera. At the beginning my mother didn't like people giving that name to the drums; then she realized that rebullones was the name given the type of birds called in Cuba *tocoloros,* the birds of Oyá. So she finally accepted the name.

The skills Felipe gained during the revolution while organizing a group to perform Afro-Cuban traditions in the theater would prove extremely valuable for him as a diasporic musician in New York City. Furthermore, his parallel trade as a craftsman of religious ritual objects would constitute one of his main sources of income as an immigrant.

• • •

Afro-Cuban traditions had been an object of reflection for the Cuban intelligentsia since the 1920s, as they sought to define Cuban identity as a creole mixture of Spanish and African elements. During this period, a movement that came to be known as *afrocubanismo* developed within the urban Cuban intellectual circles—among painters (Wilfredo Lam), writers (Alejo Carpentier, Nicolás Guillén), musicians (Alejandro García Caturla, Amadeo Roldán)—bringing many to study seriously Afro-Cuban religion and music. This group re-evaluated Afro-Cuban culture, recognizing the significant role it played in the formation of Cuban creole culture. However, this consciousness and re-evaluation did not touch Afro-Cubans like Felipe. While it inspired many artists to incorporate Afro-Cuban culture into their creative work, the movement remained limited to the intelligentsia in its effort to re-evaluate the contribution of Africans and their descendants in the process of forging a national identity.

In contrast, as a consequence of their activity as cultural workers, as informants and performers in the numerous folkloric ensembles organized after the revolution, people like Felipe began to reflect on their religious practices, their music, their everyday life. Their cultural practices become objects of reflection, "texts" that had to be explained to others. In this process, issues such as authority, authenticity, the limits of secrecy, lineages of drums began to be explored, debated, and redefined.

However, the activities of Felipe as a cultural worker, like those of many Afro-Cubans, were limited to those of an informant and performer. Management, control, selection, assessment, and judgment remained in the hands of others (government officials, musicologists, ethnographers, scholars, intellectuals). Before the revolution, cultural practices (or traditions) for Felipe were just the way things had been done in his family since he was a child. Then, as a cultural worker, he became "ethnically aware." It is ironic that Felipe's ethnic awareness comes as a result of cultural policies implemented by the Cuban government not in order to recognize ethnic diversity but to define a unified national identity in what was officially viewed as a "mono-ethnic," "multiracial" country (Eli Rodríguez 1994: 95).

· · ·

The full impact of the theatralization and secularization of the music of the Afro-Cuban religious traditions is yet to be assessed.[34] This raises a number of major topics for future study.

The groups or practitioners chosen by researchers or cultural officials to take part in the folkloric ensembles and agree to open up are those who get wide exposure (on stage, on tours, and in recordings). Those who choose to defend secrecy are excluded. Thus, certain styles and repertoires become more visible, hegemonic, and in some ways canonical. Another avenue by which the canonization of a particular style operates is written and transcribed versions of chants and dance movements, published in books that are used as study guides by the art instructors of the Casas de la Cultura. The dances and chants included in these books tend to become "standards" in a tradition that has been predominantly oral.

Also at issue is how the tradition will be affected by the training of performers in professional art schools. Many such performers have no to ties and little knowledge of the religious beliefs at the root of the musical traditions they perform, having been divorced from the traditional system of apprenticeship, which was tightly linked to religious ceremonies and rituals.

The process of theatralization and secularization also has repercussions for the secrecy that traditionally has surrounded many of the rituals and their music. While a large number of chants for the orichas are performed in the portion of the rituals open to the public, some chants accompany ritual activities that the uninitiated are not supposed to witness. This is the case, for example, with many of the chants to the oricha of herbs and plants, Osain, whose chants are sung during initiation ceremonies; santeros feel they are not to be performed in public. However, as nonreligious performers learn the chants and begin circulating them, they become part of a repertoire which is then performed in the theater. Even if this does not affect chants as music, it definitely affects their meaning. Further, it violates the secrecy and privacy important to those for whom these chants are not only music but a channel of communication with their gods and ancestors, to be performed only to accompany certain ritual gestures.

In adapting it for the stage, stylization and constraints are imposed on the Afro-Cuban musical repertoire. The theatralization of folklore implies aesthetic choices, which are now left in the hands of choreographers and musicians who decide how to offer an artistically stylized performance of the traditions. Furthermore, the stage imposes a series of spatio-temporal constraints that affect the dances and music to be performed. For instance, repetition, an essential element in ritual participative music, is not effective in stage performances; tempos are modified in order to create climaxes, and generally, changes are made to adjust to the rapport the performer has with the audience, which is fundamentally different from that of the celebrant and the practitioner.

Elements of tempo with regard to batá playing are particularly vulnerable. Even though the drums accompany dance and follow the movements of the dancers in many of the religious ceremonies, there are also ritual contexts in which the drums play alone and address the orichas. Not only do the drums talk to the orichas, but they establish a dialogue among them. This influences the tempo at which certain rhythms are performed, because one has to be able to hear the different "conversations" being carried on among the drums. In such a dialogue, tempos tend to be slower than when the drums are only accompanying a dance. Stage performances, however, tend to impose a style of drumming with faster tempos. As these stage performances become widespread, they may impose a particular style and may even affect ritual performance practice.

Many members of the professional stage ensembles are santeros themselves, and their numbers have increased since the party lifted the ban that excluded them from its ranks for religious reasons. Having to reconcile and alternate between the aesthetics and demands of stage and ritual performances will most likely bring about changes in the tradition. Inevitably, the stage experience of these performers will impact on the ritual domain.

The fixing of a text is another potential outcome of the process.

In a tradition where few people know the language used in the religious context, the words of the chants vary—sometimes considerably—from one singer to the other. Once written versions begin to circulate in the folkloric ensembles, however, many santeros who also perform on stage may decide to impose these in the casas de santos where they usually perform, relying on the authority of the written word to settle any discussion that may come up with those who only sing in the rituals. Contradictions also may arise from the fact that certain practices are accepted (e.g., teaching women to play batá) in these folkloric ensembles which in religious settings fall under a strictly respected taboo.

The changes brought about by the theatralization of these musical traditions are not altogether negative. In contrast to the critiques (many of them valuable) of what has been labeled the "folklorization" of Afro-Cuban religions, one must keep in mind that this process is a result of policies that have aimed at valuing the contributions of Afro-Cuban culture. Rogelio Martínez Furé, one of the founders and the first director of the Conjunto Folklórico Nacional, whose views are representative of the official policies adopted in Cuba with respect to folklore, sees folklore as

> the culture of a people, generally transmitted through oral tradition; the customs and habits of a human aggregate in which their life experiences, tastes, aspirations, conceptions of life and death etc. are reflected; the ways they build and decorate their houses, their oral prose and poetry, the remedies, the home cooking, the popular art, the beliefs and superstitions, the mythology, the music, dances, holidays, and traditional dress . . . in short, that which some researchers have called "popular knowledge" and others "traditional popular culture." Folklore is the opposite to the official, the bookish or the institutionalized. . . . Folklore is of the people, and for the people. (Martínez Furé 1979: 258)

By defining folklore this way, he emphasizes the difference between culture that is *generated by* the people and culture that is *given to* the people, separating folk culture from culture as what is "cultivated or learned." Folklore is not a "museum piece" but the most authentic manifestation of traditional popular culture, which should be stimulated and directed toward the construction of socialism (Martínez Furé 1979).

Alongside folklorization or aestheticization, commodification has been viewed by many critics as a strategy the Cuban government has used as an alternative to outright prohibition of Afro-Cuban religious practices. In the global economy of late twentieth century, the commodification of anything that can interest large constituencies is all but inevitable. Religious matters are particularly prone to commodification because of the ease of exploiting deeply felt emotional religious feelings; witness the flourishing industries that surround the holy sites of any religious denomination.

(*above*) **A** street corner in Matanzas where Felipe's bar (Santa Teresa) was located.

PHOTOS THIS PAGE COLLECTION OF FELIPE GARCÍA VILLAMIL.

(*left*) **F**elipe's mother and oldest sister, Maria Luisa, with the son of Felipe's niece Clarita and one of Felipe's grandchildren.

Some of the elders back in Cuba. From left to right: Emiliana (Felipe's sister), Osvaldo (his cousin), Juana (his cousin), Tomasa (his mother), Beba (his sister), and Beba's granddaughter Sonjaisy.

Bembé at Osvaldo's house. PHOTOGRAPHER: LYNDELL BROOKHOUSE-GIL © 1994.

Osvaldo with prenda.
PHOTOGRAPHER: LYNDELL
BROOKHOUSE-GIL © 1994.

(*facing page*) **F**elipe's house in Cuba was described as a house with three doors. In New York, Felipe keeps three altars (two linked to Santería and one to Palo) and an Abakuá corner. When possible, the altars are placed in separate rooms in the house.

(*above*) **T**he Santería corner: the altar where the soperas with the sacred stones are placed. This altar houses the tureens and the sacred emblems of the orichas of Felipe's family in New York. The sacred set of batá drums hangs from the ceiling. PHOTOS THIS PAGE BY ADRIANA GROISMAN.

(*top right*) **T**he espiritista corner. This altar is called *mesa blanca* (white table). Figures and lithographs of Catholic saints and a series of glasses are placed on a table covered with white cloth. This altar, found in the houses of many santeros and paleros, shows the influence of espiritismo in their religious practices.

The Palo Monte corner: the altar that houses the prendas of Felipe's family in New York. The cauldron that houses Felipe's prenda (Sarabanda–Rompe Monte) is placed in the middle, surrounded by other prendas, each placed in a separate iron cauldron.

The Abakuá corner. Traditionally, the Abakuá do not set up altars in their houses as paleros and santeros do. However, Felipe has organized an Abakuá corner where he keeps the enkomó drums and the seseribó, together with a picture of his father and the figure of an ireme, or diablito.
PHOTO BY ADRIANA GROISMAN.

(*right*) **F**elipe and his American wife, Valeria.
PHOTO BY ADRIANA GROISMAN.

(*below*) **F**elipe's American children: Ajamu, Tomasa, Miguel, and Atoyebi. COLLECTION OF FELIPE GARCÍA VILLAMIL.

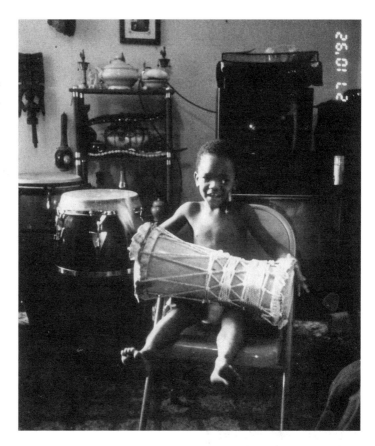

Felipe's youngest son, Atoyebi, playing batá. PHOTO BY MARÍA TERESA VÉLEZ.

Felipe's set of iyesá drums. PHOTO BY ADRIANA GROISMAN.

(*top left*) **B**embé drum decorated with mariwó. PHOTOS THIS PAGE BY ADRIANA GROISMAN.

(*top right*) **B**embé drum made by Felipe.

(*left*) **S**eseribó, one of the symbolic Abakuá drums made by Felipe.

(*below*) **F**elipe's set of enkomó drums.

(*right*) **R**eligious objects crafted by Felipe: gourd for Changó, stick for Eleguá, and statue of Eleguá. COLLECTION OF FELIPE GARCÍA VILLAMIL.

(*below*) **D**ecorated apron (bandel) for the iyá drum. PHOTO BY ADRIANA GROISMAN.

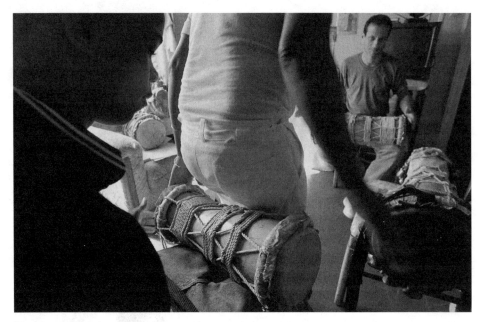

Felipe explaining a toque to his son Miguel. PHOTOS THIS PAGE BY ADRIANA GROISMAN.

Felipe teaching batá to his son Miguel and another drummer.

Felipe building a drum. PHOTOS THIS PAGE BY MARÍA TERESA VÉLEZ.

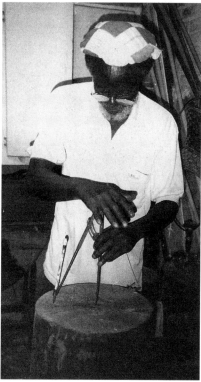

(*above*) **F**elipe decorating a gourd. COLLECTION OF FELIPE GARCÍA VILLAMIL.

(*left*) **F**elipe playing an iyesá drum. PHOTO BY ADRIANA GROISMAN.

PART THREE

Life as a Diasporic Musician

Leaving Cuba

Migration to the United States has been a recurrent feature in the history of Cuba. However, the mass movement of Cubans to the United States took place after the revolution of 1959. Migration and refugee studies divide these postrevolution migrants into several waves, each of lower educational background and socioeconomic status than the preceding one. Many of the later waves of migrants, unlike the early ones, left Cuba moved by economic rather than political motivations.[1]

Until 1980, Cubans who came to the United States were defined as refugees by the American government and received substantial help through a federal program of assistance. The preferential treatment given to Cubans changed with the events surrounding the Mariel exodus between April and September 1980. This wave of refugees came to be known as the Mariel exiles, or more commonly, the *marielitos.* (Though this term is not used in the scholarly literature, it is widely used among Cubans.) The exodus began when several Cubans sought asylum at the Peruvian embassy, and it ended with a boat lift that brought approximately 125,000 new immigrants to Key West, Florida. The open-door policy that had characterized the reception of all refugees from Cuba in the United States came into question when it became evident that most of the Mariel refugees had emigrated for economic reasons.

The situation was aggravated by the press, which concentrated on a small subgroup of refugees that included mental patients, homosexuals, and those with prison records.[2] The disturbances at various camps where the refugees were housed while awaiting resettlement contributed further to alienate sympathy (Masud-Piloto 1988: 85–86).

The Mariel boat lift turned into a major crisis for the Carter administration, which was confronting rising U.S. unemployment and widespread anti-immigration attitudes in the midst of the presidential (re)election campaign. Furthermore, during the same period a group of about twenty-five thousand Haitians who had arrived in Florida were not granted asylum and were threatened with deportation. To avoid the charges of discrimination that the preferential treatment of Cubans would have raised, the Carter administration created a new label, "entrant," to be applied to those Cubans and Haitians who had arrived before 1981. Under this classification, pre-1981 immigrants were allowed to remain in the country and adjust their status to "permanent resident aliens" after two years, making them also eligible for medical services and emergency assistance benefits.

Studies of the Mariel group of Cuban migrants show that they had similar occupational and educational backgrounds to the group that came on the "freedom flights."[3] Like the previous waves of refugees, the Mariel group came mostly from the provinces of Havana and Las Villas (Eckstein 1994: 160). However, the Mariel entrants differed in other ways: They were young (the median age was thirty-one); they were mostly male; they were drawn from sectors of the population not previously part of the Cuban migration; and they had a higher proportion of blacks than any previous refugee group. In addition, the way in which the decision to leave Cuba was taken differentiated this group of refugees, which comprised both individuals who had decided to leave and others who were sent out of Cuba (Bach 1985; Pedraza-Bailey 1985).

The latter subgroup included mental patients and people who were or had been in prison or who had problems with the local authorities. Those who left voluntarily were prompted mainly by economic considerations. During the late 1970s, the trade balance as well as the economic growth rate of Cuba had deteriorated. The last years of this decade were years of economic hardship; the standard of living had declined, food was scarce, and the housing needs of the population had gone unmet. Dissent and discontent had grown after the austerity measures the government took to cope with the emergency. Leaving their country in search for better living conditions, this group of refugees could not have anticipated the discrimination and prejudice they would suffer on arrival in the United States.

Although bad press contributed significantly to fuel prejudicial attitudes in the United States, many consider that racism played a significant role. In light of the reaction of the general public to the Mariel crisis, U.S. Cuban residents, who considered themselves a "model minority," received a great psychological blow when they found themselves grouped with the most disparaged minorities. Although many U.S. Cubans helped the newcomers, many others shared the prejudice against the Mariel Cubans and kept away from them (Pedraza-Bailey 1985: 28–29). Older Cubans blamed the Mariel exiles for the change of attitude toward the Cuban refugees and distanced themselves from them. A study carried out in south Florida concluded that the Mariel refugees in that region felt discrimination coming from their own ethnic group far outweighed that coming from native whites (Portes and Clark 1987).

The Mariel refugees represent a wave of immigrants whose experiences not only in Cuba but in the United States contrast sharply with those of previous waves. Pedraza-Bailey (1985: 29) captures an essential difference between these groups of immigrants: The nostalgia of the early refugees attaches them to the Cuba they knew, a Cuba that was; the nostalgia of the Mariel refugees is for the Cuba that is.

The fact that a majority of the postrevolutionary Cuban migrants came from the provinces of Havana and Las Villas may well have contributed to fact that the Santería practices that have developed in the United States among Cubans mainly follow the Havana tradition. To my knowledge no large network of santeros from Matanzas has developed in the United States, and the Matanzas santeros are still a minority. Thus, coming from Matanzas, Felipe found himself a minority within the Santería community.

Felipe arrived in Cayo Hueso, Miami, during the Mariel exodus. He was then sent to Fort McCoy in Wisconsin, one of the four refugee camps. He had to wait a couple months, until some friends from Cuba sponsored him, to be released from the camp. After his release, he established himself in Miami and lived for a while with the sponsoring family.

Why Felipe left Cuba when he was almost fifty, had a large family that he had to leave behind, and had a stable job exercising his trade, music, is not easy to understand, for it involves issues Felipe would rather not talk about. It is a part of his life he wants to keep to himself. From his brief references to the incidents surrounding his departure, I gathered that at the time of the Mariel exodus, he had problems (not linked to his religious affiliation) with the local party authorities and was "advised" to abandon Cuba. Most of those who came from La Marina, the neighborhood where Felipe's family lives, belonged to the group of refugees who were sent.

When the problem [arose] with the Mariel, they came to my house and told me: "You leave or you are in for four years," just like that. So I left. But many people came because they wanted to. They even pretended to be homosexuals to be able to leave. I know of a father and a son that pretended they were lovers, to be able to come out. Because the government didn't like homosexuals.

Others chose to go to prison instead of leaving their families. Felipe's niece Clarita, whose husband also left with the Mariel exodus and was murdered in the United States, told me another touching story when we spoke about the boat lift during my visit to Matanzas in 1997. She remembers one of her neighbors in La Marina who had a newborn son. When the authorities came for him, the child began crying, and he told them: "I will do what I need to do to stay in Cuba with my son"; so he went to prison.

In contrast to Felipe's reticence when it comes to the circumstances of his departure form Cuba, he narrates the story of his arrival in the United States in great detail.

I came in a boat called the Love Boat, but what love boat—it was a big iron boat. But to cross the gulf in that Love Boat—damn that boat! The captain that sailed that boat was an American woman. We were ready to leave but we had to come back to the port again. They said the weather was bad. Our captain said: "If we don't leave right now the bad weather will hit us crossing the Gulf of Mexico." She kept telling people not to be afraid, that she was a knowledgeable person. She said that in English, but there were interpreters there who would tell us what she was talking about. She was good, she really was a good captain. So when we arrived at the Gulf of Mexico she maneuvered and sailed along the coast until she had to come in. It was worse than a tornado. The waves were coming from above *buuuuu!* Others would hit the boat and again another one would come from above. Listen, that was an odyssey—I kept telling myself: "I will be left here in the sea." I climbed up to a small type of roof because the waves were coming into the boat and I tied myself up there. Then the dawn came and the captain said: "At full speed! Raise the *palenques* [tackle] that there's no problem now." Relieved I said: "Ay! we arrived, we arrived."

I arrived at Cayo Hueso in underwear, because my clothes were soaked. When the sun came everything dried, and my clothes were like stones. I had to take them off because they were tearing my skin off. I took them off and there in Cayo Hueso they gave me two pair of pants and a pair of tennis shoes. Imagine, in Cuba they had told me that: "When you arrive they are going to throw the dogs at you." So when I arrived I saw so many dogs and wondered: "What if it's really true that they throw the dogs at the black people here?" The police were there with the dogs. I thought: "Now when I get off . . . " Then they told us: "Everybody off." I said to myself: "Damn it! Here they come." The prisoners went down first and then it was our turn. I saw how they were passing by, "Stand up, stand up in line there," but in a nice way. Everyone got off the boat and I said: "They didn't throw the dogs at us after all, ha! ha! ha!" They gave us Coca-Cola and we went to see the Virgen de la Caridad who is there at the pier. For the first time in many years I saw apples and grapes, that place was full of apples and grapes. They gave us a nice soup, a nice lunch. From there we took the plane to Wisconsin.

Building the Present: Exercising His Trade in His New Home

The separation of people from their native culture has become a common experience in our century; in one way or another, we are all marked by the experience of displacement, either as protagonists (as immigrants, refugees, exiles, expatriates) or as hosts who have to learn to share with those displaced the space we have considered ours.

The displaced person faces multiple ruptures, a split between "here" and "there" and the need to rebuild a cultural identity in a new homeland, while constrained by factors that are mostly beyond his or her control. For some, this experience becomes an opportunity, while for others it is transformed into a source of frustration and pain. In Felipe's case, music is the avenue that connects, sometimes without success, the new world with the old, the "there" (Cuba) that is always present in all his narrations, always present in his memory.

Felipe was released from Fort McCoy after being sponsored by a Cuban family who lived in Miami and knew Felipe's family back in Cuba. He traveled to Miami and lived with them for four or five months. The head of the family was a batá player who was very active as a musician in the Santería community not only in Miami but also in New York; his name was Juan Silveria, though he was better known as Juan Candela.

I began playing with Juan Candela. He was one of the pioneers here, he played everywhere, in New York, in Miami, everywhere. In October he told me: "Well, we're going to New York again in case you want to come with us. You're not going to stay here alone, come to New York and you will make your way there." And it's true that I did well.

Then in New York I used to play with Renard.[4] I met Renard in Florida, and at that time I didn't have it in my mind that I was going to come to New York. But not long after I arrived here, I was invited to a tambor. Some people came to look for me and took me to that tambor. Renard was the one who was playing there and as soon as he saw me he embraced me, screaming like hell, and he told me: "Sit, sit there." And so I played and I sang. When the thing was over Renard told me: "I want you to play with me." I began to play with Renard, and one month later I rented an apartment and I was doing well. I had my telephone and everything. I was doing well because I was working with the santeros, playing here and there.

In New York, Felipe started playing in güiro ensembles, and it was this type of ensemble that he organized with some members of his family and some acquaintances from Matanzas who had also arrived during the Mariel exodus. Later, in 1983, he began using batá after he was able to bring his Añá from Cuba. However, the members of his family who lived in New York were not batá players, and frequently Felipe had to call other drummers to "fill in."

Renard left for Florida. Then people began calling me. So I bought my tum-badora [conga]—the same Americans used to come to look for me to take me around playing; they came to look for me so that I would sing and play.

Then in 1983 my things arrived, the Añá of my batá drums, and I began to play. Because even if nobody believes it, here little is still known of what batá is all about. And I had arrived with a name, I arrived with a name because Renard brought a record, and in that record you could listen to me play.[5]

I began to play with two other drummers that came from Matanzas, and things were going really well. When we arrived anywhere people would say: "Here come the *matanceros*." But that luck didn't last because one of the drummers had a problem with the law and the other one left. I kept looking for drummers but it was not easy at all to find them. Then I did something I shouldn't have done; I did it for my family. I got my family to work with me, my nephew, my brother, and a lot of other people who had come from there—I had created the drum with what I had earned working alone, but still I wanted to "make family." If anyone was to earn a penny, I wanted it to be my family because the drums were mine. But I was mis-taken, oh how was I mistaken. I thought: "Well, here are these people, if a toque comes up they can start 'grinding,' and never mind, if they make a mistake I would keep it going." But I was counting on them wanting to practice and learn. The drums were there at the house and they could play them anytime and make some progress. I was disappointed, and later I even ran into problems because everyone just wanted to earn money but nobody wanted to learn. I used to tell them: "Let's stretch the drums"—"Let's feed the drums"—"Come, take a class"—nothing! They didn't want to learn. So the fights began and I became somewhat tough.

The negative experience with his family and friends left Felipe dis-appointed, and around 1984, after trying his luck in Texas for a couple of months, he returned to New York and unsuccessfully tried to re-establish the group. It would not be until the end of the 1980s that Fe-lipe would form another batá group. During these years he continued to play for people who would call him to sit in with their groups and would sometimes form provisional batá ensembles to play for ceremonies.

Disheartened, Felipe even considered giving his batá drums to his friend Teddy Holiday, a well-known African American drummer and ba-balao. He was advised by a santero not to take this radical step and to keep his drums, but for a long period he did not play batá with others.

I almost gave Teddy my drums. I was going to call him and get rid of the drums and keep only the santos. I was upset because I couldn't do things the way they were supposed to be done. In the middle of all of this a santero called me and told me: "No, no, no, no, you're crazy, man; these drums are going to bring you benefits in the future. Cool down and wait, wait a little . . . "

Felipe was contacted then by an American drummer who wanted to learn to play rumba in the Matanzas style. From this point on, through word of mouth, Felipe's reputation as a teacher grew, and drummers began contacting him for lessons. Felipe organized a group with some of these students and gave it the same name as the group he had organized and left behind in Cuba: Emikeké.

For a while I had to look around for people who were not even drummers and "die with them." That went on until I put together this family of drummers. One came to learn tumbadoras and stayed in the drum. Gradually I became enthusiastic and: "Yes, yes, come, I'll teach you." And it's true, they would give me ten or fifteen dollars or nothing—I've never taken money from people without teaching them.

With Emikeké, Felipe began a new stage in his musical life, one that somewhat resembled what had happened to him in Cuba: a movement from private performances of Afro-Cuban religious music in sacred contexts to the performance of this music in public, in concerts and at lectures and demonstrations. The "new" Emikeké, which had only one Cuban member, Felipe (the others were Americans or Puerto Ricans), performed for such institutions as the Museum of Natural History and the Museum of African Art, at Lincoln Center outdoor festivals, and in lecture demonstrations in universities such as Yale, Columbia, and Rutgers. The group was also called for private religious ceremonies, predominantly Palo ceremonies, and, less frequently, to play batá for the orichas. The group dissolved in 1994 when Felipe went through a personal life crisis and left New York, establishing himself in California.

• • •

Felipe's experience as a cultural worker in Cuba had prepared him to deal with issues related to the "staging" of his tradition for outsiders.

This skill was useful to Felipe when he organized Emikeké in New York and began "working the folklore circuit."

In the United States, the nationalistic discourse that surrounds folk-lore worldwide is recast as "ethnicity or unity in diversity" (Kirshenblatt-Gimblett 1992: 35). In this country, even as Felipe is given a voice to stage his heritage, his traditions no longer belong to a pool of ancestors that may be used to define the cultural tradition of one nation (Cuba). Now his is one voice among many in what is defined as a pluralistic and multicultural nation. In addition, in the United States, Afro-Cuban traditions are invoked as part of the heritage of the African diaspora. Thus, through his work in the folklore circuit, Felipe established links with other African, African American, Afro-Latino, and Afro-Caribbean artists. This gave Felipe access to the Pan-African tradition based not on roots but on cross-connections, where the sense of community is built cross- and intraculturally. Therefore, in defining his identity, Felipe finds himself involved in an exchange where his "blackness" weighs more heavily than his Cubanness.[6]

Performances by groups such as the one Felipe organized (labeled "ethnic" or "folkloric") for the most part are sponsored and promoted by two types of cultural institutions in the United States: the institutions one might define as "supercultural," dominant or "official" institutions[7] whose principal aim is to present the multiplicity and assert the variety of ethnic or folk cultures that contribute to the pluralist and multicultural identity of the nation (e.g., museums, universities, folklife festivals); and institutions that are organized by members of a particular community or ethnic group to display, study, and preserve their own traditions (e.g., the Caribbean Cultural Center for the traditions of the African diaspora).[8]

In New York, with the growing popularity of what has been labeled by record companies as "world music," a third group of venues (e.g., the World Music Institute) has emerged to present and support the music of immigrant musicians. Felipe's experience has been limited to performing for concerts or demonstrations organized by the first two types of institutions.

Musicians or folk artists like Felipe are "selected" by these institutions according to their own criteria of authenticity and their political or cultural agendas. Once selected, the artist's tradition is reframed according to presentational modes, standards, and aesthetics that have been shaped by the ideology and interests of the presenting institution. Just as in Cuba, Felipe's own power to decide remains limited; choices remain in the hands of others.[9]

While Felipe, first with Emikeké and now with the group he has organized with his sons, has presented on stage the musical traditions of both Santería and Palo, it is the music of Santería that has received more attention from the American public. As it has developed in the United States, Santería music is a genre difficult to demarcate; it reflects the dynamism, complexity, interrelatedness, and transnationalism of many immigrant musical cultures. In the late twentieth century's global village, music—like people, capital, products, and so forth—moves constantly across borders, sometimes independent of the musicians or cultural practices to which it was originally linked. Thus the secularization and decontextualization of ritual music that circulates on a global circuit is inevitable.

Even in places where this music remains linked to specific cultural practices and immigrant groups (e.g., the United States), its characterization is far from simple. As ritual music of a religious practice, this music falls within the cultural practices of what is referred to as the African diaspora. Yet, from the perspective of the practitioners of the religion in New York, a characterization based on race or a shared past is not accurate. Multiple diasporic groups (African Americans, white Cubans, Afro-Cubans, Latinos, etc.) converge and lay claim to this music while diverging in their conceptualizations of and relationship to other aspects of the tradition.[10] In addition, Santería music has attracted many musicians who, although having no ties with the religion, have played an important role in the history of this musical genre in the United States. Affinity rather than heritage links these musicians to this musical genre.

The staging of Santería music takes place, then, in very different venues and with very different conceptions of how to stage it and why. Because of the ties that Afro-Cuban music (secular or sacred) has to the Latino and African American communities, Santería music is frequently featured in concerts that are not always organized as presentations of ethnic or folk music, such as jazz festivals (e.g., New Jazz at the Public Theater and concerts at the Village Gate) and popular Latin music concerts in which well known artists like Celia Cruz, Tito Puente, and Mongo Santamaría are featured. Furthermore, mainstream popular music artists such as David Byrne—who is involved heavily in staging, producing, and promoting world music—have featured the music of Santería in some of their concerts. Santería music has also acquired high visibility worldwide through the many concert tours of Cuban groups such as the Conjunto Folklórico Nacional and Afro-Cuba, and through the work of musicians based in the United States, such as the Puerto Rican Milton Cardona and the Cubans Orlando "Puntilla" Rios and Francisco Aguabella.[11]

The Tools of the Trade

Felipe could have resumed the practice of his trade in his new home country confident that most of the instruments he needed were available: chekerés or güiros, congas, and even batá drums. However, sacred batá drums (fundamento drums) are not common in the United States, and bembé and iyesá drums were nonexistent. Furthermore, Felipe wanted to own a set of drums because owning the drums is a precondition for acquiring leader status. Leaders are also expected to be familiar with the full repertoire of toques of the three drums and to have an extensive knowledge of the dance movements and the chants.

Felipe needed to become a olúbatá not to gratify his ego but to assert it at all. Inasmuch as he practiced the Matanzas style of drumming owning a set of drums was crucial for Felipe to be able to impose his style and his performance practice.

Instruments as Immigrants: Añá Crosses the Ocean

My drums were brought by Basha. She brought the outside things, the ropes, the secret, the aché, all of that, she brought all of that. Because Basha visited my mother. So the old lady liked her so much that she told her: "I have a son that is a drummer there in the United States, but he has his drums here; I would like you to do me a favor in this life, and I would be grateful to you forever: bring this to my son that my son is going to need them." And it was true, I needed the drums because without them I was nobody, I felt so empty it was incredible. Even if I don't play the drums, I look at them and that's enough. I could have gotten those batás with tuning pegs, but I needed to have a fundamento batá drum.

The package was rather big, because it had the ropes, the aché, and the secret. Well, Basha took everything and put it inside a handbag: "Well, well," she said, "and what if they take it away from me, what if something happens?" My mother told her that nothing was going to happen and that she would be able to deliver the package here to me. And Basha felt a chill because at the airport they were checking everyone but they told her: "Go ahead, madam."

This was not the first time Añá had crossed the ocean. The spirit that inhabits the drums had gone through a previous diaspora when it arrived in Cuba from Africa. According to Felipe's cousin Osvaldo, when Añá first crossed the ocean he could not have known if he "was arriving to a land of life or to a land of death."

Upon the arrival of the Añá of his drums, Felipe built a set of drums to house the spirit.

What I did here was, that I had to build only the outside part of the drums, the frame. It's the same as if now I have a santo and the tureen that contain the stones breaks. I have to get another one. It's the same with the drums. If I had a santo back in Cuba—that couldn't be brought here because it was very big—well, here I can build the house for that santo again. It happens the same with people; if I go any place, if I move, I have to look for a house in the new place. This is also the case with the santo and the drums.

Felipe is discussing here the difference between the spirit or sacred power and the receptacle that contains it. In the case of the santos or orichas, the receptacles or houses are the soperas in which the sacred stones are placed. In the case of the drums, the wooden frame is the dwelling site of Añá, the sacred power that inhabits the drum. When the wooden part deteriorates, it has to be rebuilt.

After Añá crossed the sea, a ceremony had to be performed. This was done after Felipe remade the wooden part of the drums, attached the skin and ropes, and placed Añá in its new dwellings.

So the ceremony for having crossed the ocean was celebrated. I performed a ceremony here. I did it with a babalao. Besides that ceremony, another one had to be performed to wash the outside, the wood, of the drums. And there were these babalaos that told me: "You have to bring the measurements of the drums, and this and that." They were giving me a hard time. I said: "Ay! In Cuba we don't need so many things to do this. Besides, I'm knowledgeable of all that involves the drum and you don't know about drums. I'm going to bring you the drum." So I brought the drum there, and they had a book. They took the drums, measured them, and went to the book to check. Then they said: "They can be washed now" But asked me where did I learn to build the drums. I replied: "But what are you telling me? I, who handled three sets of drums in Cuba and hung around the old people, the wise ones. Besides, my great-grandfather was Iñoblá Cárdenas, who gave the fundamento to these drums in Cuba, Iñoblá Cárdenas, a pure African. So, what stories are you going to tell me, I who come from those roots? You rule yourself by a book but know nothing about history." After that, the ceremony was celebrated and I did the bandeles [decorated beaded aprons] and all the rest.

And the drums I made! Listen, Teddy says it himself, these drums of mine talk. And the mellowness, the flavor of the drums, they have a sound that gets to the blood.

Applying "Cultural Memory": Making Instruments

Drums for Felipe represent not only his past life but also a way to approach, apprehend, and give meaning to his experience as an immigrant. They are not just the tools of his trade (a way to earn a living) but the medium through which he can establish communication with the deities that have protected and guided him since he was a child. The imperative that moves Felipe to build drums in the United States is the need to build a new life. Drums are the threads used to weave the pieces of the "there–Cuba" with the "here–United States" into some meaningful shape; drums also become a way of remembering.

The care and length with which Felipe describes how he built his drums in the United States constitutes a metaphor of the central role these instruments have played in his life. Drums are and have been Felipe's life; rebuilding a life implies, then, the need to rebuild the instruments of his trade.

Drums not only represent Felipe's experiences but also contribute to their interpretation and apprehension, because, as Babcock writes, "cultures and the individuals within them not only constitute, reflect on, and reconstitute themselves through what they say and what they do

articulations of the material world as well . . . for objects
only to represent experience but also to apprehend it and
it, to give it a meaningful shape. . . . Objects do speak and
eard as significant statements of personal and cultural reflexivity" (Babcock 1986: 317–18).

Batá Drums

Felipe not only made a set of batá drums to house Añá but also built
a set of unconsecrated drums to use for public performances and lecture demonstrations. Likewise, he has made drums for his students and
for sale to percussionists who are interested in owning batá drums with
the traditional tuning system (tensioned ropes). When he was making
an okónkolo for me, Felipe interrupted our regular chanting sessions
to explain how a batá set is built and consecrated, and through what
type of initiations drummers have to go in order to be able to play a
fundamento set of batá drums.

In New York, Felipe's sources of wood were limited, and he was
forced to work with whatever type of wood he could get hold of (oak,
birch, and others). Traditionally, batá drums are made of a trunk of
cedar cut after a series of ceremonies have been performed. Although
the ceremonies to prepare the already cut trunk before proceeding to
build the drums are still performed, the ceremonies to ask permission
from the spirits before cutting the trunk, which regularly took place in
the monte when Felipe lived in Matanzas, are usually not performed in
New York. Even in Cuba nowadays, most of the drummers buy the
wood from specialized stores.

You get the three tree trunks to perform the ceremony. When you go to
cut the trunk from the tree, you have to ask permission to the spirit of the
tree before cutting it. You have to explain what you are using the tree for:
"We come here to look for this *iki*, because we need it to make a drum."
We also ask Osain, the owner of all the plants, if he authorizes us to cut it.

Then you do the ceremony to the trunk. You feed it an omiero of trees,
not of herbs. Because there are plants like the *siguaraya*, like the *guanábana*,
like the *piñón dulce*, the *palo de caja*, *platanillo de Cuba*, and some other
logs—plants that are big. You also use all the fruit trees. So you prepare an

omiero and you wash the logs there. Then you throw the coconuts to consult the santos and you proceed to feed the logs.

Omiero is a sacred liquid used in different rituals. It is prepared using diverse plants, herbs, parts of trees, and other elements such as pepper, honey, and cocoa. The composition varies according to the ritual use. In the preparation of some omieros only plants and herbs are used. However, some require the leaves and fragments of trees. Sacred objects have to be fed also with the blood of ritually sacrificed animals. The coconuts—one of the systems of divination—are thrown to consult the orichas about the appropriateness of the sacrifice offered to them.

You feed the logs with the blood of a rooster. Then you place the fees that go with it: aguardiente, honey, *jutía,* smoked fish, and corn—because it's an osain [a talisman]. You also have to offer a pigeon to the Osain in order to clean all the logs. So everything from that omiero remains in that tree trunk. Why? Because that tree trunk has to continue living. By cutting it you took away life from the trunk, so through these ceremonies you are bringing back the spirit of the wood.

Well, then you proceed. You bring the drum to where the artisan is. And here there are different opinions, because there is a book that says one thing but I say what I know—I'm not interested in what books say—I tell you what the book says for you to know what's around. So there's a drum that has to be set up first and the book say it's the iyá [Canizares 1993: 71], but I say it isn't the iyá, it's the smaller drum, the okónkolo, because that is the oldest drum. By oldest we mean the first one to be made.

You hollow the tree trunk with a gauge—by hand you bore it—you begin working with the gauge, taking wood out, taking wood out. Making like a funnel. You begin with the bigger part first, then go toward the edge so you can continue downward.

Then the same shape the drums have outside has to be given to them inside. If you go to Matanzas you'll see that all the drums are like that. It means that, for the *chachá* [smaller head] you have to have a third of the measurements you are using. The larger part of the drum is two times the smaller part. You measure three parts. I take a third part and then make a mark in the wood—then—I cut with the saw, *rararararará,* and then I begin coming from one end to the other, from the bigger to the smaller part, *kan kan kan kan.* I begin cleaning with the saw and I start shaping it, *ran ran ran ran,* and then *pa pa pa pa,* sandpaper, and the drum is finished.

For the measurements of the head of the drums, the chachá and the *enú* [larger head], I decide by using my ear. The enú of this drum here sounds like a pipe. We call "pipe" those things where you used to keep wine before. The chachá is higher [pitch], it has a different sound.

In Matanzas we don't like the chachá to be very small, because a small chachá cracks your hand and doesn't sound the way it's supposed to. I also made a small sole, a *chaguala,* to play in the style of Matanzas, but here nobody uses it, so it was left around someplace.

Batá drums are played with the bare hands, placing the drums on the knees and holding them in position with a strap. However, in Matanzas some drummers use a rawhide strap in the shape of the sole of a shoe to play the *chachá* of the omelé (small drum) and the itótele (medium drum). This technique of playing is exclusively used in Matanzas; in Havana, drummers have always played the drums beating both membranes with the bare hand. It is interesting to note that in western Nigeria the two largest drums of the batá ensemble (which has four instruments instead of three) are played striking the large membrane with the open hand and the smaller one with a narrow rawhide strap, whereas the batá from Adja Were, Dahomey, are played like those in Havana, using only the bare hands (Rouget 1965; Thieme 1969).

• • •

Once the wood part is finished, the skin has to be placed on the drums. The two heads of the drum are then surrounded by hoops made of rattan, around which the skin of the drums is wrapped. The skin is then stretched with a system of longitudinal leather ropes (in Havana) or cords (in Matanzas). The cords or ropes are pressed to the body of the drum by wrapping and interlacing transversal cords around the waist of the drum.

In Cuba, when I was small and began seeing the drums, they used to tie them with skin. Later they discarded that, because the problem is that you go through more trouble with the leather than with the *cáñamo* [cord]. To tune the drums if you use leather, you have to take all the leather cords out, dampen then, stretch them, and all that nonsense, until it's ready again. After the leather they began using *corojo*. Do you know what corojo is? Well, is made from a plant. It's a cord that had a color similar to that of the drums. Later, fishing cord was used because it's strong so it pulls well. If you use this type of cord you can stretch the drums and play them that same day.

For the skin of the drums I use goat. Goat, chosen by me. Male goat for all the three drums.

I prepare the skin myself because I don't want other people to get my stuff. I go to look for it myself in a place in New Jersey. It's a farm, far away, where they sacrifice goats to sell them. I go and pick the skin, because they throw it away anyway. They are authorized to do that. I have my secret of how I prepare the skin. I clean them, I stretch them, I put my secret "chemistry" on them. Some people use lime, but I don't; I have another system that doesn't smell bad or anything and that dries fast.

The skins of the drums have a signature. The "mouth," which is the one that talks, has to have a seal; and the chachá, which is the potency of the drum, the strength of the drummer, also has to have a seal. Those seals are called *osun* and are found on each side of the drum; osun is a painting.

This type of mark or painting is also used in the initiation of neophytes, each of whose head is ritually painted with *osu* or *osun*.

Then you make the hoops—with wood, with the rattan used for baskets. Here in New York you find a lot of it, they make furniture with it. Basket rattan which you cover with fabric . . . you open the holes in the leather to pass the cords through them. It has to go in pairs. I use sixteen, eight and eight. There are eight lines of cord but you have to make two turns, one inside the skin and another one outside. It's like weaving. Then the cords have to be knotted, with knots that we call *gangá* and *mariposa* [butterfly]. Some say that the one we call butterfly has a N shape.

When you run out of cord and have to use another piece of cord, you tie the two pieces together. I try not to use ties. But if you have to tie there is a type of tie done close to the enú that is called "pig's ass."

But before you do all of this, Añá has to be prepared. Añá has to be there so it can be introduced into the drums. You need then three babalaos and you need an oriaté—an oriaté and a contingent of santeros afterward. Because the babalaos are going to do their share and when they give you the drum back, you have to untie it again and do the santero stuff. Añá has a lot of things, a lot of minerals; everything that is consumed in the earth and a lot of secret things.

After you feed Añá, you put it inside the drums and you close the drums. From then on, if Añá is to receive any spirituality, if we are going to feed Añá, it has to be done through a small metal ring placed close to the chachá.

An iron ring is placed on each drum close to the smaller head and is used to hang the drums and to feed them ceremonially. After Añá is placed inside the drums, the drums are sealed, so when the spirit of Añá has to be fed, this is done through this exterior metal ring.

The drum is made by hand but is made using iron, and in anything that uses iron, Ogún has to participate. In the drum his participation is shown in that ring. Because whenever Ogún works you have to give him a participation. The drum is mainly Ogún, because Ogún is the one who made it. The tools used are all in iron so iron was what made the drum. Besides, you have to go to el monte, where Ogún lives, to look for the tree trunk and the plants. Because Osain gave Ogún a power in his house: "You are the one in charge here because if you don't come to the woods nothing can be opened up here." To walk through the woods one needs a machete or a knife made of iron. If Ogún doesn't work, there will be nothing in the forest. So he has a power there. Then to cut the tree trunks, if you're using a saw it's Ogún, if you are using a drill it's Ogún, if you are using any machine made of iron it's Ogún who is working. So he has to have a participation in the drums, which is that ring. Through that ring is where you say: *Ogún choro choro.*[12] Because the drums don't have a small hole to feed the inside, so through that ring you do all the mimic so that Añá receives the spirituality that is being sent from outside. Only every seven or twelve years you do take Añá out and feed it directly.

Then you wash the drums, wash the vats. What this means is that the drums when they are empty, without the skin, they resemble the soperas where you place the santos. The empty drums are going to receive a secret inside. So we call it a vat. So you have the vat, you wash it; then the babalaos make a mark outside and inside the two heads of each drum. But before they do this they have to ask [the oracle] about the name for Añá, they have to find Añá's name.

The babalaos do their work and then they bring the drums into the cuarto de santo. They finish doing their work, and finding the name for Añá. Then they bring the drums to the cuarto de santo because here is where the skin is going to be marked—the osun of the skin. That cannot be done by the babalaos. You need an oriaté for that job. You need an oriaté for making the osun, giving the aché to the drums, and finding the name in santo of each drum. Because each individual drum has a name—an example can be Adé Kolá—that's the name of my small drum. Another example is Ogundei—Odúfora; the santo names; each drum has a santo name that is found using the dilogún. That way each drum has a name, and Añá the set of drums has another.

After all of this is done, inside the cuarto de santo, you begin to tie the skin. This takes about seven days, because after you feed Añá, you have to clean everything, and put it inside the drums. For these steps you only have drummers, there are no babalaos or anything of that sort, only drummers. It's going to take about seven days because you're going to have to wet the skin and do each drum one by one. You can't do three drums at the same time. Besides, you have to look for people to work with you—people you trust, because Añá is already there. It's not only stretching the drums, one has to practically build them again. Then you have to wait for the skin to dry, and leave them without stretching them too much. You wait for two or three days for the skin to dry; it takes time. So then you loosen them and stretch them again. Then you have the presentation.

The power of a set of batá drums to communicate with the orichas has to be received from an older, previously consecrated set of drums. Before this is done, the newly built set is considered "silent"; it has no voice.

In New York before the arrival of the exiles from Mariel in 1980, sacred batá drums were rare, if there were any at all. But as batá drumming developed and santeros began to use this type of ensemble in their rituals, consecrated batá sets were needed. It took several years before many of the drummers who arrived with the Mariel boat lift were able either to bring their set of drums or to have the Añá of their set of drums sent from Cuba. Meanwhile, in 1982 a group of babalaos who had organized a temple in New Jersey decided to build a set of batá drums. Sixteen babalaos, during a period of five months, made a set of sacred batá drums "from scratch."[13] These babalaos either were not familiar with the secrets and restrictions of the transmission of power between sets of drums or were limited by the absence of other sets of consecrated drums in New York. As the leadership of the temple felt the "use of unsacred drums or alternative ensembles was unsatisfactory" (Brown 1989: 130), they "created" a new way of giving birth to sacred drums. This practice might have become a tradition and replaced the Cuban manner of consecrating drums. However, with the arrival of drummers such as Juan "El Negro" Raymat, Orlando "Puntilla" Rios, Felipe García, and Alfredo "Coyude" Vidaux, who used drums consecrated in the Cuban practice, the New York community of religious drummers began to acknowledge this as the authentic way of placing Añá in the instruments. Moreover, santeros began to question drummers about the origin of their sets, inquiring into what set of drums each had been born from. Lineages of drums therefore regained the importance they have had in Cuba.

In New York, a situation parallel to that Ortíz described in Cuba began to occur frequently: As the number of sacred batá sets increased, rivalry, competition, and misinformation led many to question the fundamento (sacred character) of various sets of batá drums. Nowadays, in New York as well as in Miami, a lot of disagreement exists over who owns "real" fundamento drums and who doesn't.

In Cuba, even though babalaos play an important role in the preparation of a set of sacred batá drums, their duties are limited and cannot replace the role of the olúañá, a priest who belongs to a separate and independent priesthood within the liturgical system of the Lucumí. According to Ortíz's findings, which coincide with the practices of the drummers in New York who came with the Mariel boat lift: (1) The fundamento batá are born one from another; (2) only the priests of Añá can transfer this spirit from a pre-existing Añá to a set that is still unconsecrated; and (3) not even the babalaos can consecrate a trio of batá, because they do not have the power to do so (Ortíz 1952: vol. 4, 285–310).

The presentation is a ceremony to give power to a thing that is asleep, that is very young. With the ceremony you are going to move it, to awaken it. You have to bring those drums in front of an older set, because they are going to be born, and nothing is born from nothing. An example: People come here and want to make a set of drums; they have to rely on me because I'm the one who has a real fundamento set of drums, or count with someone who has a real set of batá. From my drum another drum will be born, because my drum will give birth to that drum.

During that ceremony the old set of drums is playing, and the new one has to come, with the drummers and a basket with three liters of aguardiente, three roosters, candles, coconut, and the fee. You present them the same way you present a *yawó* [an initiate]. The old drum begins to play—plays for a while, plays for all the santos. Then, without stopping, other drummers come and begin to play the new drum. When this drum begins to play, the older drums begin to go away softly, softly, softly. . . . The new drum continues to play. It's new, so maybe it won't sound too good, but it keeps on playing. It has been given a "transmission," a power. It plays for a couple of hours, three or four. It plays an oro for all the santos, and then it takes leave.

Bembé Drums

Around August 1992, Felipe got the wood to make a bembé drum similar to the one he had made for Oyá in Cuba.

The bembé is a free drum.[14] I can make a bembé drum right now and say: "Well I'm dedicating this bembé to Eleguá, or to Ochosi, or to whomever I want." When the drum is finished I would—ask Eleguá, ask Oyá, ask here, ask there. I wanted Oyá to give me permission to make a different drum here but connected to those I made in Cuba for her.

Bembé drums are *bembé oro,* which means for everybody. They are used to cleanse and for many other uses. You, who are an aberikulá—not baptized in the religion—can hire a bembé drum to play. If you feel like it you can say: "Well, I don't have a godfather, I don't have a godmother, I have nobody, but I like Felipe's house. Felipe, I'm going to give a toque with bembé to your santo." You can do it, because we are all children of santo even if we have no santo made. You understand? But if now you go and get crowned with your santo [get initiated], it's like a kingdom that you have. After that you can't celebrate a ceremony with a drum that isn't baptized, because now you are baptized. If you do it: Who do you think you are honoring with that? Because your santo can't accept it, much less Olofi. So, what you have to do is to bring a drum with Añá. Only then will the santo answer to you.

Felipe made the bembé drum and dedicated it to Osain. When he finished the work, he had a dream in which the words and music of a chant to Osain were given to him. This was the chant that was used to dedicate the new drum to this oricha.

I was sleeping, you see? And this chant came to me in a dream. I woke up at around two o'clock in the morning: "Valeria, Valeria, write this down for me, the way I'm putting it"—and I had the music in my mind and everything. Look:

> ewe ayé osain babamí
> ewe ayé osain babamí
> osain alámofinye 'ra ewe iyá mi
>
> tiwi tiwi
> kukurú kukurú
> tiwi tiwi
> kukurú kukurú
>
> tiwi tiwi
> kukurú kukurú
> tiwi tiwi alámofinye 'ra[15]

Osain is my father, and without herbs ocha cannot be made. The chant talks about ocha, you see? From seven plants on, there is already a spirituality. Osain is the spirit of the plants, that is why you say: Osain *alámofinye 'ra*, because you are calling the spirituality, the spirituality of the herbs, to come and accomplish something for you. Osain's personality is reflected in the chant—Osain is an oricha that is missing a foot, an eye, an ear, an arm. "Well, I'm an imperfect person but I come to do good to humanity. I have one eye, I have one nose, one ear only, one arm only, but I come to do good to humanity, so that the world may be perfect, so that it's not like me."

Iyesá Drums

As a son of Ogún, every twenty-fourth of August, Felipe celebrates the feast of his santo with a big fiesta. When his finances allow it, he gives a separate fiesta to the Palo deity Sarabanda, who is the Palo syncretic equivalent of Ogún. It was for the fiesta of Ogún that Felipe made the iyesá drums. These drums belong to two orichas in particular: Ogún and Ochún.

Because in 1981 I gave my fiesta here, at the house of the Candelos, and it was the end of Troy [i.e., of mythical proportions]. In Renard's house I met an American woman who was a banker. So she told me: "Don't worry, the fiesta for Ogún will take place, I'll provide for whatever is needed." So we prepared everything and I made the iyesá drums.

To get that first wood, it was at Orchard Beach; it was as cold as it is now and I was freezing. We had a machine to cut the wood, but it seems that it got stuck and it didn't want to work. So the "chasers" [police] came. The guy who had taken me there, the Niche, knew how to speak English well. So he began to talk to that policeman: "I have been working for the Ford corporation, and now that these Cubans arrived I want to help them because we want to do a theater presentation, we went to the ministry . . . " He made such a mess that he drove that white guy nuts. Then the white guy stared at us for a while and said: "OK, see if you can start that machine—I'm giving you thirty minutes and then you have to leave." So we put some oil into the machine and we started it, and began to cut—it was so cold! Then we took everything, and I did the work. Diodado who helped a bit, Danilo and I with a carving knife, and nothing else—Oh! Yes, and a handsaw.

My iyesá drums were born from Ogún, because they are linked to Ogún's cabildo [in Cuba]. Ogún is the one who knows and he gave me the secret. Listen, these are transcendental things that one cannot take into the open [things that should be kept secret]. Ogún is a warlock, Ogún is the one who invents all the *Añáses*. If I want to do something, just by having some of the things from the Iyesá cabildo in Cuba, I would be able to do things here. In Matanzas there is only one set of iyesá drums, from which my set was born.

When the drums were finished, Felipe painted them green and yellow, the colors of Ogún and Ochún. This set of drums became the first iyesá set to be made in the United States. The special bond these drums have with the above mentioned orichas is explained by Felipe through a *pataki* (a Lucumí legend).

When Ochún went to the land of the *Yesá* to dance, she was shaking and moving a lot. So Ogún said: "What the hell is going on with this one? With her pretty face she thinks that—I'm going to see if she really can shake." He then placed five iron bars, a load of iron, on her waist. "Shake now!" he told her. But this time it was even worse, because Ochún was shaking like a whirlwind, ha! ha! ha! *Ladé* is the handkerchief Ochún has underneath her crown. So when Ogún placed the iron bars on her waist he told her: "I want to see if you can move your waist the way you move the handkerchief, the ladé, that you have on your head." According to the patakís that's what happened. Then Ogún told her: "Well, now I'm going to make you the queen of that drum." That's why the drum is green and yellow, the colors of Ochún and Ogún. That's the story behind the chant that says:

> *tá ladé yeyé*
> *obasoma ogue dé*
> *Ogún tá niwo*

Drums as an Extension of the Self, as a Source of Living, as Life Itself

Music is life itself. Because I'll tell you this, look, look, right now, the guys come here, and people aren't the same, right? I have one drummer who likes the drums a lot but he doesn't know, he has no love for the drum—and for me the drum is like—like an extension of my body, no? Any of those drums is like a part of myself—not because they belong to me, they can belong to anybody else. According to the way you hit the drum you are going to make me happy or you are going to upset me. So I have this student who comes here, brings down all the drums and begins hitting them in a way that hurts me. He gives these blows to the drums but I'm the one in pain. Because he's hitting them wrong. That's not being a professional, one has to have affection for the drums. Because at my age, I've been playing drums longer than I've been alive. So the skin and the drum, that structure has been my life. Because it has given me life, it has given me food, it has given me everything. Some days I haven't earned enough, but other days I've earned a lot and it has even helped me to feed my children. Sometimes I tell this drummer: "Why are you mistreating the drums?" You have to just pass your hand softly over the skin, you caress it, then you give it a small strike—listen, it sounds sweeter, it sounds better." But he pays no attention and continues hitting the drums and *piketi pan.* So I go to the kitchen and start talking to myself—Valeria [Felipe's wife] comes in and tells me: "But why don't you go out and—?" "Because I already told him once and I don't want to teach more. Let him go on hitting it." And my other students know I'm hurting, they know. They don't do that. They take the drums and greet them. I've told them, the drummer who comes here and brings down one of those drums and begins to punch them isn't a drummer; he has no sense, he has no love, he has nothing. You are supposed to go to the drums and salute them softly—*pakiti kiti*—you give them some soft strikes, just like if you were talking to them. The way someone who knows that this is his culture and has to take care of it with love will do. You really have to teach those who want to learn; but if someone doesn't want to listen to me, I would let them go on hitting the drums anyway. But I know tomorrow they're going to be sorry. They're going to be sorry because the drums are transmitting something, the skin is transmitting a message. If we believe in something, well, we believe. If we're not going to believe, well, we won't.

Viewing the drum as a person, as an interlocutor with a will of its own who has to be treated with the utmost respect, is not merely a philosophical consideration for Felipe; rather, it encapsulates the approach that guides his playing technique.

I hit the drum strongly, I hit it strongly but with technique. It's strong but not to break the skin, not to get your hand from one side and to bump it to the other. It's knowing how to hit. If you struggle with the drum, you won't be able to conquer it. You have to relax and hit it a little softer . . . try to be a little bit more intelligent with the drum. He doesn't want to give in to you, but just wait and you will see. When a rhythm doesn't come out, you have to hit it softer, without tightening the skin. Only when you have it under control you can say: "Now I am going to play this."

The Artisan Transformed into an Artist

When Felipe was having financial difficulties, he began to make sets of miniature batá drums and sell them as "souvenirs." With the money he made he was able to acquire tools, materials, and supplies that enabled him to build standard sets of drums.

There in front of our building they knocked down a beam and left a log of four by four. It was a time when I was going through a bad situation and had no money, had nothing—I was standing at the window and something told me: "Go take that log so you can make some drums from it." And I went out—and it was cold like it is right now. I took the log and when Ajamu [Felipe's son] saw me coming in with it he told me I was bringing garbage into the house. That same night I cut it and cleaned it, and whatnot—I began making the drums by hand. I took a hammer and got all the nails out; and I had a piece of a saw and I began cutting the small drums, the little ones, the souvenir type—and I cut and made about five sets. I worked fast, but I made them really beautiful—but working by hand. Opening the holes with a very fine cutting gauge. I hollowed them really well, I placed the skin, and a week later I went out to sell them. I went out to the streets and people snatched them from me. Then Valeria began buying tools and—listen: from that which Ajamu called garbage we got money to buy more logs, and I made some three hundred sets of small drums and sold them all! Then I stopped the production of small drums and began making the big drums.

Felipe was gaining a reputation as a palero, and many people had visited his house to see the altar in a closet where he had set his prendas. Some of the visitors were moved by simple curiosity, others by interests that ranged from the religious to the anthropological to the aesthetic, yet others by the belief they shared with Felipe in the power and force of the spirits that were housed in that altar. Elements of the prenda were "smuggled" out of Cuba and into the United States, and Felipe reconstructed other elements that had to be replaced, using materials he found in New York. The results were impressive, powerful, and stirring. Many people approached Felipe for help in setting their own prendas. By 1993 there were at least a hundred prendas in New York like Felipe's, many of which he made and ritually prepared (Thompson 1993: 288).

As his reputation as a religious artisan grew, Felipe began to be approached by people who wanted him to manufacture religious objects for them: beaded gourds, beaded hooks, canteens, hats, pouches, *collares de mazo* (beaded necklaces), and other types of collares for the different orichas.[16]

In 1993, Felipe was approached by Professor Robert Farris Thompson, a scholar in the field of African art from Yale University, to build an altar for Sarabanda at the Museum of African Art in New York. This altar was to become part of an exhibit of altars of Africa and the African Americas called "Face of the Gods," which Thompson curated. Felipe installed this altar in the museum, and *Sarabanda* was visited by thousands of New Yorkers during the five months the exhibit lasted; it then traveled to several other museums in the country.[17]

Thompson looked for the resources and the prenda was made. But when I made it, when I fed it here in the house, I fell so much in love with that prenda that I didn't want to give it away. Because it was born under a good sign. And it was a big deal with Valeria—because Valeria values the religion and she was saying: "How can it be possible for these people to make a prenda and then not to have someone who understands and knows about that in the place where they are going to keep it?" Because up to this day the people from the museum don't believe in that, they study it because it's their job, but they don't believe in any of those things. But I'm going to tell you something, I did it because I asked Sarabanda and he told me: "Do it because it's going to be something that will give you strength." So I was doing that as a job commanded by my things.

·   ·   ·

The transition from the house shrine to the museum and the transformation of an artisan into an artist are both consequences of a recent movement to open the doors of Western museums to objects and artists that until recently had been excluded. The distinction between objects valued as ethnology and those valued as fine art has been broken, and the dividing line that clearly separated the art museum from the ethnographic museum has blurred with the appearance of numerous museums that belong to either (or neither) camp: ethnic, tribal, and local cultural museums.

The problems associated with the representation and exhibition of these objects are widely discussed among museum and art curators, anthropologists, and art historians. Two opposite approaches to representation—one in which contextual information about the objects is considered fundamental, the other with limited or no contextual information, in which the objects are to be viewed and judged as pure form–are the extremes of a range of practices adopted by museums and art galleries, which frequently used an approach that combines elements of both. Irrespective of the representation approach adopted, the end result is always an exhibition filtered through the ideas, tastes, and political and artistic views of those who organize it.

Even museums of the ethnographic type adopt a particular strategy of representation to address the museum-going public. Thus, even when museums exhibit works that are not considered "for sale," by highlighting them in an exhibition the museums contribute not only to the creation of value but to the process of commodification of the works.[18]

On the transformation of utensils, ritual objects and talismans into museum pieces, Octavio Paz (1979: 8) writes:

> Many of the objects that are accumulated in our museums and private collections belonged to that world where beauty was not a distinct and self-sufficient value. Society was divided into two great territories, the profane and the sacred. In both beauty was subordinated, in one case to usefulness and in the other to magical efficacy. Utensil, talisman, symbol: beauty was the aura of the object, the consequence—almost involuntary—of the secret relationship between workmanship and significance. The workmanship; the way a thing is made; the significance, for what it is made. Now all these objects, torn from their historical context, their specific function, their original meaning, offer themselves to our eyes like enigmatic divinities and demand adoration.

Felipe's "There" Faces His "Here"

When Felipe arrived in the United States, he encountered a practice of Santería that had undergone a series of transformations and developed into a set of diverse and sometimes conflicting approaches to ritual matters and religious beliefs. The history of Santería in the United States has been marked by debates over beliefs and ritual practices that reflect the contradictions and competition of the different groups that adhere to it. Not governed by a strict orthodoxy, Santería continues to elicit and accept new interpretations and accommodate the needs of diverse, multiethnic groups of practitioners.

Although there were Santería practitioners in New York by the early

1930s, the first Santería priest or babalao, Pancho Mora, is said to have arrived in New York only in 1946.[19] During the 1930s and 1940s, people in the United States who wanted to be initiated had to travel to Cuba, a practice that continued through the 1950s. With the advent of the Cuban revolution, however, becoming initiated in Cuba became quite difficult; therefore, people began traveling to Puerto Rico, and in the early 1960s initiations began to be performed in the United States. By the 1970s, Santería has spread beyond its ethnic boundaries and had numerous adepts among African Americans, non-Cuban Latinos, immigrants from other Caribbean islands, and even white Americans.

Coming from Matanzas in 1980, Felipe found himself a minority within a practice of Santería that, among the Cuban practitioners, primarily followed the Havana tradition. (The fact that the majority of postrevolutionary immigrants came from Havana and Las Villas may well have contributed to this.) Among Afro-American practitioners it had developed into a practice known as "Yoruba religion," and among Puerto Rican practitioners it had incorporated practices of *espiritismo*. The latter two practices led to the formation of house-temples that have developed independent religious practices.

Yoruba religion was the product of a movement led primarily by African Americans, who sought to purify Santería of its Spanish and Catholic elements and bring it closer to its "Yoruba roots." This movement began to unfold at the time of the civil rights movement and was linked with the black nationalist movement. In the 1960s this push for return to African roots in Santería led to the foundation of the Shango Temple in Harlem (later called Yoruba Temple). Members of this temple emphasized a direct connection with Africa; they wore African dresses, adopted African names, and promoted Yoruba social practices such as polygyny. They also brought the practice of the religion into public view through interviews, parades, television performances, films, and concerts—a clear contrast to the tradition of secrecy that most Cuban practitioners maintained. In 1969, some of the Temple's members, led by Walter King (one of the founders), left New York for South Carolina, where they established a Yoruba village called Oyotunji.[20] When the temple dissolved, the members who had remained in New York organized their own house-temples, joined pre-existing house-temples, or became members of predominantly Cuban or Puerto Rican houses. However, the movement to restore Santería/Yoruba religion to its "African essence," bringing it back to its Yoruba roots, has continued and spread, even among Spanish-speaking santeros. Among the best-known figures of this movement are the founders and organizers of the Yoruba Theological Archministry, John Mason and Gary Edwards. They call their approach "Yoruba revisionism," which, according to Edwards, fosters "a philosophical approach to the study of Yoruba culture which is based on the idea that the religion should return to its origin" by promoting the use of modern Yoruba language in the ceremonies and by returning the concepts that relate to the orichas to the "pre-slavery status minus the influence of the Catholic saints" (Mason and Edwards 1985: iv–v).[21]

Espiritismo (spiritism) is a movement based in the writings of a French schoolteacher, Leon Rivail (pen name Alan Kardec), that became very popular in Latin America after the arrival of Kardec's books (from 1856 on). The doctrine of spiritism includes belief in the possibility of communicating with the spirits of the dead, a hierarchy in the world of the spirits (which is a world where spirits evolve and reincarnate temporarily in human bodies) and that spirits may intervene in the human world by helping, hindering, or giving advice. In Cuba many practitioners had already incorporated some practices of spiritism into Santería and Palo. In New York, espiritismo became exceedingly popular among Puerto Rican immigrants, and from the 1960s on, many of its practices have been mixed with those of Santería. Nowadays, among Spanish-speaking practitioners it is not rare to find people who are both *espiritistas* and santeros. However, there are many espiritistas who resent any identification with Santería, as well as many santeros who prefer to keep Santería free from the influence of espiritismo. When the marielitos (some of whom were paleros) arrived, many began to interact with the spiritist mediums, sharing with them their Palo spirits and teaching them how to prepare a nganga.[22]

Ideological differences that one encounters among various U.S. Santería groups not only are a product of the encounter between Cubans and other ethnic groups but reflect existing disagreements among Cubans themselves. Not all Cubans were reluctant to include other ethnic groups in their religion. A major source of conflict among Cuban santeros was the power assigned to the babalaos in the different houses of ocha. Because of the small number of babalaos in New York's Santería community in the 1960s and the privileged position they enjoyed—which they strove to preserve by refusing to train or initiate other priests—a concentration of power had developed that is unusual for Santería. The early priesthood in New York was very selective about the admission of new members into the religion, and this applied not only to people outside their ethnic group but also to Cubans who did not belong to their "network." The babalaos claimed their authority on the basis of "authenticity," which became an important issue and was measured by asserting ritual ties to old and important house-temples in Havana. Furthermore, at this early stage ritual knowledge was transmitted orally, and the few *libretas* (notebooks) that contained religious information were in the hands of this group of priests who had established a niche in the different social clubs that were important centers for religious networking at the time (Morales 1990).

The wave of Cuban immigrants known as the "freedom flights" (1965–1973) saw the arrival in the United States of many important elders and ritual specialists who could perform many of the ritual functions that had been monopolized by the babalaos. This situation created the necessary conditions for the emergence of many houses of ocha that were not directly connected to or dependent on an Ifá priest. Thus, two types of ocha house arose: those that still relied on the babalaos and did not question any of their prerogatives, and those that became independent of the babalaos for most of their ritual activities. Interestingly, many of the houses that became independent from the control of the babalaos were headed by women (Morales 1990).

The arrival of the marielitos contributed further to the struggles and debates within the Santería community, this being the first wave of immigrants to include a large percentage of blacks—some of whom came directly from Matanzas, where the rituals and practices of Santería historically differed from those of Havana.[23]

Dissension, debate, controversy, disjuncture, fissures, and schism have demarcated the history of the main religious movements in the West. Competing groups of practitioners have sustained contrasting versions of myth and ideology. This dynamic also characterizes lesser-known religious traditions such as Santería and has to be taken into account when trying to unravel its historical development. Santería, a religion born from the encounter of two different worlds, has proved resilient, able to adapt to changing circumstances and environments and to answer to the sometimes-conflicting yearnings of the groups that have identified with it. The incorporation over time of new gods, new beliefs, and new rituals bespeaks a flexibility that has enabled Santería's deities, the orichas, to survive through two diasporas.

Felipe's Concept of Tradition

In Cuba before the revolution, Felipe had exercised his trade and practiced his religion without feeling the need to question or justify his practices. It was an integral part of his life, and as such it was lived, not spoken about. With the arrival of the revolution, he became a cultural worker and began to drum to the orichas not always to praise them or invoke their presence. In a new setting—the theater—he demonstrated his tradition to a public that frequently did not share his religious beliefs. He began to be involved in questioning or debating issues of culture, tradition, authenticity, and so forth. This "awareness"—trying to verbalize and define practices that used to be part of the way things always were—became even more important when he left his country and re-established his musical and religious practices away from home, distanced from all the familiar things that served to validate them. In the United States these traditions had been integrated into the legacy of the African diaspora among people of African descent in the Americas and as such had been reinterpreted, re-created, and shaped to construct a Pan-African identity, in ways that sometimes seemed alien to Felipe when he first encountered them (although after many years in the United States he began to accept some of them).

We are going to perform a ceremony, and you do it one way and I do it another. Which means that everyone learned a way, a point of view, according to the way they were taught. That creates a habit, and that's a tradition. Why should I talk about what I don't know? My ancestors taught me a way, which was good for them, and that was the way. That's why in Cuba they say: "I belong to this branch—" We understand that there are no such branches, but we still say: "I belong to this branch." We understand that there are not really different branches, but different habits that are created in the different families, even to sit at the table. For example, in a ceremony you have to use water from the sea and from a river, but in some houses they say you also need water from a lake, from the mountain and whatnot, a cave, a well—some houses used blessed water. The same things happen with the plants. You go to houses where they tell you: "Don't put that plant in because we don't use it." However, Osain is in every plant, the good plants and the bad ones. Because the world is like that, it has good and bad things.

Those who came from Africa had a different way of thinking, as well as a different way of speaking. When they were brought to Cuba, everything changed: the climate, the plants, everything. So they began to see how they could continue to do their things, because in Africa it was different from Cuba. When we arrived to the religion, well, the new generation began "de-purating," doing new things, using new vocabulary . . . in many of the chants we began to use many words in Spanish, because we couldn't speak their language, and the chants remained like that.

I'm a person who's here and who does things the way he was taught to. And who taught me? People of nación, a Lucumí—or a Yoruba, which is the way they call them now—taught me about the things I do. I work the way they taught me to work—one ceremony more or less doesn't determine things. What determines things is that they are done, giving an account to Olofi, because without Olofi nothing works.

Syncretism

Syncretism is a term used in the social sciences to describe the reconciliation or union of different religious practices or beliefs. Although frequently applied to Afro-Cuban religions, for many it has acquired negative connotations. Some deem syncretism a criticism that the religion is "impure" or "inauthentic," while others consider that applying it with reference to religious practices places the less well known religion in a subordinate position.

Although the slaves brought to Cuba were forced to adopt Catholicism, through the institution of the cabildos they were able at the same time to re-create some of their African religious practices, adapting them to their new environment and to their circumstances as a marginalized, repressed, and enslaved group. This forced encounter of different Afro-Cuban religious practices with one another and with Catholicism was not a smooth process of synthesis but one in which coercion and imposition coexisted with resistance and agency. The outcome was a religious practice that gathered and sometimes fused together rituals, practices, and beliefs of diverse origins. Was the adoption of elements from

Catholicism just a subterfuge, a way to disguise native religion? Were the saints just masks, or did they fuse with the orichas to give rise to creole deities? Did Afro-Cuban religions develop in resistance or in respect to Catholicism, or both? These are questions that are still being debated by scholars of Afro-Cuban religion.[24]

Although aware of the debates over syncretism that are taking place among the practitioners of Santería in the United States,[25] Felipe has not been involved in them and continues to live his religious practices in a way that fuses, combines, mixes, overlaps, or uses in parallel rituals and beliefs that he learned from his elders in Cuba. He incorporates into his religious life a plurality of hybrid religious practices (Palo, Santería, Abakuá, Catholicism) in what could be called *metahybrid practice*.[26]

Below I describe two incidents that illustrate better than any theoretical explanation the hybridity, or metahybridity, of Felipe's religious practices.[27]

When I visited Felipe during Holy Week in 1992, he had covered all his saints and his batá drums in the same way the saints are covered in Catholic churches during this week in Latin America. When I asked him about this, he described to me the following:

Already on a day like this they begin to prepare for the *romerías* [pilgrimages].[28] In the casa de santo, all the santeros, all the godchildren get together to go to the romería. Because what they are really doing is like an egbó [santero offering or sacrifice]. They begin to prepare on Holy Friday, because they go to church. Then on Saturday, with all the food and all the other things, they go out to a place in Matanzas that is called Monserrate. The Church of Monserrate is there; it is on a hill and from there you can see the whole valley. So they go to prepare the food. They begin to cook—because they leave very early. At five or six in the morning people are already there, waiting for it to be ten in the morning. Because they say that at ten in the morning is when God goes back to the Glory. The Church bells begin to ring and people begin to *rumbiar*, to play rumba. From Saturday on, when He rises up to Glory, the rumba, and the food and the whole thing, begins. Then on resurrection Sunday the fiesta continues—everyone dancing at Monserrate. It's a very beautiful tradition. If you see it, it combines the church with Santería. Because then everybody goes back and uncovers their santos, gives water to them, and the fiesta continues. The Abakuá groups do the same thing. They place their manifesto, and then Saturday at ten, they do their plante helping the Holy One, God, rise up to Glory. And then Sunday, the big fiesta. They all party because it is a combination. It is beautiful, beautiful, beautiful.

Then he explained to me his position on the rejection of the Catholic saints by santeros in the United States.

Here they want to eliminate the statues, well, they may do it if they want to but we can't. If I find out that in Cuba they begin to do the same I'm going to protest, because that would be a lack of respect for our ancestors. What happened was that our ancestors used the statues to be able to manifest the power of their things—the stones were below those statues. Even if they were Catholic figures and at the time may have had no spirituality, our ancestors gave them a spirituality by using them the way they did. Then when we came along the saints were already there. We were born seeing that the Virgen de la Caridad del Cobre is Ochún. So how can they come now and tell us it isn't Ochún? Those things have roots that cannot be unearthed. Doing so would be mocking our ancestors.

Let me now describe another ceremony that I witnessed when Felipe's brother Nino died. It took place at a funeral home in the Bronx. For someone brought up Catholic, what was taking place at this funeral parlor seemed utterly familiar: the prayers, the ritual, the behavior of the visitors, the setting. However, not long after I arrived, Felipe came in accompanied by other members of the family and some Cuban friends. In one corner of the room hidden behind the place where people sat, were some bags I had not noticed when I entered. From them Felipe took out the Abakuá drums, and each of the newcomers took one as he approached the coffin, where they began to play and sing chants I had never heard Felipe sing. One of the men took out his keychain and began to play a bell pattern, using the candelabra as an instrument. As the tension grew, Felipe gave the drum he was playing to another member of the group and began to play a parallel rhythm, using Nino's coffin as a drum. I was too immersed in this daunting and sorrowful ritual to understand fully why suddenly the drumming stopped and the drums were hastily brought back to the bags in the back of the room. I asked the person next to me what was going on, and she replied: "The priest is coming!." At this moment a priest walked into the room. No traces were left of the ceremony that had taken place only a few seconds before. The scene that followed was quite familiar again. Most of the people present made the sign of the cross and followed the prayers and invocations. When the priest finished and left, the drums were brought back. However, this time they used the batá drums. The traditional salute to the orichas was followed by a series of chants, after which some Palo chants were sung, accompanied by conga drums and bell. The departure of Nino's spirit was guided by a ritual that combined all the religious practices that had been part of his life: a Catholic, santero, palero, and Abakuá farewell.

The Marielitos

One of the difficulties Felipe has had to face in the exercise of his trade in his new country relates to the fact that he is a drummer of religious music. This music is strongly tied to ritual: There is a prescribed sequence in which chants and rhythms are performed; certain chants, rhythms, and dance movements are linked to specific deities; specific occasions call for certain ceremonies; and so forth. When Felipe arrived in the United States, he found a community where a lot of ritual practices differed from and sometimes conflicted with his. Many of the santeros in New York—especially the babalaos, who had acquired power and control that was not exclusively theirs in Cuba—felt that the wave of Cuban immigrants known as the marielitos would disturb the religious practice in New York with their "innovations." Two of Felipe's experiences clearly illustrate this clash between the "here" and the "there."

A lot of people with more experience arrived, with more knowledge. Because before we came there were a lot of problems here. We were able to give more knowledge to people but many times they didn't want to accept it. They trusted more what they heard on a record or what they read in a book. They didn't want to accept what we brought; those who came here before didn't want to accept that. They said: "No, you marielitos came here to mess everything, because you came with your things, saying this and saying that." But we didn't come to mess anything, we came with what's real.

Look, a babalao calls me once because he wants a *toque de muerto*. When he told me a *tambor de muerto* [dead]—because I already know how the cards are played here—I said: "Do you want a toque of *égun* or do you want a Palo toque?" He replied: "No. No. No. I want a tambor de muerto. And added: "*Coño,* since you marielitos arrived here in 1980 everything is called differently."

I did not argue with him, but when I went to his house after I had finished playing I said to him: "Look, a toque for muerto is called a toque for Ikú, because Ikú is when the coffin is there, when the body is there, and you perform a ceremony; that it's a toque for Ikú. It is a toque to bid farewell to the deceased. Once the dead body is buried after nine days you do a ceremony for the spirit; a ceremony in which you have to make an offering of white doves—that represent the Holy Spirit. After a series of ceremonies, then the dead person becomes an égun, because he begins to gain spirituality, to loose the skin, to become a spirit. So a toque for égun is when you are playing without the dead person being there, without the cadaver; you are playing to the spirit of that body. Because égun for us in the jargon, in our language, means to play to the spirit. And a toque for Ikú is playing for the cadaver, that the body is there, the coffin and the dead person inside it." Ha! Ha! Ha! That's what I told him. Then I continued: "What we just played today is a toque de Palo, which has nothing to do with a dead person being or not being there. The chants are different because Palo is Congo and the rituals are different. [Égun chants belong to the Lucumí-Yoruba traditions. Palo chants belong to the Congo tradition.]

Another time I went to play for a Palo ceremony and a woman there complained about the chants I was singing. Then the owner of the house, who knew me well, explained: "The chants you sing nobody knows them here, because those are fundamento chants and those prendas are what they call *prendas espirituales.*" But what is this of prendas espirituales, I never saw anything like that before. They just go to a *botánica,* buy a bunch of sticks, a pile of iron things, take some earth and throw everything into a pot. They spray holy water and place it on an altar and then call you to play for it. But that isn't right. Then they sing all kinds of songs to that prenda, that in Cuba if you sing them they send you to hell! They sing songs from the radio, and they get "mounted" [become possessed] while playing *tambora* [drum used to perform *merengue*], with a merengue, with whatever. For us that is a profanity. All the things of the Congo have a way, they have to be well fundamented, following all the steps. It's the same as when you work in construction. If you are making a mix to just bind something you don't have to use gravel. But if you are using it for a floor you have to add gravel of certain dimension. Or like food, every dish has its own condiments and those who do not know about these things should learn first. Because if you are trying to create a "spirituality," you have to do things right.

Many Cubans who arrived in the United States during the Mariel exodus or after and were familiar with the music of the Afro-Cuban religions had gained this familiarity not necessarily through religious affiliation but through the concerts and demonstrations of groups such as the Conjunto Folklórico Nacional (either as performers or spectators). For many, this music was not any different from secular genres like the rumba, which were also performed in the concerts of these ensembles. Many musicians—members of these ensembles—who came with the Mariel boat lift were not santeros in Cuba and became initiated into the religion after their arrival in the United States.[29] Thus, the religious background and knowledge of the marielitos varied considerably, and generalizations with respect to this group are bound to be problematic.

Felipe acknowledges that the controversy surrounding the marielitos and the prejudice against them were in part justified by the fact that many of them invoked religious knowledge and credentials they did not possess, and many were not even linked to any Afro-Cuban religion back in Cuba.

Of course many have come who took a pot and threw four sticks there, four goat bones or whatever, and it's now to be considered a prenda. And they have luck, and people come and whatnot, but they aren't doing anything right. To go by the little book, you do this and you do that. Lies! They saw there was money there so they started it as a business. Like many santeros also, who have just commercialized the religion.

Reticence toward the changes brought about by the arrival of the marielitos was not limited to matters of ritual but was also felt in the field of sacred music and drumming in New York, where some of the "elder" drummers felt that the style of drumming brought by the marielitos was too "liberal."

When Santería began to develop in New York in the 1940s and 1950s, although there were no consecrated drums and people had to travel to Cuba to undergo the major religious initiations, there were musicians familiar with the Afro-Cuban religious repertoire. Some of this repertoire was included in performances at the clubs where Puerto Rican and Cuban immigrants used to socialize, which were particularly popular during this period in East Harlem (Morales 1990: 132–33). Teddy Holiday, who was born and raised in El Barrio, recalls how the famous Cuban musician Arsenio Rodriguez and his brothers, one of them named Quique, used to perform bembés and Palo ceremonies in this neighborhood using congas to replace the traditional drums.[30] The first religious ceremony where batá drums were used took place in 1961 in the Bronx (New York). Julito Collazos led the ensemble using non-sacred (aberikulá) drums for the occasion.

Julito Collazos, a drummer from Havana, has been credited as the key figure in the introduction of batá drumming to New York. Julito came to the United States as a member of the dance company of the renowned African American choreographer and dancer Katherine Dunham. On one of her trips to Cuba, Dunham had met another famous Afro-Cuban drummer, Francisco Aguabella, a drummer from Matanzas, who joined her company in 1953. At that time Aguabella was the head of a group of drummers of the Orquesta de Rafael Ortega that included Candito, Trinidad Torregosa, Raul Diaz, Raul "Nasakó," and later Julito Collazos. At the recommendation of Aguabella, Collazos joined Dunham in 1954, and both drummers toured the world with her company for several years. In 1957, Aguabella left the company and settled for a few months in New York, later leaving for the West Coast, where he still resides.[31] Julito remained in New York, where he led an active life during the 1950s and 1960s as a freelance musician for club and recording dates while performing occasionally for religious ceremonies. In the late 1960s he began teaching batá drumming to a select group of students, but at this time he did not have a set of batá drums (he used makeshift double-headed drums as substitutes); he acquired a set in 1975 (Friedman 1982: 107–8). The drums he acquired in 1975 were not sacred drums and therefore had limited ritual use. That the drummer, who is deemed by many to be the most important figure in the introduction of ritual drumming in New York, did not own a sacred set of drums may explain why unconsecrated drums came to be accepted and continued to be used by drummers for some ceremonies in the United States. However in Matanzas, Cuba, these types of drums are not accepted as appropriate for any ritual.

Collazos was also an active popular musician who was well known by many of the Latin musicians in New York. This may explain the importance assigned to him in the introduction of ritual drumming, while the role played by other religious drummers, who only performed in rituals, is not widely recognized. Such is the case of Juan "Candela" (Fire), a drummer who was active also in Miami, who by 1962 had built his own set of batá drums and was recognized in some segments of the community as the one who "broke the thing wide open." Juan "Candela," his son "Papito" and his nephew Angel used to perform with Julito Collazos and Ornelio Scull when batá drumming was just being introduced in New York.[32]

Parallel to the need for sacred batá drummers, which increased as the religious community expanded and as trips to Cuba were restricted after the revolution, an interest in batá drumming solely as music (not always tied to religion) grew among Latin musicians and other drummers in New York.[33] Thus, many non-Cuban musicians such as Louis Bauzo, Milton Cardona, Franky Malabé, Steve Berrios, and John Amira began to learn and later perform this music. Not all these drummers were able to learn with Collazos, who was very selective in taking students.

The drummers who were not able to study with Collazos had to look for alternative sources of information. Some of these drummers, instead of following the traditional road of the apprentice, used a combination of sources, mainly published transcriptions found in the works of Ortíz and commercial recordings (Cornelius 1991: 146–49). One of these drummers, Louis Bauzo, acknowledges the importance written transcriptions and recordings had for him in learning this music, since he was not accepted as "part of Julito's clique." After getting hold of Ortíz's books, which were difficult to find and were not readily shared by those who owned them, he began to gather with other drummers at a place located at 13th Street and Avenue A in New York, to try to reconstruct the rhythms of the three drums and practice them. Bauzo remembers that at least fifty drummers began to participate in these workshops but not many remained after a few months.

Some of the participants in these workshops, among them Steve Berrios and Milton Cardona, were drummers who had access to Collazos, whether to play with him or to watch him perform.[34] Thus the sources available to the participants in these workshops were not exclusively written transcriptions and recordings. Many had access to oral sources (other, more knowledgeable drummers) and occasions for traditional apprenticeship (by attending religious ceremonies) to acquire knowledge, which later they shared with others. While some drummers had access to Ortíz's books, many did not read notation or have the skills to interpret the transcriptions. Therefore, it was only drummers like Bauzo and Amira, who had considerable expertise with rhythm notations and were not involved in performing with Julito Collazos, who relied extensively on these transcriptions and on recordings for learning. Other drummers followed the traditional road, learning from more-experienced drummers.

The 1980s represented a watershed in the history of sacred batá drumming in New York. During this decade, fundamento drums, unavailable previously, began to make their voices heard at religious rituals. With the exiles from Mariel four olúbatás, three from Havana and one from Matanzas, arrived: Alfredo "Coyude" Vidaux, Orlando "Puntilla" Rios, Juan "el Negro" Raymat, and Felipe "Mazo de Yerba" García. Each of these drummers was able to get a set of fundamento drums to perform in ritual ceremonies. As mentioned earlier, when the drums consecrated according to the Cuban practice began to be used in New York, the concept of lineages was introduced and became essential in defining the religious credentials of a set of drums. This did not come about immediately, however, and in the interim many houses of ocha continued to perform ceremonies using aberikulá drums, while others, such as the Bonifacio Valdéz Temple in New Jersey, built their own sets of drums (without a godfather to transmit to them the voice).

Exiles from the Mariel not only reconstructed the tradition of the "transmission of the voice" among sacred drums but were also instrumental in making the knowledge of batá drumming more accessible by taking under their guidance groups of apprentices and even teaching more experienced drummers. However, some of the elder local drummers deemed the style of drummers like Puntilla too liberal and felt it showed many differences when compared to the older sources (Cornelius 1991: 149). In principle this could be explained by different training lineages or an accelerated evolution. I believe the first possibility can be ruled out. The purported sources of the New York–trained drummers were Julito Collazos and Ortíz's transcriptions. Both of these sources stem directly from drummers Pablo Roche and Jesús Pérez, who represented the standard of the Havana tradition. Collazos, once a member of Roche's group, had also drummed on the set known as Los Machetones, the drums of Nicolás Angarica, later inherited by his son Papo Angarica. On the other hand, the "newly imported" styles were those of Coyude, who was sworn to the drum of Nicolás Angarica, and Puntilla, who was sworn to the drums known as the drums of Pobolotti, on which Pérez performed. Thus, the sources in Cuba for all these styles of drumming are not only closely related but also stem from the Havana style of drumming. That leaves the accelerated evolution hypothesis. Making allowance for possible exaggerations on the part of New York drummers, I tend to believe that the stylistic changes stem from the transformation batá drumming may have undergone after the revolution, as a result of the involvement of many sacred batá drummers in professional and amateur folkloric ensembles.

Felipe's case is different because he comes from Matanzas, with a drumming tradition that most considered a separate one. The Matanzas style was not known in New York, and an interest in it developed only recently with the arrival of recordings and visits (through organized tours and workshops) of musicians from Matanzas, in particular the group Afro-Cuba.

Another development that took place in the 1980s was the organization of "folkloric" groups that began to stage selections of the Afro-Cuban religious repertoire for the public. At present, there are two types of batá ensemble in New York: those who perform exclusively for ritual purposes and those who alternate between ritual drumming and public, staged performances. Whereas the leaders of both types of ensemble remain fixed, the drummers who play the other two drums (itótele and okónkolo) tend to change in some of these ensembles. (Some play in two different ensembles.) The dominant style of batá playing continues to be the Havana style, and Orlando "Puntilla" Rios, one of its representatives, is considered at present the most important ritual drummer in New York.[35]

Given that most house-temples in New York are familiar with the Havana repertoire of chants and style of drumming, it has been difficult for Felipe, as a drummer from the Matanzas school, to open a space for himself within this network. He has limited opportunities to perform and has had to train the drummers who play with him, since New York's batá drummers are not familiar with the Matanzas style of playing. Teaching has thus become an important avenue for Felipe to continue to exercise his trade as a batá drummer. However, as was the case in his early years in Cuba, the batá drumming that has been central in his life is not his main source of living.

"The Orichas Behave Different Here"

Many of the differences Felipe has encountered in his new country have to do with ritual practices he will not discuss for a published source that can be read by anyone. However, he considers that the behavior of the orichas during the part of the rituals that everyone can witness may be discussed freely. Felipe finds that the orichas and Palo deities do not conduct themselves in the way they used to in Cuba, where, when an oricha mounts (takes possession) one of his or her horses, the recipient dances and moves in a way that portrays certain characteristics of the deity or that responds to what is being said in the chant.[36]

I will give you a few examples. There is a chant for Changó that says in Lu-cumí: "I have a goat here for you, but first I want you to do like the goat and take three steps back, and do three somersaults." No Changó here in New York does this when you sing this chant.

Here, many of the Eleguá chants are danced with one foot; that's not right. Eleguá dances with two feet unless he is commanded to dance with one foot, as in the chant:

> *eribo eribo*
> *ago metá metá*
> *motimore elese kan . . .*

Elese kan is one foot; so the chant is saying get one foot up and go and run with one foot only.

There is another Eleguá who lives in a crosspiece up in the ceiling. Years ago in Cuba, houses used to have ceilings in the form of a triangle connected by a beam. Up there lives an Eleguá who, when you sing

> *ago ibara*
> *ago ibara*
> *Eleguá agukeño*
> *ago ibara*

jumps, wanting to go up to the ceiling. When you sing this here, nobody jumps or anything.

When Yemayá [oricha of the sea] dances the agolona she mimics that she is combing her hair. Then she begins to take steps backward like the waves of the sea. When she comes forward she jumps in front of the drums. So that crash, that movement, you have to signal it with the drums. Three times she does like the waves of the sea that come crashing against the cliffs. Here they don't do that. Then, with a handkerchief, she imitates the movements of a boat, that handkerchief turns around and around, as she continues to do that. I've never seen here a Yemayá doing this.

Felipe has also encountered horses that are not mounted by their orichas after he entices them with chants that, in Cuba, always bring those orichas down.

Once in a fiesta I sang a chant for Oyá that says: *Oyá kokoroooo; Oyá kamade,* and the woman was not being mounted. So this other lady that was with her comes and says to me: "You are singing *puyas* [chants sung to goad or poke fun at the orichas] to Oyá; Oyá is not coming because you are not singing to her properly." I told her: "But what the hell do you know about what I'm singing? Because I'm singing *Oyá kokoro Oyá kamade,* and I'll say what it means now in Spanish. It means that Oyá is a little animal, an insect as we call it in Cuba, that cannot be eaten by anybody—there's no animal, not the lion, not the tiger, the panther, nothing that can eat Oyá; Oyá is poison. If when I sing that Oyá doesn't come, she won't come with anything else."

Instead here they sing a chant for Oyá that is really a puya and you have to know when to sing it, otherwise Oyá gets offended. It's a chant that asks Oyá: "What are you doing here dressed that way, with your cloths made of pieces of fabric of different colors?" You cannot sing that chant to the Oyá of my old lady. My mother, if you sang that chant to her Oyá, she would change colors and would be fuming in anger.

According to Felipe, Palo deities such as Mamá Chola and Tiembla Tierra also act differently in New York. In Cuba, when these spirits possess a devotee, the person falls to the floor and begins to crawl like a snake. He can rise to his feet only after a series of ritual gestures are performed, which involve, in part, placing some gunpowder (fula) on the soles of his feet and setting fire to it. After this, the spirit who has taken possession of the body of the palero stands up and addresses those present, giving them advice, revealing secrets, predicting their futures, and cleansing them of bad influences and energies. Felipe finds that in the United States, when people fall in trance they remain standing, a behavior that in Cuba would be considered unusual and raise suspicions about the authenticity of the possession.

If we go to a fundamento de Palo [a Palo ceremony], when the perro de prenda is possessed, the spirit comes to the floor, it doesn't come up straight, it doesn't stand up. It cannot stand up until the necessary things are done to order him or her to stand up. Because if it's a muerto [dead person], from where is that spirit coming? It's coming from the earth, because it's the spirit of a dead person, it's coming from below. That's why when the perro de prenda is possessed by a spirit [he or she] has to drop to the floor. That's understood in Cuba. But here it isn't like that. You see here that the muertos come—and always they come standing up. And Mama Chola comes and Tiembla Tierra comes and Siete Rayos come, and all the ones they want come. But it isn't like a real toque de palo. Here you remain astonished. You don't even know where you are.

Not only do some of the deities seem to Felipe to behave differently across the ocean, but some of the orichas Felipe knew in Cuba seem never to have crossed the ocean.

Sometimes I mention one of those saints that are less well known in Cuba and people look puzzled and ask me: "What kind of stories are you making up, because that is an invention of yours." But it is not an invention; in Cuba there were many, many santos that people here do not know about.

Confronting the Written

In prerevolutionary Cuba, books were not sources santeros would turn to in order to learn about their religion, nor were they ever quoted as sources of authority in matters of tradition. Instrument makers knew the measurements of the drums because they had learned them in the process of building instruments; singers learned the texts of the chants by attending ceremonies and listening to other singers.

After the revolution, as the aesthetic side of the tradition (music and dance) was decontextualized and learned by many outside the religious context, knowledge began to be transmitted in a formal way, through lessons taught by instructors. In this environment, the written (i.e., printed texts of chants, sketches of dance movements, transcriptions of rhythms) began to take hold in the transmission of knowledge. The publication of books on various aspects of the religious traditions increased, accompanied by new editions of the works of Ortíz and other researchers that were unavailable during the 1960s. One may assume that these publications have had an impact (which is yet to be evaluated) on a population with the level of literacy of postrevolutionary Cuba.[37] However, in families like Felipe's (at least until Felipe left in 1980), the younger generations continued to be taught by the elders, orally and through apprenticeship.[38]

In the United States, because of the increasingly public nature of Santería and the shift among certain sectors of the practitioners toward institutionalization, the religion has been moving gradually away from the oral and into the written. Concurrently, the secrecy that had characterized these religious practices has been abandoned by many who have decided to bring the religion into the public view. Thus issues such as the development of texts and the authority of texts have become crucial among certain groups within the religion (Murphy [1988] 1993: ix). Moreover, many people who joined the religion in the United States have acquired their knowledge of many religious matters through books. Therefore, in his new country, Felipe has frequently been confronted by people who question his knowledge based on information they have gathered from books.

Thus, Santería is undergoing a process of change from what could be considered "mixed orality" to a "secondary" type of orality. Mixed orality is the type of orality that coexists with writing, but where the influences of the written remain external to it. Secondary orality, by contrast, is an orality that has been (re)composed based on writing, one where writing determines the "value of voice" (Zumthor 1990: 25). However, whose version will be singled out for transmission, who will do the singling out, and what weight will be given to the written word are still in the process of being defined.

Felipe's first encounter with the "authority of the written" was when he was making his drums in the United States and the babalaos checked in a book to see if his drums had the appropriate measurements. After this first encounter with the written authority, Felipe found himself frequently questioned in matters of ritual by people who would invoke books as the source of knowledge and authority.

They all have to go to the book and look for what's there. And we don't go by the book, we follow our inheritance, because that's the way we were taught. What I sing is what my nephew is singing, what my daughter is singing, you understand? Because that's what I used to listen to in my house. In my house, from the moment they wake up, they wake up singing santo. Then someone would ask: "So what is the meaning of this, what is the meaning of that?" "Well, that means this and so on." That is the way we learned. Not with the book, because the book—Now, sometimes I take a book and I see that a chant is wrong. Sometimes I think it is wrong because maybe there was a difficulty in writing it. Or maybe they didn't want to give the right information, they wanted to keep it secret so they changed the words. The fact remains that there's a book. This book that says: What you see is what it is. Then what should you do? What you should do is, don't abandon what you learned but learn other things, learn the other things but keep also yours, keep the positive things that you learn; that's what I do.

The Struggle of Memory over Forgetting

Teaching as a Way of Remembering

Back in Cuba, Felipe gave formal batá lessons only to tourists at the time of the revolution, when he was performing at Varadero, an important resort in the province of Matanzas. Felipe taught tourists who remained in the country for only one or two weeks and wanted to familiarize themselves with the different styles of Afro-Cuban drumming. He never took this teaching experience seriously, because trying to convey in three lessons what had taken him a lifetime to learn seemed to him quite preposterous. Yet it was work, and work brought an income, which he always welcomed. However, during these years he continued to hand down the tradition of batá drumming to members of his family and other drummers in Matanzas, in the way in which he had acquired it from his elders: a process of observation and playing where a lot of the learning is done alone. Only when you already can play a little are you allowed to sit with others, have comments made on your progress, and receive help with your playing. This is a way of learning that characterizes many oral musical traditions.

When Felipe organized his own musical group, Emikeké, in Cuba, many aspiring drummers would learn, by playing, the different toques for the orichas during the group's rehearsals. The concepts of a paid lesson with a set schedule, of layering information and skills so as to present them to students in a way they could tackle them, were foreign to Felipe.

In the United States, during his early years as an immigrant musician, Felipe played with people who were already familiar with batá drumming and who knew some of the repertoire of Santería chants. It was only around 1989 that Felipe was approached by an American drummer who wanted to study with him.

Jess, who is not into Santería, came, and he wanted to learn only rumba. I used to say to him: "*Chico,* you can play the drum," and he: "No, because I'm white—and people—" "Go to hell with that." And one day he came and told me: "I think I'm going to play the drum." I gave him the drum and he began. And he became so eager to learn that he would come two, three times. Paying ten dollars, or whatever he could. He would come, two, three, four, and even five times; sometimes he would come the whole week. Back then I used to tell him: "*Chico,* come even without paying, come as you please, without money or with money, but come." Because I saw that he was making progress and had the will to learn. He used to come just to learn one toque, if he didn't know it he would come every day until he learned it. Then Jessy brought Greg, and so on.

Since then, Felipe has incorporated teaching into his overall musical activities. He worked in a way similar to what he was used to in Cuba. Students would listen, observe, imitate, and play or sing. His first students formed part of the group he organized in the 1990s, and instead of receiving formal lessons, they "rehearsed" once a week. Other students called Felipe and went every week or even just once in a while for a lesson. Most, if not all, the students that approached Felipe were drummers or musicians who were already familiar with Latin percussion, and many of them already had some knowledge of the Afro-Cuban musical traditions. When Felipe moved to California in 1995, teaching remained one of his main activities as a drummer (together with drum making).

Teaching not only provided income for Felipe; it became a weapon for him in his struggle for memory over forgetting.[39] Teaching gave Felipe the opportunity to play the toques the way they are performed in Matanzas, and to play toques that were used only in Matanzas and were unknown in the United States.

We have a toque in Matanzas that I taught the drummers of my group in New York to play, that is called *amalá,* but commonly they refer to it as the *harina* [flour]. It is a toque that you play for the dancers to make a circle. And everybody has to dance turning around in that circle. All the santeros get into the circle and it is a beautiful dance. Because they do as if they were stirring a cauldron where the flour is cooking. Then they do as if they were taking the flour out of the cauldron and throwing it up. According to the changes in the toque, the movements of the dancers change. And it is done in a circle because anything that has to do with the santos is rounded, like the earth, there is nothing squared. So as the dancers keep turning around, the rhythm begins to rise and rise. That's when people begin to get mounted, because that toque is played precisely for that. It is a toque addressed to all the santos. In a toque when the santos are not coming down, you play that toque, and the "real" santos have to come down. Here in New York you don't hear about that, they don't mention it in those books they write. But we in Matanzas, we have a lot of things, because Matanzas was really the strong cradle of all of that. In Matanzas a lot of slaves were brought, and they remained there, and they had a lot of knowledge.

Teaching Women to Play Batá

Gender plays a crucial restrictive role in the world of batá drummers. Only males are allowed to be sworn as drummers, and the barring of women from this ritual world goes as far as not even allowing women to touch the drums. Drummers cannot have sexual relationships with women some number of days before they play a ceremony, and during the rituals women are not allowed to stand behind the drummers or among them.[40] Even the skin used for the drums cannot be of a female animal.

The explanations of these restrictions, which are based in menstrual taboos, are at best ambiguous.[41] This may be explained in part by the fact that it is always drummers (men) who are questioned about the rationale of this taboo and called on to explain it. Drumming is male territory, and many drummers consider even questions about issues of drumming an invasion and handle them as such. One might assume also that a subject related to women's menstruation could create uneasiness and contribute to the simplistic explanations the drummers tend to offer. However, I suspect the vagueness of the answers does not come from uneasiness or tact but rather from unfamiliarity with the religious basis of a taboo that has been maintained just because "this is the way things have always been."

When questioned about this taboo, some drummers argued that women presented a threat to the drums (the drums could lose their voice or power), yet they could not explain why. Others just believed women should "learn to keep their place," which in this case means not touching or playing the drums.

Felipe's explanation links the interdiction to how Añá, the source of power of the drums, is made. Though he offered no details on the composition of what is placed inside the drums to serve as the vehicle for Añá, he made it clear that something in it could harm women. The importance of blood in Santería has already been discussed. Spirits are fed with blood; thus a sacrifice is offered to the spirit that inhabits the batá drums before playing any ceremony. According to Felipe, women are kept from playing the drums in order to protect them, not the drums. It is believed that the spirit that inhabits the drums, desirous of blood, may cause women to bleed to death.[42]

At present, opinions about women playing batá drums are divided. In Cuba a debate on this continues that began after the revolution, when foreign women began to be taught batá at workshops organized by the revolutionary government; the instructors were members of groups such as the Conjunto Folklórico Nacional and Afro-Cuba. Felipe tells me that many Cubans used to comment: "If we teach foreigners, why not teach our own women here in the solar?" In fact, some of the women who performed with the Afro-Cuban folkloric groups played some batá, though not openly. Since Felipe left Cuba in 1980, however, things have changed. There are at present at least two all-women batá ensembles, which perform only in concerts. However, women continue to be banned from playing in religious ceremonies.

In New York, drummers are more conservative than in Cuba when it comes to teaching women to play batá. They do not make the distinction between fundamento and unconsecrated drums. By refusing to teach women to play batá, they are in practice extending the taboo from the drums that house Añá, to include the toques to the orichas played in any type of batá drum. What is surprising is that many of these drummers, aware of the changes that are taking place in Cuba and not being religious themselves (not all the drummers in New York are initiated santeros), have clung to the prohibition more for personal than for religious reasons. Moreover, these restrictions are not carried out uniformly; certain practices, such as drumming styles of Abakuá traditions, where secrecy and exclusion of women have been the rule, are taught to women. The choice not to teach women batá appears in many cases to be inconsistent and arbitrary.

We know that the batá is a fundamento drum, and as a fundamento it can injure women who play it. But the music has nothing to do with the fundamento. The music is the roots that have to be taught because otherwise they would be lost. Rhythm has nothing to do with it, the rhythm is music. When women are playing they are not performing a ceremony. Because a woman can perform in a theater but with drums that are not baptized. Those drums for me are not batá, they are like regular drums because they don't have a fundamento. For example, it is like a car without a motor, you can get into the car, but the car doesn't move. Yes, you are in the car, but the car doesn't move.

In the fundamento drum, what is important is what the drum has inside; that is what gives the drum a power. That drum is not played for pleasure, it is played only because there is a ceremony.

. . . There are still many bataleros who don't agree to teach women, I am one of the ones that agrees to it. I agree because we have to give life to our tradition. Because if a woman, as we say, *se sube* [is possessed or mounted], well then she has the power of being a sanctuary. So, why should we inhibit them from playing the drums? Isn't this backwardness, isn't this practicing machismo?

. . . I just keep on going and this culture, I teach it. If a dog comes and tells me to teach him the culture, I am going to teach him, because I believe the dog has a guardian angel because it is a creature that has life. If the dog can do it even with one leg, I would teach him. Why shouldn't I? God commanded me so, and I don't care about what people have to say.

Singing as a Way of Remembering

Singing has also become an important strategy in Felipe's struggle against forgetting. Batá playing requires a lot of concentration from the drummers because of the permanent changes in the rhythmic patterns and the "conversations" that go on between the drums (in particular, between the iyá and the itótele). Because of this, it is rare to find an iyá player who can sing while he drums. However, in New York, Felipe encountered the need to sing while he played when performing with the group he organized with his students. Many of these students were not familiar with the repertoire of Santería chants as they are sung in Matanzas.

Santería chants, which may be sung *a cappella* or with instrumental accompaniment, are performed in a call-and-response style by a solo singer (*akpwón, akpón,* or *gallo*) and a chorus composed of the participants in the ceremony who know the chants and join in the singing. Variations (textual and musical), when introduced, take place in the solo section, while the response tends to be fixed. The response follows diverse iterative modalities: The chorus repeats the whole strophe or only a phrase of the strophe, answers with a refrain, answers with a different strophe or phrase, and so forth. The way in which the call and the answer follow each other also varies: One part might wait to begin until the other is finished, or one part might begin to sing while the other is still performing, thus crossing each other. Thus, the system of alternation lends itself to a large number of variations.

As we sat during many months recording chants for the orichas, Felipe's face would lighten up, and with more than a tinge of nostalgia he would tell me how since he left Cuba, he had not heard many of the chants he was singing for me.

There are many chants that are never sung here. Sometimes I sing one and nobody knows what I'm talking about. Then I don't use them and I begin to forget them. Sometimes when I am drumming I remember a chant but then it goes away again. Other times I feel as if the santos themselves are taking the chants out of my mind so I won't remember them. Now, while singing to you, I remember a lot of chants from back there. But they are not related to the quotidian. If I were back in Matanzas it would be different. There, you sing every day so you always remember the chants. Here, it is different, they sing the same chants over and over.

As we progressed through the repertoire, I would identify a chant as one I had heard in New York, and frequently he would correct the words I was singing and complain about how often the words of the chants were changed in the United States. He also lamented that many chants which were supposed to be sung only in the igbodu when a ceremony was being held were being sung outside for people to dance to, something Felipe found sacrilegious.

Commonly, chants are classified by the oricha they belong to. Each oricha has a repertoire of chants, toques, and dance movements, of varying numbers and complexity, that are performed during the public part of the ceremony. There are also chants that accompany certain rituals (some open only to the initiated). Such is the case of the body of sixteen chants (*suyeres*) that are sung for Osain while preparing the herbs in the rituals of initiation, and in the case of the chants for the *matanza,* used during the ritual sacrifice of animals.

Another group of chants is known as *puyas* (literally, a sharp point), and these are used to criticize or joke with the orichas as a way of coaxing them to join the ceremony. Singers also use puyas when they compete with each other in performance, competitions that are known as *controversias*. Puyas have been compared to the African American speech act known as signifying (Castellanos 1977: 147), with which they share the tactic of verbal dueling and the element of indirection. In Cuba, puyas still signal the ability of a singer to cope with the different challenges of performing in a bembé. A singer has to be knowledgeable in order to use a puya against an oricha successfully. He or she needs command of the repertoire to "play" the game of the double entendre with the oricha: For example, if, after a strong puya, an oricha descends infuriated, the singer has to be able to placate the deity and play (signify) with the meaning of the puya he sang, making it appear as praise to the oricha.

In New York puyas are rarely used, and competition (controversias) among singers in the context of a ceremony is infrequent. Felipe misses the excitement of the ceremonies in Cuba, where the presence of many knowledgeable singers competing contributed to building the atmosphere of the ceremony. In New York, frequently only one solo singer is familiar with the repertoire. This singer, who is hired with the drummers, usually does not allow or want other singers to call for chants.

Singing santo is really like a controversia [literally, "controversy"], that is what makes it beautiful. It's not like here where everything is commercialized, and if you come in they don't let you sing because there is a singer there hired and paid for singing. Back there in Matanzas, four, six, seven singers come to the fiesta. It all depends on how good people think the fiesta is going to be. In some places where the fiestas are good and the santeros are strong and popular, then the house is crowded with singers who go there to sing, to enjoy, to eat, to have a beer after the fiesta is finished, to hang out. So . . . among those singers the controversias take place. Discussions take place, with a singer challenging another. Never real fights, but clarifying things about the religion. They say things to each other with the chants, but once the santo is there then "the move" gets different. You have to be careful not to say something that would offend the santo. Because the santo may think you are talking to him directly and not to the other singer. Sometimes the puyas are really addressed to the santos. Then it may happen that the santo stops the chant or comes up with a chant of his own. The santo begins to say: "I am so and so, and in the world I have these powers, and I will prove them to you by making this happen. . . . " You understand? Because the singer is trying to prove the santo, checking if he is really there. And if he is there he answers back. But at the end nothing bad ever happens, because if the santo is upset, then the singer offers a "fine," he offers him something to appease him.

That is the way santo is sung. It is an exchange, not this thing that I am the owner of the drums and decide who sings or who doesn't. In Matanzas you cannot refuse a singer the right to sing. There is a word—agó—that has to be respected. Once a singer says that word, he is asking permission to sing, and the one who is singing at that moment has to give it to him.

The competence of a solo singer is also judged by his or her knowledge of the repertoire and how he or she uses it within the ritual context. Even though the singers are not part of the batá ensemble, they work closely with the drummers in creating a festive atmosphere, charged with energy powerful enough to induce the orichas to descend. The qualities most frequently praised in a singer do not include the beauty of his or her voice but rather the ability to be heard (over the drums and the background noise); the capacity to induce the audience to participate through singing and dancing; the capacity to fuse the participants together, engendering a corporate spirit (thus strengthening the communitas); and the ability to "bring the orichas down."[43] Furthermore, in the part of the bembé known as fiesta, the singers are responsible for directing musical changes by switching from the chants of one oricha to another (changes that are then followed by the drummers), in accordance with what is happening in the audience. To manipulate adequately the repertoire of chants, singers have to be aware (or be made aware) of the socioreligious relations of the participants: who the children of a particular oricha are and what their ritual family relations are.

There is no formal training for singers. Knowledgeable singers acquire their expertise by participating in as many rituals as possible. However, folklore ensembles, both in Cuba and in the United States, have introduced another learning avenue for singers and drummers: rehearsals. Frequently during these rehearsals, leaflets with the words of the chants are distributed. Another such venue is dance classes with live music, which many drummers and singers use to strengthen their knowledge of the repertoire outside the demanding context of rituals.

Singers, like drummers, are paid a fixed fee for performing in a ritual. They also collect additional money during the performance in a basket or a similar container that is placed in front of the performing musicians. As they call chants for the various orichas, the participants whose oricha is being praised at the moment may approach the basket and make a money offering. Money is also placed in the basket by members of the audience as a token of appreciation for the quality of the performance.

The chorus's knowledge of the repertoire may limit a solo singer's choices in introducing chants. When a singer introduces a chant the chorus doesn't know, he sings the refrain with the chorus until they feel comfortable enough to continue answering by themselves. However, this limits the number of unfamiliar songs that may be introduced during a ceremony. If participation and the energy level of the devotees are to be kept high, singers have to rely mainly on the songs the participants know. This has been one of the major problems Felipe has encountered in New York. Many of the chants he sings are unknown in New York, where the repertoire of chants comes largely from Havana.

Encountering a practice that differs in many ways from his, Felipe has adopted two strategies. When he goes to a ceremony where other musicians have been hired to perform, he usually does not sing, opting instead for silence; he sings only when he performs with his own group. However, this limits his possibilities of remembering through singing, because many chants in the repertoire call for complex rhythmic batá accompaniments, making it very difficult for an iyá player to sing them while playing the drum. In these cases, Felipe chooses not to perform the more complex chants.

· · ·

In one way or another, Felipe continues to follow his beliefs, adapting himself to the challenges his new country presents him with the flexibility, persistence, and resilience that were exhibited by his ancestors when they re-created their traditions in Cuba.

If you are a real believer you have to continue hammering there. Because I see many santeros that live better then I do, they have their houses full of people bringing them money and flowers, gold and prendas and everything, and I don't receive anything. I don't care, I hang on to my beliefs. He was born for that luck and I wasn't and that cannot be changed. That is what God has destined for me. And there I continue "biting" to see if someday He loosens up and gives me something before I die. But I continue my beliefs, I can't change. I think like this: This is my religion and I adore it and love it with my soul.

EPILOGUE

This story has followed Felipe's activities until the end of 1994. That was a trying and difficult year for Felipe. He had left the apartment in the Bronx where I had met him in search of a safer environment for his children and more space for his activities. The family found a big house in a better neighborhood in the Bronx, with a backyard and a huge basement that became the new home for Felipe's prenda. There was even a separate room on the first floor that was used to house the altars of the santos, while the family settled comfortably in the three bedrooms upstairs. This was a dream house for Felipe, but it implied financial commitments that became increasingly difficult to attend to.

He also had another dream: going back to Cuba, going back to a place he had left fourteen years before, a place he had dreamed of and longed for, a place that had been adorned with all the trappings of his imagination, a place that represented the "there" to which he always longed to return—an imaginary return that made his present more bearable. Going home for an immigrant from Latin America who has been living in the "land of opportunities" is not an easy return. One is expected—and expects—to return a winner, defined almost exclusively in terms of economic success. One is expected to return, hands filled with all sort of goods, with money to buy land, to build a house, to help those who were left behind. Felipe's finances did not offer him the opportunity for such a return.

However, the often-imagined trip back home took place in 1994, when one of Felipe's godchildren decided to be initiated in Cuba and helped finance his trip. At the time Felipe was facing a personal crisis, which was exacerbated after his return from Cuba. In Cuba, Felipe had to face loss in many guises. Some of the older members of his family were dead; the death of his godmother in santo, Agustina, in particular affected Felipe strongly. Also lost was that "there" which was always present in Felipe's remembrances, that imaginary world he longed to come back to some day. The difficult conditions Cuba was going through during the "special period"—the austerity measures, the economic hardships, the lack of medicine and food—had exacted a toll on the neighborhood and on the family. The houses were falling apart and the strain of the struggle to make ends meet in such difficult economic conditions and in a two-tier economy—where those who have access to American currency have an open door to a world beyond the reach of the rest of the population—were affecting family life and relationships.[1]

When Felipe returned from Cuba, just as things "here" (in the United States) were falling apart, "there" in Cuba, the home he had dreamed of going back to, was not anymore. During the unfolding of the crisis, while Felipe neglected many of his activities, he maintained, with a regularity and discipline otherwise uncharacteristic of his behavior during these months, our weekly sessions of batá playing. I find it significant that as things fell apart, the drums were what he held onto the longest. At the end of 1994 and the beginning of 1995, Felipe's crisis peaked, and he was unable to keep up with his activities and his daily obligations. With the support of some of his godchildren and students, he was able to pull through this difficult period, and he left New York. He established himself in California, where gradually he went back to work. He began teaching private lessons, became very active again as a ritual drummer, built several sets of batá and iyesá drums, and resumed his work as an artisan. He also participated in several seminars as a teacher of batá at the University of California. In one of those seminars, which lasted for three months, Felipe worked with a Nigerian professor, Francis Awe. While in California, Felipe's beadwork was chosen for inclusion in an exhibition at the UCLA Fowler Museum and was featured in the book that was published as part of the exhibition.[2]

Felipe had left his family in New York. After several trips to visit them, when he felt he had exorcized the ghosts that haunted him, he returned. It was a new beginning in the sense not of a fresh start but of having to build everything all over again. Since the batá group he led had dissolved before his trip to California, Felipe organized a group with his children, to whom he had been teaching batá all these years. With this group Felipe has begun again to play for museums and art festivals. They also play for religious rituals, although not frequently. Felipe's work as an artisan, which has earned much recognition, has also become an important source of income for the family. Felipe continues to be sought, for his knowledge of and familiarity with many aspects of the Afro-Cuban religious practices, in particular those of Palo Monte.[3] He also has done some studio recordings of Afro-Cuban drumming and participated as a percussionist in the recording of tracks for the film based on Toni Morrison's novel *Beloved*.

He is back in the Bronx, living again in a difficult neighborhood, trying to find a better place to move with his family. However, when I saw him again and talked with him for many days during the summer of 1998, something had changed. Cuba had become a place to remember and to visit—not to return to. New York, with all its difficulties, was home, although a home quite different from the one he had expected to find when he left Cuba in 1980.

I left Cuba expecting to find a better life, in search for work, looking for the conditions to bring my family here, in search of many other things . . . but that was not meant for me. Something very different was expecting me. However, a part of me was prepared for the disappointment because when I came I was aware of what José Martí used to say. I had learned about Martí back in school. Martí talked about how he lived here in the "monster" [the United States] and how things were not as good as they seemed or as people said they were. But my experiences here have served a purpose, they have given me something . . . knowledge. Now I can live in any other city in the world and survive because I have learned a lot of things here. In the university of the street, ha! Ha! I speak here with a lot of professors, and I am no one, I just hold the professorship of the streets, I didn't learn from books, I learned with my heart, I learned by practicing.

I want for me only what God wants to give me; I don't desire or envy what he gives to others. After eighteen years in this country I find myself still feeling positive about life. I just hope to have the strength not to be attracted by any force that will go against what I believe, what I keep in my mind. However, there is a difference. When I arrived I was perhaps more enthusiastic with this country and whatnot. Today I know this country better, I know where I'm standing, I know what I want and where I am going. I have had many problems, even with my family here, and I have made many mistakes, I lost my house, I lost my things. But this is my life and this is my family and I have learned to accept them.

In this second stage of my life I have learned to live with all the mixtures I find in this country, without abandoning my tradition. I want to keep my tradition without being dissuaded away from it. I don't want my tradition to die but I also know things have to be taken easy. Besides, I also see that some things are changing. Before, people used to say what I sang were chants from the countryside, and now I hear people singing the chants I sing. Frustrations? Yes, many, but life is like that. Life has been hard but not always bitter. What I have to do is survive and let people understand who I am. I have to keep on drumming, I need to drum, even when I was alone I drummed. Drumming has always helped me to keep everything going. In Matanzas, he who is born to play the drums will end up playing them. For me it was fate, it was marked in my life. The drums called me, so I went out and looked for them.

· · ·

This is Felipe's story, or rather, my retelling of his story; a story without an "ending" as Felipe, who is now sixty-seven years old, eighteen years into his exile continues to play drums, build drums, craft religious objects, and assemble altars, still struggling to make ends meet.

Why Felipe chose to have his story told by me is a question I cannot answer with certainty. The reasons may have been many: a way to fight against invisibility; a tool for remembering; an opportunity to let people know the way things really were "back there"; an access to the power of the written word; participating in divulging his tradition as he saw it being "told around" by others; a way to confront the written in a tradition that is moving gradually from oral to written; a chance to claim his right to participate in the negotiations and struggles to define the "canon" through written texts; or simply a sign of friendship and trust.

· · ·

Memory—the struggle against forgetting—works as the binding element that brings the pieces of this mosaic of stories together. The use of memories in keeping and rebuilding a sense of identity, the role music plays in evoking and organizing these memories, the way in which musical instruments and a repertoire of chants embody and trigger memories. In Felipe's efforts to rebuild his life in the United States; in his struggle against invisibility, poverty, and marginality; in his search to keep continuity with the past while coping with the shock of displacement and the pain of abandoning his dear ones, remembering is a strategy one always sees at play—while he tells stories, plays the drums, sings chants, performs, teaches, and crafts drums and religious objects.

However, Felipe's memories should not be viewed only as fragments of a personal life story but as located within the mental and material space of the groups that have contributed to build Felipe's identity. Individual memory is an aspect of group memory, connected with the whole material and moral life of the societies of which an individual is or was a part (Halbwachs 1992; Connerton 1992). As such, individual memories are an important part of the history of these groups.

Undeniably, in the narratives people spin from their memories, an important role is played not only by the imagination but by what I would call "the editing machine of our remembrances," which selectively forgets what in some way clashes with our present ideas of the self or with the exigencies of our present lives. Granted the presence of a fictional component, those narratives still open a window onto the aspirations, dreams, fears, anxieties, strategies, values, and mentality not only of an individual but of the groups that have contributed to shaping them.[4]

For Felipe, remembering is not just a nostalgic recollection of how things used to be but a struggle that has cultural and existential implications. When Felipe notes that the orichas in New York do not dance the way they used to in Cuba, he is not just longing for something to be as it once was; he is struggling against forgetting—forgetting rituals, gestures, bodily postures, the script of his cultural memory. What is missing for Felipe is a matter not simply of choreography but of bodily gestures that have been considered by a social group (the santeros from Matanzas) as the proof of the presence of the orichas among them. When an oricha takes possession of an initiate in ritual, he or she is expected to move according to prototypical gestures that portray the personality traits of and aspects of the myths relating to that oricha. What is inscribed in these gestures is a cultural construction that is given religious meaning and content in and through ritual behavior.

The type of memory that allows one to reproduce a certain performance (a ritual in this case) Paul Connerton has called *habit-memory* (1989: 22). I find Connerton's ideas on the importance of the body as a repository of cultural memories particularly apt to understanding the role of bodily gestures in the rituals of Santería called bembés, where these gestures act as markers of the presence of the oricha that has been invoked through music.[5] The ritual gestures of the dancers not only represent the orichas but cause to reappear that which has disappeared; the possessed initiate "becomes" an oricha. Thus, in these rituals, "gestural repetition enacts the idea of bi-presence; the inhabitants of the other world can reappear in this one without leaving their own, provided one knows how to recall them" (Connerton 1989: 69).

This knowledge of how to recall the orichas is tightly linked to habit-memory: "For if the ceremonies are to work for their participants, if they are to be persuasive to them, then those participants must not be simply cognitively competent to execute the performance; they must be habituated to those performances. This habituation is to be found . . . in the bodily substrate of the performance" (Connerton 1989: 71).

•   •   •

How much of our experiences are encoded in music, in a particular tune or song; how much of our past and what is sometimes called our "identity" is recalled to us through music was made evident to me after having visited Cuba. One day, while visiting Felipe's sister Beba, as we were chatting in the living room and she kept answering all the questions I poured on her, she suddenly stopped talking and began to sing a song. This was a song I had learned from my mother in Colombia when I was very young. I looked at Felipe's sister, smiling, and began to sing with her. She would sing one phrase, and I would answer with the next one. When we finished the song I asked her why she had suddenly begun to sing, and especially a song that was not Cuban but Ecuadoran. She told me it had been our talk about Felipe that had brought this song back to her; it used to be one of Felipe's favorite songs. On my return from Cuba, I visited Felipe in New York to give him the tapes his family had sent him. As we sat there talking about his family and about Matanzas, I suddenly began to sing the song for him. I will never forget the look in his eyes. We didn't need to talk; the song was saying more than words could convey, it was bringing back a world with a strength and vividness words could not rival. At once the song brought much of Cuba back to Felipe and so much of Colombia to me. Two different pasts, two different worlds, two different identities—one song.

NOTES

PART ONE

1. This is an edited version of part of a letter that Felipe dictated to one of his stu-
    dents in New York when he had to present his credentials as a drummer. As
    the narration of Felipe's life proceeds, the meaning of these titles will become
    clear; however, I give a brief description here:

    Balogún: a name given to the sons of Ogún. This name is also used
        to refer to a head drummer (Cabrera 1986).
    Olúañá: Olú is the name given to a wise man. Olúañá is the name
        given to those who know all the secrets of añá, the secret power
        the inhabits the batá drums.
    Omóañá: child of añá, name given to batá drummers who have un-
        dergone a special initiation.
    Olú Iyesá: he who knows the secrets of the Iyesá drums.
    *Tata Nganga, Amasa Nkita, Rompe Monte Quinumba Maria
        Munda:* This is the name Felipe has as a practitioner of Palo. Usu-
        ally, part of this name coincides with the name given to the prac-
        titioner's *nganga,* the spirit with whom the *palero* works.
    Yo Clava Lo Taca a Rubé: Yo clavo la estaca a Rubé *[el diablo],* "I
        thrust my 'stick' in Rubé [the devil; this word is pronounced with
        a soft *r*]," meaning, "My powers are used against the devil, against
        evil."

    The other names are explained when the Abakuá are discussed.

2. During the early decades of the twentieth century, the Abakuá societies had a lot of power among the workers on the docks in Matanzas. They also represented a strong electoral force. Their members were therefore approached by numerous politicians to participate in their campaigns. See Sosa 1982 and López Valdés 1966.

3. Pérez de la Riva 1974: 78–79 and 1976: 108. Statistics about the annual numbers and the total number of slaves brought to Cuba vary considerably. Furthermore, the trade is divided into two periods: a legal one, until 1820 (Spain signed the first treaty with England to abolish the trade in 1817); and an unofficial, clandestine one, for which extant reports are not trustworthy (Aimes [1907] 1967: 145).

4. On the cabildos in Cuba, see Castellanos and Castellanos 1988 and Ortíz 1984.

5. Moreno Fraginals 1978: vol. 2, 9.

6. The name Yoruba was first used by the Hausa to refer to their neighbors the Oyo. This name assumed its modern sense only in the early nineteenth century, when missionaries used it to designate the diverse and heterogeneous tribes in southwestern Nigeria, Benin and Togo. At this time it competed with Aku as the authoritative ethnological designation (Waterman 1990: 369). For convenience, I continue using Yoruba when referring to the cultural and geographical origins of the group of slaves known in Cuba as the Lucumí and in Brazil as the Nagos.

7. Daniel Dawson, in his introduction of Felipe at a concert on August 9, 1992, at the Caribbean Cultural Center in New York.

8. The fourth religious systems is the Regla Arará of Dahomean origin, closely related to Santería. At present almost unknown in the rest of the island, it is credited with a considerable number of followers in the province of Matanzas.

9. A description of Santería, Palo, and Abakuá follows this section.

10. Short descriptions of the most important characteristics of the major orichas are presented in the Glossary. For an extended account on the Cuban orichas and the extensive body of myths that surrounds them, see Bolívar 1990; Cabrera 1974 and 1975b; Castellanos and Castellanos 1992; Sandoval 1975; de la Soledad and San Juán 1988.

11. According to Ortíz, *enkomó,* in the Efik language, refers to a small drum that belongs to a secret society similar to that of the ñáñigos of Cuba, called Egbó or Ekué (1952: vol. 4, 34).

12. At the funeral of Felipe's brother (see Part 3 on syncretism), only these three drums were used. However, the coffin was used as a resonating board to substitute for the fourth drum (*bonkó*), which Felipe does not own at present. This was a ceremony performed in public, which may have differed from the esoteric funeral rituals that took place after Nino's death and to which I had no access.

13. Iñoblá, or Ñoblá as some members of the family call him, is a contraction of el señor Blás (Mr. Blás).

14. When Felipe uses the word *güiro,* he refers to a type of celebration for the orichas where beaded gourds (*chekerés*) and conga drums are used instead

of the batá ensemble; it is also the name given to the chekerés. However, in Cuba the word *güiro* is also used to refer to a kind of rattle used in secular dance music.

15. The word *bembé* is also used to refer to a Lucumí ensemble of single-headed drums and to the music played by them.

16. See Martínez Furé 1979: 137–56.

17. "Moor" in Cuba is used to refer to a Turk or to a street vendor.

18. These stories not only portray the importance Ogún has in Felipe's life but also illustrate the relationship santeros have with their parent oricha. Santeros usually know more stories about the oricha that governs their head than about the other orichas. They use these stories to underline the power and importance of their own oricha.

19. The recipient or cauldron that the spirit worshiped by the palero inhabits.

20. Cabrera 1986b: 20.

21. *Prenda* is defined in the Spanish dictionary as an object that is given to guarantee a contract or an obligation. It is also used figuratively to refer to something that is loved intensively, something that serves as proof of another thing, or the moral qualities of a person (García Pelayo, *Pequeño Larousse ilustrado* [Buenos Aires: Ediciones Larousse, 1964]).

22. A visit to a graveyard was an important step in the preparation of a prenda. Graveyard earth and bones were always included in the cauldron as a way of tying the spirit.

23. Police repression of the Afro-Cuban religions was an aspect of the pervasive racial discrimination practiced against black Cubans during the early years of the republic, after the end of American occupation of the island. These attitudes were fueled by sensationalist press reports that fed people's prejudices and fears of the "black menace." For a description of discrimination during the early years of the republic, see Castellanos and Castellanos 1990: 303–27.

24. In Cuba, *ritos cruzados* was the name given to practices that mixed Catholic elements and those of the several Afro-Cuban religious practices (Arará, Lucumí, Congo, etc.). The mixing of diverse beliefs and rites through a process of transculturation gave rise to new hybrid, creole religious practices. See the section on syncretism in Part 3.

25. The members of an Abakuá juego belong exclusively to it and cannot join another group, unless they establish a new one. The old juego authorizes the founding of a new juego and acts as the godfather for the new group.

26. Peasants who came from Galicia in Spain. Here Felipe uses the term *gallego* to refer to peasants with no education. It is also used, in general, to refer to a white person. Afro-Cuban musicians use the word to refer to music that does not swing: "It sounds gallego" and "You are playing like a gallego" are common evaluations of a performance.

27. To make this book accessible to a wide readership, the more technical aspects of Afro-Cuban religious music have not been included. For those interested in my views and findings on the subject, see Vélez 1996.

28. It was customary for black people to straighten their hair by ironing it.

29. When Felipe talks about drumming, he frequently demonstrates the sound through syllables. I have kept them in his dialogue and transcribed them using both boldface and italics.

30. The orichas not only organize and group the repertoire of *toques* but are also important in matters of performance and interpretation. Thus, the tempo and the interpretation of the toques are shaped by the characteristics of the oricha being addressed with a particular rhythm. When trying to convey a matter of interpretation to an apprentice, experienced drummers frequently refer to the movements of each oricha that are related to the oricha's personality and attributes. Therefore, the orichas play an important role in the music theory of batá drumming.

31. Santeros learn about the behavior that characterizes each oricha both during their apprenticeship for their initiation and from attending rituals and observing others. Stories about possession are also frequently shared among santeros.

32. Batá drums, like the stones in the soperas of santeros, are fed with the blood from ritual sacrifices.

33. According to Felipe, Amado Díaz's full name is Amado Manuel Díaz Guantica. Ortíz mentions Manuel Guantica as the owner of one of the sets of batá drums made by the famous Atandá. See the section on the "History of the Drums" below; see also Ortíz 1952: vol. 4, 317.

34. Quintín Banderas was a black leader who participated in the struggle against the Spanish for the independence of Cuba.

35. Ortíz, a well-known Cuban researcher and ethnologist, wrote extensively on Afro-Cuban culture and was responsible for bringing batá drums out of the temples and to the stage; he organized, in 1936, a concert/demonstration (with a conference included) of batá in Havana, where Pablo Roche, Jesús Pérez, and Aguedo Morales, famous drummers at the time, performed. Since then, many unconsecrated sets of drums (*judíos* or *aberikulá*) have been built for use in secular contexts.

36. Except for minor discrepancies, the account Felipe gives concurs with what I gathered from conversations and interviews with musicians who had visited Matanzas, and with the information I compiled when I visited Felipe's family in Cuba, where I had the opportunity to meet and talk with Estéban Bacayao "Chachá," one of the most famous olúbatás in Matanzas.

37. This mistakenly states that four people were involved in building this set of drums. In fact, Iñoblá Cárdenas and Oba Enkolé, or Obankolé, name the same person. This point came out in recent conversations with Felipe and, separately, with his cousin Osvaldo, whom I met in my trip to Cuba. The error came about because the original statement was dictated, not written, by Felipe, who, as is customary with him, used interchangeably the two names (Iñoblá Cárdenas and Obankolé, which is the santo name of his great-grandfather). Unaware of this, the person who wrote the letter for Felipe

edited the text incorrectly. I myself had no knowledge of this when I wrote my dissertation.

38. From this point on, Felipe's letter is mixed with information he gave me during our conversations and classes.

39. The highest priest of the Abakuá, who plays the sacred drum.

40. Carlos Alfonso was the owner of two sets of batá drums that are mentioned by Ortíz, one of them built by the famous Atandá (Ortíz 1952: vol. 4, 317).

41. Felipe's cousin Osvaldo remembers a different version of what happened to the drums during this persecution. According to what one of the family elders told him, the bodies of the drums were burned by Tomasa's father (Felipe's grandfather), and while he was burning them a raging storm broke out.

42. *Antología de la música afrocubana,* vol. 2: *Oru de igbodú* 1981.

43. Estéban Vega Bacayao (Chachá), personal communication with the author, September 9, 1997.

44. One set was made for Miguel (Michael) Spiro, and the other, still in the process of construction, belongs to Bill Summers. Chachá, personal communication, September 9, 1997.

45. The name given to the iron bells varies according to the sources: Ortíz calls them *ekón,* which is also the name of the Abakuá bells, and Martínez Furé calls them *agogó.* Felipe just uses the Spanish word for bell, *campana.*

46. Generally, the name given to each drum, in order of size, is: *bajo* (played with a stick), *caja, segundo,* and *tercero.*

47. The recordings of Iyesá music made for the already-mentioned *Antología de la música afrocubana* were done at this cabildo. In the liner notes to this record, written by Argeliers León, Loreto García, who at the time of the recording was one hundred years old, is credited as one of the "veteran" drummers of this cabildo (*Antología de la música afrocubana,* vol. 3: *Música iyesá* 1981).

48. Felipe's family had close ties with the cabildo Iyesá in Matanzas, going far back in time. In fact, one of the performers who appears in the picture of the iyesá ensemble that Ortíz included in his book (1952: vol. 4, 371) is the husband of Felipe's sister Beba. He is the father of the nephew Felipe mentions here.

49. The texts of the mambos use Spanish sprinkled with some Congo words but follow the syntactic structure of Spanish. However, one encounters in them a general use of a form of Spanish known as *bozal,* which was spoken by the slaves and later survived among the rural blacks.

50. The terms *makuta* and *yuka* are not always used in the literature to refer to the same type of dance. Ortíz, for example, ascribes the *vacunao* only to the dance called yuka, while León maintains that the dance known as makuta includes the vacunao. Makuta and yuka are also names used to refer to a drum ensemble (Ortíz 1952, vol. 3, 455; León [1974] 1984: 73).

51. According to Cabrera, for the Congos *yuka* and *makuta* were the same thing: a trio of drums that accompanied a profane celebration (see Castellanos and Castellanos 1994: 318).

PART TWO

1. Felipe uses the expression "rebel army" to refer to the state army, not to anti-Castro rebels.
2. The speeches and documents published by the different Cuban cultural institutes that I consulted in researching the official cultural policies of the revolutionary government were compiled in several anthologies: *Pensamiento y política cultural cubanos,* 4 vols., 1986 (abbreviated PPCC); *La cultura en Cuba socialista,* 1982 (abbreviated CCS); *La lucha ideológica y la cultura artística,* 1982, which contains the resolution of the First and Second Congresses of the Cuban Communist Party, along with other official resolutions (abbreviated LICA); and, on the report presented by the Cuban government to UNESCO in 1972, Lisandro Otero, *Cultural Policy in Cuba.* I have also relied on the official newspaper of the Central Communist Party, *Granma;* a general weekly, *Bohemia;* and *Cuba internacional,* a publication aimed at audiences outside of Cuba.
3. During this period rock music and long hair were banned, a black cultural movement was accused of black separatism, and the famous Padilla affair became an international scandal in which numerous Latin American and European intellectuals intervened (Manuel 1985: 3; Stubbs 1989: 770).
4. The JUCEI were regional planning boards with the task of facilitating the decentralization of some administrative and economic activities.
5. On the systems of incentives, evaluation, and employment of musicians after the revolution, see Robbins 1991.
6. Felipe always uses the word *Cultura* (culture) to refer to governmental cultural agencies in general.
7. The Organizaciones Revolucionarias Integradas (Integrated Revolutionary Organizations), formed in 1961, runs the provincial and basic schools and played an important role in the campaign against illiteracy. ORI was formed by a number of revolutionary organizations: the Communist Party, the Revolutionary Directorate, the 26 July Movement, the United Youth Movement, and the Young Pioneers. An office of the ORI was established in almost every town, and the secretaries of the planning boards (JUCEI) in most cases became the provincial secretaries of the ORI. The ORI disappeared in 1963 and was succeeded by the PURS (Partido Unificado de la Revolución Socialista), which in turn became the Communist Party of Cuba in 1965 (Thomas 1971: 1372, 1373, 1453).
8. Robbins (1991: 242) offers the example of an instructor who wanted to impose the use of *batá drums* (Lucumí drums) on a group whose members played music of Congolese origin. The group was dissolved when the members refused to use the *batá* drums and asked for permission to build their own traditional drums.
9. León, who died in 1991, was for many years the director of the Music Department of the Casa de las Américas. He was Cuba's best known musicologist and the teacher of most of the new generation of Cuban music scholars. A classical music composer himself, he participated actively in the intellectual movement

afrocubanismo of the 1920s and 1930s, which inspired the use of Afro-Cuban musical elements in the works of such composers as Alejandro García Caturla and Amadeo Roldán (Manuel 1991: 1, 268). He had been active in the field of folklore before the revolution, having worked closely with Fernando Ortíz. In 1946 he replaced María Muñoz as teacher of the course on Cuban folkloric music that the University of Havana had begun to offer in 1943 (parallel to a course on Cuban ethnography taught by Ortíz). In 1948 his wife, musicologist María Teresa Linares, replaced León in this position (CCS 1982: 188).

10. Cuban scholars divide Cuban music into folk, popular, and artistic music. Within the realm of folk music they distinguish two categories: the music that has remained close to its pre-Cuban sources, such as the ritual Afro-Cuban music and the *campesino* (peasant) music, and the secular, urban folk musics (León 1991a: 3).

11. Many scholars and artists opined that the religious beliefs that were part of the Afro-Cuban cultural heritage would eventually disappear. Thus ethnographer Jesús Guanche writes:

> The process of disintegration of the religious beliefs and in particular of the syncretic cults increases during the construction of socialism . . . because as the individual acquires real freedom and enlarges his cultural horizons . . . his ideological dependence on animism and the ancestral cults begins to dissolve. On the other hand the artistic manifestations of these groups are an integral part of our cultural patrimony, due to their definitive traditional popular character. The cultivation of these values from the scientific point of view, that is to say, eliminating the mystical halo and preserving the positive traditions, is part of the present job of the projection of socialist culture. (Guanche 1983: 449–51)

Similar statements are found in Guerra 1989: 6; Martínez Furé 1979: 259–62; Sosa 1982: 15; Sotonavarro in Sosa 1982: 325–28; Vinueza 1988: 56. This was obviously the "official" position, not shared by everyone and at times not held privately by those who advocated it publicly. Since the 1980s there has been a major change in the official position of the government with respect to the Afro-Cuban religions.

12. By 1964 there were 1,164 such groups; the number grew to 18,000 in 1975 and by 1980 had multiplied to 33,000 (PPCC 1986: 90). These groups not only were viewed as important vehicles to promote the artistic practice and the aesthetic education of peasants, workers, and students but also were considered a "significant factor for social integration" (Otero 1972: 21).

13. This is an important Cuban ethnologist, who was one of the founders of the Conjunto Folklórico Nacional. He is the author of many essays on Afro-Cuban music and culture, some of them compiled in a well-known book, *Diálogos imaginarios* (Martínez Furé 1979). Until recently he was in charge of giving the lectures and talks offered at the performances and workshops of the Conjunto Folklórico.

14. Benny Moré is the "king" of the music genre known as *son,* a legend in the field of Cuban popular music.

15. René López, well known in the world of Latin music as a record collector, researcher, producer, and folk panelist for the New York State Council on the Arts, brought a recording of Felipe's group Emikeké to New York as part of the field recordings López made in Matanzas in 1978. According to López, at that time the group was considered "the best in Matanzas province" (René López, letter, New York, 1986).

16. Los Muñequitos de Matanzas is one of the most famous Cuban ensembles. The group, considered the world's best performers of rumba, was founded in 1952 and began touring the United States in the past two years for the first time since the revolution. Afro-Cuba, a group from Matanzas that performs a repertoire similar to that of the Conjunto Folklórico Nacional, was founded in 1980. Many of its members belong to Felipe's family, among them Sara Gobel Villamil, Bertina Aranda Villamil, Reynaldo Alfonso García, Reynaldo Gobel Villamil, and Ramón García Pérez.

17. Osvaldo is the oriaté in Felipe's ritual family, and he is also Felipe's consanguineal cousin. He is a ritual expert and a deeply spiritual and knowledgeable man who has dedicated himself to the study of his religious tradition (Santería) and its ritual language (Lucumí). He inherited the *libretas* of the elders of his ritual family. Once Felipe told me a story about the handwritten notebooks Osvaldo used to spend days studying; Felipe described one of them as being such a large notebook that it had to be read laying on the floor.

18. For practical reasons I use only the word *santeros* here, but I am also referring to the practitioners of other Afro-Cuban religions, i.e., paleros and ñáñigos (or Abakuás). When Felipe mentions the older santeros, he is referring to the santeros of his mother's generation.

19. What is commonly referred to as the *cuarto,* or room, is the *igbodu,* the sacred space where the secret ceremonies take place.

20. In Santería as well as in the Abakuá rituals, a section of the ritual always takes place in a sacred room, closed to the eyes of the uninitiated, while a public part is open to everyone and has the character of a fiesta (party), a celebration in which food abounds and even the uninitiated are welcome to participate.

21. Felipe here makes a difference between playing for rituals and playing in concerts. After the revolution, many musicians performed ritual music of religious practices that were not their own. Before the revolution, ritual drummers performed within the bounds of their religious affiliation.

22. Arcadio, the famous santero ritually linked to Lázaro Peña, led a house-temple in Guanabacoa named La Asociación de los Hijos de San Antonio that still operates in Cuba today, under the leadership of Ramón Valdés Guanche. In an interview (Luis and Cuervo Hewitt 1987) published in the *Afro-Hispanic Review* Arcadio talks about the Great Egbó, which he describes as three months of religious celebrations that took place after the triumph of the revolution.

23. I did not find any reference to a bureau of religion at this time. Felipe may here be referring to an office set up by the Ministry of the Interior to grant permission to hold meetings.

24. In an interview (Luis and Cuervo Hewitt 1987: 11), Arcadio states that his religious practices were never repressed after the revolution. According to him, whenever he wanted to celebrate a ritual, he was allowed to.

25. Felipe refers to the beaded necklaces ritually bestowed to santeros during a special ceremony, which they continue to wear for protection.

26. It has been estimated that 40 to 50 percent of the troops present in Angola were black and mulatto Cubans (Taylor 1988: 32). Miguel Barnet asserts that the practitioners of Afro-Cuban religions (he does not make definitions by race) were the ones sent to fight in Angola and Ethiopia (Barnet 1988: 5–7).

27. Many aspects of Pan-Africanism and black nationalism were criticized by Fidel and other members of the political establishment in the 1960s as being divisive and racialized. Alberto Pedro, writing in *Casa de las Américas* 53 in 1969, emphasized that "to pretend and/or state that 'all blacks are brothers' would be tantamount to accepting the strictly racist premise that 'all blacks are equal' " (quoted in Moore 1988: 258). Even though Fidel has been criticized for not fully supporting Pan-Africanism at a local level (Moore 1988), he has nonetheless embraced Pan-Africanism at an international level.

28. It is interesting to follow these developments through the press clippings of publications such as Granma and Cuba Internacional, which are kept by subject in the Center for Cuban Studies in New York. Under file no. 675, the center keeps all the articles on Afro-Cuban religions featured in these publications. Few, if any, date before 1980. However, after 1980 the articles on these religions (not exclusively on their music and dance) proliferate, along with interviews with practitioners and pictures of religious altars and paraphernalia. By the end of the 1980s, *Cuba Internacional* had initiated a new section called "Costumbre y Tradiciones," which includes myths about the orichas, information about the use of plants, and other issues related to the Afro-Cuban religions.

29. These views are not held by all Cuban specialists on Afro-Cuban religions. Many researchers consider these traditions, although rooted in Nigeria, as something Cuban; as traditions that developed independently and should be studied as such. For them, Lucumí is not equivalent to Yoruba; Lucumí is a Cuban reinterpretation and re-creation of Yoruba traditions that encountered and incorporated elements of other African religions and of Catholicism (Professor Lázara M. Menéndez, Facultad Artes y Letras, Universidad de la Habana, personal communication with the author, September 1997).

30. Afro-Cuban culture has become a major attraction for two different types of tourists in Cuba: (1) those in search of a learning experience, among whom are many African Americans and Afro-Caribbeans who travel to Cuba in search of information (religious and musical) about their "shared" cultural past; and (2) those attracted by nature, that is, beach, mountains, and so forth, many of whom attend shows at nightclubs and cabarets that feature Afro-Cuban music

and dances and buy Afro-Cuban handicrafts in famous resorts such as Varadero. The former type of tourist takes advantage of the numerous courses offered by the various folkloric ensembles, the organized visits to the ethnographic museums, the arranged tours of Afro-Cuban religious ceremonies, and the like. However, within this group are those who consider organized "cultural tourism" inauthentic and plan visits to house-temples in Havana and Matanzas independent of the official tours, through a series of private networks. Many, in fact, travel to Cuba for religious purposes and have ritual links to various Afro-Cuban house-temples and ritual families.

31. Members of ensembles such as Afro-Cuba and Conjunto Folklórico Nacional have taken part as teachers in these workshops (*talleres*). The workshops, still offered and very popular, last approximately fifteen days and include visits to specialized museums and participation in a religious ceremony. Here, foreign women, who according to religious tradition ought to be excluded from playing batá, participate side by side with men in the percussion workshops. This has placed many of the drummers, who are practicing santeros, in an awkward position. They teach foreign women to play batá while, for religious reasons, they exclude their own women from this practice.

32. The use of the term *bembé* can lead to confusion because *bembé* also refers to: (1) a religious celebration accompanied by batá drums; (2) a religious celebration accompanied by bembé drums, called in Matanzas *bembé Lucumí;* (3) a secular celebration to honor the orichas, called *bembé criollo;* and (4) a secular party that is exclusively for enjoyment, called *suncho* (Ortíz 1952: vol. 3, 376).

33. Israel Moliner Castañeda at present is president of the Sociedad de Antropología (Society of Anthropology) de Cuba.

34. See Hagedorn 1995 for a study of the Conjunto Folklórico Nacional that examines some of these issues.

PART THREE

1. On the waves of Cuban immigrants to the United States after the Cuban Revolution, see Bach 1985; Pedraza-Bailey 1985; Fagen, Brody, and O'Leary 1968.

2. Using samples of the biographical information forms that the U.S. Immigration and Naturalization Service filed on each entrant, combined with the profiles developed by the Cuban/Haitian Task Force and the records of each of the four military bases to which the refugees were sent, Bach, Bach, and Triplett concluded that despite contrary claims, most of the emigrants were "neither marginal to the Cuban economy nor from the social fringes." Although the exact number of criminals, deviants, and mental patients will never be known, only 16 percent of the refugees in the resettlement camps admitted to having spent time in prison (Bach, Bach, and Triplett 1981/82: 28–46). Of those with prison records, 69.71 percent had been in prison for minor crimes or acts not considered crimes in the United States, and 40 percent reported that their imprisonment was due to involvement in illegal economic activities (black mar-

ket, tax evasion). Only 7.4 percent were considered serious criminals (Fernández: 1982: 189–92, Pedraza-Bailey 1985: 26–29).

3. Those who arrived in the flights from Varadero to Miami that began in 1965 and ended in 1973 (Pedraza-Bailey 1985: 16).

4. Renard Simmons, an African American santero who was very active as a musician in the 1970s and at present is a priest of Orula (a babalao). He belongs to the santo house of Sunta Serrano, a Puerto Rican santera who initiated a lot of African Americans into the religion.

5. He refers here to the recording made by René López in Matanzas, Cuba. López also presented one of the first groups Felipe's organized, Tradición Matancera, at Rutgers University and included Felipe as part of a Cuban music documentary, *Drums across the Sea,* directed by Les Blank.

6. See Rushdie's analysis of the identity building of Indian writers in England (Rushdie 1991: 124).

7. I use the word *official* in the sense given by Cantwell, who defines it as "the sum total of those august institutions with which we identify our historical moment and level of civilization: the state, its governing bodies, its educational and business establishments, its corporate structure, commercial interests, its systems of transport, communication, production, and exchange, and so on" (Cantwell 1992: 274).

8. These type of nonmainstream organizations, however, rely heavily for their funding on official sources of support, ranging from private corporations and foundations to government institutions at the federal, state, and local level, including the National Endowment for the Arts.

9. For the policies on folklore of official institutions such as the Smithsonian, see Cantwell 1991 and 1992; Kurin 1989 and 1992; Sheehy 1992a and 1992b. See also Wilcken 1991, for a discussion of staged folklore in New York.

10. For the history of Santería in New York, see the section "Felipe's 'There' Faces His 'Here,' " below.

11. See Vélez 1994 for the role musicians such as Milton Cardona have played within this musical tradition.

12. Ritual words pronounced as the blood of the sacrificed animal begins to fall on the stones, or in this case, on the ring of the drums.

13. For the history of this temple and a complete description of the building of this set of drums see Brown 1989.

14. See Part Two, "Crafting a Bembé Drum."

15. When asked about the meaning of a chant, Felipe never gave a word-for-word translation. He did explain what the chant was saying, sometimes with a long story based on only two short lines of text. This way of translating the chants is common among Cuban practitioners of Santería and is the type of translation I subscribe to here. (See, for example, the *libretas de santo* published in Menéndez 1990.) I disagree with those who consider Lucumí just a modified version of standard Yoruba (Hopkins 1992). In my view, a language that developed independently for almost a century cannot be translated by "correcting" it and

assimilating it to another one (in this case, standard Yoruba). For more on the problems of translating the Santería chants, see Vélez 1996. See also Matory 1996: 168.

16. Specific objects are attributed to each oricha and then placed in the altar or sometimes used during the rituals (e.g., a sword and a double-edged ax for Changó, a hooked tree branch called *garabato* for Eleguá, a horsetail with a beaded handle for Babalú-Ayé). Some of these objects are decorated with elaborate beadwork.

17. This altar has also been included in exhibits in Japan, Berlin, and several cities in Latin America. For the exhibit in New York, Robert Farris Thompson wrote a book (1993), in which a picture of one of Felipe's altars is included. This book was dedicated to Felipe and to Daniel Dawson to acknowledge their collaboration in the project.

18. See, among others, Ames 1986 and 1992; Hooper-Greenhill 1992; Karp and Levine 1991; Marcus and Myers 1995.

19. For more on the practice of Santería in the United States, in particular in New York City, see Brandon 1983 and 1993; Brown 1989; Cornelius 1989; Curry 1991 and 1997; Dean 1993; Friedman 1982; Gregory 1986; Morales 1990; Murphy 1993.

20. For a complete history of Oyotunji, see Hunt 1979.

21. On the reinterpretation of Santería in the black community, see Curry 1991 and 1997.

22. For studies of the connections between Puerto Rican espiritismo and Santería in New York, see Brandon 1993; Morales 1990; and Pérez y Mena 1991.

23. Gregory (1986: 320) found that among practitioners in New York, the Havana practice was associated with "the more affluent and cosmopolitan residents of that city, who 'cleaned-up' Santería and made it more acceptable to white, middle-class Cubans." The practice from Matanzas is "reputed closer to the religious practice of the Lucumí" and considered "more potent" and "less refined with respect to ceremonial decor." However accurate this evaluation of the different practitioners may be, there is an acknowledged difference between the Afro-religious practices of the two regions.

24. See, among others, Brandon 1993; Dean 1993; Morales 1990; Murphy 1993.

25. For simplicity's sake I continue to use the name Santería, although in the United States, as the practitioners have divided along different ideological lines, other names have been adopted.

26. *Hybrid* is used here to avoid the problematic term *syncretic*.

27. Although Brandon (1993), in his analysis of syncretism in Santería, argues that practitioners tend to be unaware of the hybridity of their practices, he does not specify if he is applying this to a particular period of the history of Santería. Judging from practitioners like Felipe, such a lack of awareness does not seem to be the case in the latter half of this century especially.

28. The word also is used to describe a picnic or an excursion.

29. This is the case for drummers Orlando "Puntilla" Rios and Alfredo "Coyude"

Vidaux (who became important figures in the history of batá drumming in New York) and dancer Xiomara García, among others.

30. During the mid 1950s, Arsenio Rodriguez lived in an apartment at 23 East 110th Street, between Madison and Fifth Avenue (Salazar 1994: 12).

31. Varela 1994: 26–27. On the West Coast, Aguabella has led an active career as a drummer in jazz and Latin music ensembles. His work was recognized with the National Heritage Fellowship, awarded in 1992. Many consider Aguabella to have been, together with Collazos and Ornelio Scull (who established himself in Puerto Rico), a pioneer of Lucumí ritual drumming in the United States.

32. Teddy Holiday, personal communication with the author, New York, September 12, 1991.

33. Other non-Latin drummers were also attracted by this music. Batá drumming has a considerable degree of prestige among Latin music drummers, who consider it the ultimate test for a good drummer.

34. Milton Cardona, personal communication with the author, New York, April 18, 1991.

35. In Cuba, after the conference organized by Ortíz in 1936, when batá drums were first played outside a ritual context, secular batá drums began to be built and used in popular music recordings, radio shows, and concerts. In the United States, batá drums have also crossed over to the field of popular music and jazz. Many recordings not only use batá drums but include toques and arrangements of chants for the orichas.

36. See the epilogue for a commentary on the behavior of possessed initiates.

37. By 1962, the revolutionary government reported the adult literacy rate to be 96 percent. See Louis A. Pérez, Jr., *Cuba: Between Reform and Revolution,* 2d ed. (New York: Oxford University Press, 1995), 359.

38. Ortíz's books are extremely popular in the United States among students of Afro-Cuban traditions and culture. Many copies have even been stolen from libraries. In Cuba they are also well known, mainly among intellectuals and students. However, they mean very little to people like Felipe's family in Matanzas. When I visited Matanzas, I was taken by Clarita, Felipe's niece, to visit the director of the folkloric ensemble she was working with. He was a drum maker and an intellectual and owned all Ortíz's books. When we were talking about the iyesá drums, he took out one of the books to show me something. Clarita, who was looking over my shoulder, suddenly exclaimed: "That's my father!" Indeed, her father was part of the Iyesá ensemble whose picture Ortíz had included in his book. She had never known her father had appeared in a book and had no idea of the importance these books were given outside the world of La Marina.

39. The theme for this section on Felipe's life is drawn from Milan Kundera, *The Book of Laughter and Forgetting* (New York: Knopf, 1980), 3.

40. This exclusion also extends to homosexuals.

41. For example, I was told by a babalao that Añá was a jealous female deity who resented the presence of other women in her "territory." However, Ortíz in his

research found that Añá is a male spirit. Even the drum called the "mother" drum, the iyá, is a male drum; in Spanish, drummers refer to it as "el iyá, *el* being a masculine pronoun. (See Ortíz 1952: vol. 4, 305.)

42. Estéban Vega Bacayao (Chachá) also offered an explanation that emphasized the aspect of protecting women from danger. He said the skin of the goat (used to build the drums) is the worst enemy one may have (Estéban Vega Bacayao, personal communication with the author, September 9, 1997).

43. I have noticed that a nasal, tense vocal quality seems to be highly and frequently praised.

EPILOGUE

1. A driver with an unauthorized car can make the equivalent of a university professor's monthly salary with a single trip to the airport.

2. J. Henry Drewal and John Mason, *Beads, Body and Soul: Art and Light in the Yorùbá Universe* (Los Angeles: UCLA Fowler Museum of Cultural History, 1998).

3. Recently he participated in a video for the BBC, with Professor Robert Farris Thompson, on the use of tobacco in the Afro-Cuban religions.

4. Appadurai, talking of the role the imagination plays in the biographies of ordinary people, points out that this role is not a simple matter of escapism, "for it is in the grinding of gears between unfolding lives and their imagined counterparts that a variety of 'imagined communities' is formed, communities that generate new kinds of politics, new kinds of collective expression and new need for social discipline and surveillance on the part of elites" (Appadurai 1991: 198).

5. Connerton is concerned with the formal aspects of rituals. He sees rituals as sharing two basic characteristics, formalism and performativity. The performativity of rituals is encoded not only on more or less invariant sequences of speech acts but also on a set of postures, gestures, and movements, which act as effective mnemonic devices. However, Connerton argues that if there is such thing as social memory, it is likely to be found in commemorative ceremonies, which he considers distinguishable from all other rituals by the fact that they refer explicitly "to prototypical persons and events" (1989: 61). In my opinion Santería ceremonies, inasmuch as they refer to prototypical persons and events that are understood to have both historical and mythological existence, may be considered under the category of commemorative ceremonies.

BIBLIOGRAPHY

Abu-Lughod, Lila. 1991. "Writing against Culture." Pp. 137–62 in *Recapturing Anthropology: Working in the Present,* ed. Richard G. Fox. Santa Fe, N.M.: School of American Research Press.

Acosta, Leonardo. 1983. *Del tambor al sintetizador.* Havana: Editorial Letras Cubanas.

Aimes, Hubert H. S. [1907] 1967. *A History of Slavery in Cuba: 1511 to 1868.* New York: Octagon Books.

Ames, Michael. 1986. *Museums, the Public and Anthropology.* Vancouver: University of British Columbia Press.

———. 1992. *Cannibal Tours and Glass Boxes: The Anthropology of Museums.* Vancouver: University of British Columbia Press.

Amira, John, and Steven Cornelius. 1992. *The Music of Santería.* Crown Point, Ind.: White Cliffs Media Company.

Antología de la música afrocubana. Volume 1: *Viejos cantos afrocubanos.* N.d. Liner notes by María Teresa Linares. EGREM. Areito LD-3325.

Antología de la música afrocubana. Volume 2: *Oru de Igbodú.* 1981. Liner notes by María Teresa Linares. EGREM. Areito LD-3995.

Antología de la música afrocubana. Volume 3: *Música Iyesá.* 1981. Liner notes by Argeliers León. EGREM. Areito LD-3747.

Antología de la música afrocubana. Volume 4: *Música Arará.* 1981. Liner notes by María Teresa Linares. EGREM. Areito LD-3996.

Antología de la música afrocubana. Volume 5: *Tambor yuka.* 1981. Liner notes by Martha Esquenazi. EGREM. Areito LD-3994.

Antología de la música afrocubana. Volume 6: *Fiesta de bembé.* 1981. Liner notes by Carmen María Saenz Copat. EGREM. Areito LD-3997.

Appadurai, Arjun. 1991. "Global Ethnoscapes: Notes and Queries for a Transnational Anthropology." Pp. 191–210 in *Recapturing Anthropology: Working in the Present,* ed. Richard G. Fox. Santa Fe, N.M.: School of American Research Press.

Babcock, Barbara A. 1986. ""Modeled Selves: Helen Cordero's 'Little People'." Pp. 316–43 in *The Anthropology of Experience,* ed. Victor W. Turner and Edward M. Bruner. Urbana and Chicago: University of Illinois Press.

Bach, Robert L. 1985. "Cubans." Pp. 76–93 in *Refugees in the United States. A Reference Handbook,* ed. David W. Haines. Westport, Conn.: Greenwood Press.

Bach, Robert L., Jennifer B. Bach, and Timothy Triplett. 1981/82. "The Flotilla 'Entrants': Latest and Most Controversial." *Cuban Studies* 11 (2)/12 (1): 28–48.

Barber, Karin. 1981. "How Man Makes God in West Africa: Yoruba Attitudes toward the *Orisa." Africa* 51 (3): 724–45.

Barnet, Miguel. 1966. "Biografía de un cimarrón." *Etnología y Folklore* 1: 65–83.

———. 1988. "Algunas palabras necesarias." *Areito* 1:5–7.

Bascom, William R. 1950. "The Focus of Cuban Santería." *Southwestern Journal of Anthropology* 6 (1): 64–68.

———. 1952. "Two Forms of Afro-Cuban Divination." In *Acculturation in the Americas,* ed. Sol Tax. Chicago: University of Chicago Press.

———. 1969. *Ifa Divination: Communication between Gods and Men in West Africa.* Bloomington: Indiana University Press.

———. 1972. *Shango in the New World.* Austin: University of Texas, African and Afro-American Research Institute.

———. 1980. *Sixteen Cowries: Yoruba Divination from Africa to the New World.* Bloomington: Indiana University Press.

Behar, Ruth. 1995. "Rage and Redemption: Reading the Life Story of a Mexican Marketing Woman." Pp. 148–78 in *The Dialogic Emergence of Culture,* ed. Denis Tedlock and Bruce Mannheim. Chicago: University of Illinois Press.

Bolívar, Natalia. 1990. *Los orishas en Cuba.* Havana: Ediciones Unión.

Brandon, George E. 1983. "The Dead Sell Memories: An Anthropological Study of Santería in New York City." Ph.D. diss., Rutgers University.

———. 1993. *Santería from Africa to the New World: The Dead Sell Memories.* Bloomington and Indianapolis: Indiana University Press.

Brenner, Louis. 1989. "Religious Discourses in and about Africa." Pp. 87–103 in *Discourse and Its Disguises: The Interpretation of African Oral Texts,* ed. Karin Barber and P. F. de Moraes Farias. Birmingham University African Studies Series 1. Birmingham: Birmingham University Center of West African Studies.

Brenner, Philip, William LeoGrande, Donna Rich, and Daniel Siegel, eds. 1989. *The Cuba Reader: The Making of a Revolutionary Society.* New York: Grove Press.

Brown, David Hilary. 1989. "Garden in the Machine: Afro-Cuban Sacred Art and Performance in Urban New Jersey and New York." Ph.D. diss., Yale University.

Bunck, Julie Marie. 1994. *Fidel Castro and the Quest for a Revolutionary Culture in Cuba.* University Park: Pennsylvania State University Press.

Burton, Julianne. 1982. "Folk Music, Circuses, Variety Shows and Other Endangered

Species: A Conversation with Julio García Espinosa on the Preservation of Popular Culture in Cuba." *Studies in Latin American Popular Culture* 1: 217–24.

Cabrera, Lydia. [1959] 1970. *La sociedad secreta Abakuá narrada por viejos adeptos.* Miami: Ediciones C & R.

———. 1974. *Yemayá y Ochún.* Madrid: C & R.

———. 1975a. *Anaforuana: Ritual y símbolos de la iniciación en la sociedad secreta Abakuá.* Madrid: Ediciones R.

———. [1954] 1975b. *El monte.* Miami: Ediciones Universal.

———. 1983. *La Regla Kimbisa del Santo Cristo del Buen Viaje.* Miami: Ediciones Universal.

———. 1984. *Vocabulario congo: El bantú que se habla en Cuba* Colección del Chicherekú en el exilio. Miami: Daytona Press.

———. [1957] 1986a. *Anagó, vocabulario lucumí.* Miami: Ediciones Universal.

———. [1975] 1986b. *Reglas de congo: Palo monte mayombe.* Miami: Ediciones Universal.

Calleja Leal, Guillermo. 1989. "Estudio de un sistema religioso afrocubano: El palomonte mayombe." Ph.D. diss., Universidad Complutense de Madrid.

Canizares, Raul. 1993. *Walking with the Night: The Afro-Cuban World of Santería.* Rochester, Vt.: Destiny Books.

Cantwell, Robert. 1991. "Conjuring Culture: Ideology and Magic in the Festival of American Folklife." *Journal of American Folklore* 104 (412): 148–63.

———. 1992. "Feasts of Unnaming: Folk Festivals and the Representation of Folklore." Pp. 263–305 in *Public Folklore,* ed. Robert Baron and Nicholas R. Spitzer. Washington, D.C., and London: Smithsonian Institution Press.

Carpentier, Alejo. 1946. *La música en Cuba.* Mexico City: Fondo de Cultura Económica.

Casal, Lourdes. 1989. "Cultural Policy and Writers in Cuba." Pp. 506–12 in *The Cuba Reader: The Making of a Revolutionary Society,* ed. Philip Brenner et al. New York: Grove Press.

Castellanos, Isabel. 1977. "The Use of Language in Afro-Cuban Religion." Ph.D. diss., Georgetown University.

Castellanos, Isabel, and Jorge Castellanos. 1988. *Cultura afrocubana.* Volume 1: *El Negro en Cuba, 1492–1844.* Miami: Ediciones Universal.

———. 1990. *Cultura afrocubana.* Volume 2: *El Negro en Cuba, 1845–1959.* Miami: Ediciones Universal.

———. 1992. *Cultura Afrocubana.* Volume 3: *Las Religiones y las Lenguas.* Miami: Ediciones Universal.

———. 1994. *Cultura Afrocubana,* Volume 4. *Letras—Música—Arte.* Miami: Ediciones Universal.

Castro, Fidel. 1961. *Palabras a los intelectuales.* Havana: Editorial Política.

Clifford, James, and Georges Marcus. 1986. *Writing Culture: The Poetics and Politics of Ethnography.* Berkeley and Los Angeles: University of California Press.

Colina, Ciro. 1991. "A Cuban Best-Seller: Understanding Afro-Cuban Religion." *Granma International,* March 10.

Connerton, Paul. 1989. *How Societies Remember*. Cambridge and New York: Cambridge University Press.

Cornelius, Steven H. 1989. "The Convergence of Power: An Investigation into the Music Liturgy of Santería in New York City." Ph.D. diss., University of California.

————. 1990. "Encapsulating Power: Meaning and Taxonomy of the Musical Instruments of Santería in New York City." *Selected Reports in Ethnomusicology* 8: 125–141.

————. 1991. "Drumming for the Orishas: Reconstruction of Tradition in New York City." Pp. 137–55 in *Essays on Cuban Music: North American and Cuban Perspectives,* ed. Peter Manuel. Lanham, Md.: University Press of America.

La cultura en Cuba socialista. 1982. Havana: Editorial Letras Cubanas.

Curry, Mary. 1991. "Making the Gods in New York: The Yoruba Religion in the Black Community." Ph.D. diss., City University of New York.

————. 1997. *Making the Gods in New York: The Yoruba Religion in the African American Community*. New York: Garland.

Dean, Diana Maitland. 1993. "Dreaming the Dead: The Social Impact of Dreams in an Afro-Cuban Community." Ph.D. diss., University of Minnesota.

de la Soledad, Rosalía, and María J. San Juán. 1988. *IBO (Yorubas en tierras cubanas)* Miami: Ediciones Universal.

Drewal, John Henry, and John Mason. 1998. *Beads, Body and Soul: Art and Light in the Yorùbá Universe*. Los Angeles: UCLA Fowler Museum of Cultural History.

Eckstein, Susan Eva. 1994. *Back from the Future: Cuba under Castro*. Princeton, N.J.: Princeton University Press.

Eli Rodríguez, Victoria. 1994. "Cuban Music and Ethnicity: Historical Considerations." Pp. 91–108 in *Music and Black Ethnicity: The Caribbean and South America,* ed. Gerard H. Béhague. New Brunswick, N.J., and London: Transaction Publishers.

Fagen, Richard R., Richard A. Brody, and Thomas O'Leary. 1968. *Cubans in Exile: Disaffection and the Revolution*. Stanford, Calif.: Stanford University Press.

Fernández, Gastón A. 1982. "The Freedom Flotilla: A Legitimacy Crisis of Cuban Socialism?" *Journal of Interamerican Studies and World Affairs* 24 (2): 183–209.

Finnegan, Ruth. 1970. *Oral Literature in Africa*. Oxford: Clarendon Press.

Fox, Richard. 1991. "For a Nearly New Cultural History." Pp. 93–113 in *Recapturing Anthropology: Working in the Present,* ed. Richard Fox. Santa Fe, N.M.: School of American Research Press.

Friedman, Robert Alan. 1982. "Making an Abstract World Concrete: Knowledge, Competence and Structural Dimensions of Performance among Batá Drummers in Santería." Ph.D. diss., Indiana University.

García, Pedro Antonio 1992. "The Freedom of Worship and Respect for All Religious Traditions." *Granma International,* June 14.

Gilroy, Paul. 1989. "Cruciality and the Frog's Perspective." *Third Text* 5: 33–44.

————. 1993. *The Black Atlantic: Modernity and Double Consciousness*. Cambridge, Mass.: Harvard University Press.

Granma International. 1988. "Fourth Congress of Orisha Tradition and Culture Scheduled to Take Place in Havana." February 28.

Gregory, Steven. 1986. "Santería in New York City: A Study in Cultural Resistance." Ph.D. diss., New School for Social Research.

Guanche, Jesús. 1983. *Procesos etnoculturales de Cuba.* Havana: Editorial Letras Cubanas.

Guerra, Ramiro. 1989. *La teatralización del folklore y otros ensayos.* Havana: Editorial Letras Cubanas.

Hagedorn, Katherine Johan. 1995. "Anatomía del proceso folklórico: The 'Folkloricization' of Afro-Cuban Religious Performance in Cuba." Ph.D. diss., Brown University.

Halbwachs, Maurice. 1992. *On Collective Memory,* ed., trans., and with an introduction by Lewis A. Coser. Chicago: University of Chicago Press.

Hooper-Greenhill, Eilean. 1992. *Museums and the Shaping of Knowledge.* New York: Routledge.

Hopkins, Tometro. 1992. "Issues in the Study of Afro-Creoles: Afro-Cuban and Gullah." Ph.D. diss., Indiana University.

Hunt, Carl M. 1979. *Oyotunji Village: The Yoruba Movement in America.* Washington, D.C.: University Press of America.

Johnson, Ragnar. 1997. "The Extent of Representation, the Relationships of Artifacts and the Anthropology of Art." *Visual Anthropology* 9: 149–166.

Karp, Ivan, and Steven D. Levine. 1991. *Exhibiting Cultures: The Poetics and Politics of Museum Display.* Washington, D.C., and London: Smithsonian Institution Press.

Kirshenblatt-Gimblett, Barbara. 1992. "Mistaken Identities." Pp. 30–43 in *Public Folklore,* ed. Robert Baron and Nicholas R. Spitzer. Washington, D.C., and London: Smithsonian Institution Press.

Klein, Herbert S. 1986. *African Slavery in Latin America and the Caribbean.* New York and London: Oxford University Press.

Kurin, Richard. 1989. "Why We Do the Festival." Pp. 8–21 in *Smithsonian Festival of American Folklife Program Book,* ed. Frank Proschan. Washington, D.C.: Smithsonian Institution.

———. 1992. "Presenting Folklife in a Soviet-American Cultural Exchange: Public Practice during the Perestroika." Pp. 183–215 in *Public Folklore,* ed. Robert Baron and Nicholas R. Spitzer. Washington, D.C., and London: Smithsonian Institution Press.

León, Argeliers. 1966. "La expresión del pueblo en el TNC." *Actas del Folklore* 1 (1): 5–7.

———. 1982. "El folklore: Su estudio y recuperación." Pp. 182–93 in *La cultura en Cuba socialista.* Havana: Editorial Letras Cubanas.

———. [1974] 1984. *Del canto y el tiempo.* Havana: Editorial Letras Cubanas.

———. 1991a. "Notes toward a Panorama of Popular and Folk Music." Pp. 3–23 in *Essays on Cuban Music: North American and Cuban Perspectives,* ed. Peter Manuel. Lanham, Md.: University Press of America.

———. 1991b. "On the Axle and the Hinge: Nationalism, Afro-Cubanism, and Music in Pre-Revolutionary Cuba." Pp. 267–82 in *Essays on Cuban Music: North American and Cuban Perspectives*, ed. Peter Manuel. Lanham, Md.: University Press of America.

Levinson, Sandra. 1989. "Talking about Cuban Culture: A Reporter's Notebook." Pp. 487–96 in *The Cuba Reader: The Making of a Revolutionary Society*, ed. Philip Brenner et al. New York: Grove Press.

López Valdés, Rafael L. 1966. "La sociedad secreta 'Abacuá' en un grupo de obreros portuarios." *Etnología y Folklore* 2: 5–26.

———. 1985. *Componentes africanos en el etnos cubano*. Havana: Editorial de Ciencias Sociales.

La lucha ideológica y la cultura artística. 1982. Havana: Editora Política.

Luis, William, and Julia Cuervo Hewitt. 1987. "Santos y Santería: Conversación con Arcadio, santero de Guanabacoa." *Afro-Hispanic Review* 6: 9–17.

Manuel, Peter. 1985. "Ideology and Popular Music in Socialist Cuba." *Pacific Review of Ethnomusicology* 2: 1–27.

Manuel, Peter, ed. 1991. *Essays on Cuban Music: North American and Cuban Perspectives*. Lanham, Md.: University Press of America.

Marcus, George, and Fred Myers, eds. 1995. *The Traffic in Culture: Refiguring Art and Anthropology*. Berkeley and Los Angeles: University of California Press.

Marshall, Peter. 1987. *Cuba Libre: Breaking the Chains?* London: Victor Gollancz Ltd.

Martínez Furé, Rogelio. 1979. *Diálogos Imaginarios*. Havana: Editorial Arte y Literatura.

Mason, John. 1992. *Orin Orisa: Songs for Selected Heads*. New York: Yoruba Theological Archministry.

———. [1985] 1993. *Four New World Yoruba Rituals*. New York: Yoruba Theological Archministry.

Mason, John, and Gary Edwards. 1981. *Onje Fun Orisa (Food for the Gods)*. New York: Yoruba Theological Archministry.

———. 1985. *Black Gods: Orisa Studies in the New World*. New York: The Yoruba Theological Archministry.

Masud-Piloto, Félix Roberto. 1988. *With Open Arms: Cuban Migration to the United States*. Totowa, N.J.: Rowman & Littlefield.

Matibag, Eugenio. 1996. *Afro-Cuban Religious Experience: Cultural Reflections in Narrative*. Gainesville: University Press of Florida.

Matory, J. Lorand. 1996. "Revisiting the African Diaspora." *American Anthropologist* 98 (1): 167–170.

Matthews, Herbert L. 1975. *Revolution in Cuba*. New York: Charles Scribner's Sons.

Menéndez, Lázara, ed. *Estudios afro-cubanos: Selección de lecturas*, vol. 3. Havana: Facultad de Artes y Letras, Universidad de La Habana.

Moore, Carlos. 1988. *Castro, the Blacks and Africa*. Los Angeles: University of California Press.

Morales, Beatriz. 1990. "Afro-Cuban Religious Transformation: A Comparative Study of Lucumi Religions and the Tradition of Spirit Belief." Ph.D. diss., City University of New York.

Moreno Fraginals, Manuel. 1978. *El ingenio: Complejo económico social cubano del azúcar*. 3 vols. Havana: Editorial de Ciencias Sociales.

Murphy, Joseph M. [1988] 1993. *Santería: African Spirits in America*. Boston: Beacon Press.

Myerhoff, Barbara G. 1978. *Number Our Days*. New York: Simon & Schuster/Touchstone.

Ortiz, Fernando. 1952. *Los instrumentos de la música afrocubana*. 5 vols. Havana: Dirección de Cultura del Ministerio de Educación.

————. 1970. *Cuban Counterpoint*. New York: Vintage Books.

————. [1906] 1973. *Hampa afro-cubana: Los negros brujos*. Miami: Ediciones Universal.

————. [1906] 1975a. *Hampa afro-cubana: Los negros esclavos*. Havana: Editorial Ciencias Sociales.

————. 1975b. *La música afrocubana* Madrid: Ediciones Júcar.

————. 1981. *Los bailes y el teatro de los negros en el folklore de Cuba*. Havana: Editorial Letras Cubanas.

————. [1921] 1984. "Los cabildos afrocubanos." *Ensayos Etnográficos*. Havana: Editorial de Ciencias Sociales.

Otero, Lisandro. 1972. *Cultural Policy in Cuba*. Paris: UNESCO.

Paz, Octavio. 1979. *In/Mediciones*. Barcelona: Editorial Seix Barral, S.A.

Pedraza-Bailey, Silvia. 1985. "Cuba's Exiles: Portrait of a Refugee Migration." *International Migration Review* 17 (1): 5–33.

Pensamiento y política cultural cubanos. 1986. Compiled by Nuria Sánchez and Graciela Fernández. 4 vols. Havana: Editorial Pueblo y Educación.

Pérez de la Riva, Juan. 1974. "El monto de la inmigración forzada en el siglo XIX." *Revista de la Biblioteca Nacional José Martí* 16: 77–110.

————. 1976. *Para la historia de las gentes sin historia*. Barcelona: Editorial Ariel.

Pérez y Mena, Andrés. 1991. *Speaking with the Dead: Development of Afro-Latin Religion among Puerto Ricans in the United States*. New York: AMS Press.

Portes, Alejandro, and Juan M. Clark. 1987. "Mariel Refugees: Six Years After." *Migration World* 15: 14–18.

Rabkin, Rhoda P. 1991. *Cuban Politics: The Revolutionary Experiment*. New York: Praeger.

Robbins, James. 1989. "Practical and Abstract Taxonomy in Cuban Music." *Ethnomusicology* 33 (3): 379–390.

————. 1991. "Institutions, Incentives and Evaluations in Cuban Music-Making." Pp. 215–47 in *Essays on Cuban Music: North American and Cuban Perspectives*, ed. Peter Manuel. Lanham, Md.: University Press of America.

Rouget, Gilbert. 1965. "Notes et documents pour servir à l'étude de la musique yoruba." *Journal de la Société des Africanistes* 35 (1): 67–107.

Rushdie, Salman. 1991. *Imaginary Homelands: Essays and Criticism 1981–1991*. New York: Viking.

Salazar, Max. 1994. "Arsenio Rodriguez: Life Was Like a Dream." *Latin Beat Magazine* 4 (2): 12–17.

Sandoval, Mercedes. 1975. *La religión afrocubana*. Madrid: Playor S.A.

Scott, Rebecca J. 1985. *Slave Emancipation in Cuba: The Transition to Free Labor, 1860–1899*. Princeton, N.J.: Princeton University Press.

Sheehy, Daniel. 1992a. "Crossover Dreams: The Folklorist and the Folk Arrival." Pp. 217–29 in *Public Folklore*, ed. Robert Baron and Nicholas R. Spitzer. Washington, D.C., and London: Smithsonian Institute Press.

———. 1992b. "A Few Notions about Philosophy and Strategy in Applied Ethnomusicology." *Ethnomusicology* 36 (3):323–36.

Sosa, Enrique. 1982. *Los ñáñigos*. Havana: Ediciones Casa de las Américas.

Stokes, Martin, ed. 1994. *Ethnicity, Identity and Music: The Musical Construction of Place*. Oxford and Providence, R.I.: Berg.

Stubbs, Jean. 1989. *Cuba: The Test of Time*. London: Latin American Bureau.

Taylor, Frank. 1988. "Revolution, Race and Some Aspects of Foreign Relations in Cuba since 1959." *Cuban Studies* 18: 19–40.

Thieme, Darius L. 1969. "A Descriptive Catalogue of Yoruba Musical Instruments." Ph.D. diss., Catholic University of America.

Thomas, Hugh. 1971. *Cuba: The Pursuit of Freedom*. New York: Harper & Row.

Thompson, Robert Farris. 1984. *Flash of the Spirit*. New York: Vintage Books.

———. 1993. *Face of the Gods: Art and Altars of Africa and the African Americas*. Munich: Prestel.

Varela, Jesse. 1994. "Sworn to the Drum." *Latin Beat Magazine* 4 (2, 3): 27–28, 16–18.

Vélez, María Teresa. 1994. "Eya Aranla: Overlapping Perspectives on a Santería Group." *Diaspora* 3 (3): 289–304.

———. 1996. "The Trade of an Afro-Cuban Religious Drummer: Felipe García Villamil." Ph.D. diss., Wesleyan University.

Vinueza, María Elena. 1988. *Presencia arará en la música folclórica de Matanzas*. Havana: Casa de la Américas.

Waterman, Christopher Alan. 1990. " 'Our Tradition Is a Very Modern Tradition': Popular Music and the Construction of Pan-Yoruba Identity." *Ethnomusicology* 34 (3): 367–80.

Wikan, Unni. 1996. "The Nun's Story: Reflections on an Age-Old, Postmodern Dilemma." *American Anthropologist* 98: 279–89.

Wilcken, Lois E. 1991. "Music Folklore among Haitians in New York: Staged Representations and the Negotiation of Identity." Ph.D. diss., Columbia University.

Zumthor, Paul. 1990. *Oral Poetry: An Introduction*. Minneapolis: University of Minnesota Press.

GLOSSARY

For simplicity, non-Spanish words used in the Afro-Cuban religious practices are labeled as Lucumí, Congo, or Abakuá, though the linguistic origin of some words may not be clear. Key: **(L)** Lucumí; **(A)** Abakuá; **(C)** Congo; **(S)** Spanish.

Abakuá	(A)	Name of the secret societies of Carabalí origin.
Aberikulá	(L)	In Santería, the name given to a person who does not belong to the religion, a "nonbaptized."
Aché or Ashe	(L)	Power, force, strength, luck, energy, blessing.
Acheré or Atcheré	(L)	Rattle.
Agallú, Agayú, or Aganyú	(L)	Oricha, owner of the river and the deserted plain. Patron of porters and travelers. The volcano.
Agogó	(L)	Metal bell.
Ahijado, Ahijada	(S)	Godson, goddaughter.
Akpón or Akpwón	(L)	Solo singer in Santería rituals. Also called *gallo,* Spanish word for rooster.
Aláña	(L)	Owner of a set of batá drums. Also called *olúañá.*
Amalá	(L)	Corn flour.
Añá	(L)	The power or force that inhabits the batá drums.
Anaforuana	(A)	The pictographic writing system used by the Abakuá.
Arará	(S)	Name given in Cuba to slaves and traditions coming from the area of Dahomey.

Asiento	(S)	The major initiation ceremony in Santería.
Avatares	(S)	See *camino*.
Awó	(L)	Diviner.
Babalao or Babalawo	(L)	High Santería priest who reads and interprets the divination system known as Ifá.
Babalocha	(L)	Name given to men who are initiated in Santería.
Babalú-Ayé	(L)	Oricha of sickness, in particular those illnesses that affect the skin (smallpox, leprosy, etc.). Protects against disease and want. Syncretized as San Lázaro (Saint Lazarus). This deity was adopted by the Arará in Matanzas, and its cult became central to their ritual practices.
Banté or Bandel	(L)	Beaded liturgical garments used to decorate the batá drums during ceremonies.
Batá	(L)	The set of three double-headed sacred drums used in the rituals of Santería.
Batalero	(LS)	Batá player.
Bembé	(L)	Name given to a religious celebration (a ritual party). Known also as *tambor* and *güemilere*. Name given to a set of single-headed drums and to the music played on them.
Binkomé or Biankomé	(A)	The highest-pitched enkomó drum of the Abakuá drum ensemble used for public celebrations.
Bonkó Enchemiyá	(A)	Largest drum in the Abakuá drum ensemble used for public celebrations.
Botánica	(S)	Place that sells the religious paraphernalia used by santeros.
Cabildo	(S)	Mutual-aid organization of free blacks and slaves that were said to belong to the same ethnic group, or *nación*. Name given later to house-temples in Santería.
Cachimbo	(S)	Name given to the smallest drum of the Congo yuka ensemble.
Caja	(S)	Literally: box. Name used to refer to the biggest drum in the batá ensemble. It is also used to refer to the second largest drum of the iyesá ensemble.
Camino	(S)	Literally: road. The different aspects, sometimes contradictory, of the orichas, also know as *avatares* (avatars).
Casa de Ocha or Casa de Santo (see Ilé)	(S)	House-temple. Basic social unit that groups the practitioners initiated by the same godfather or godmother.
Chachá	(L)	The smaller head of the batá drums.
Chaguala	(L)	A rawhide strap in the shape of the sole of a shoe, used in Matanzas to play the smaller head of the omelé and itótele drums.
Chamalongo	(C)	Name given by the paleros to the shells used for divination.
Changó	(L)	Oricha of fire, thunder, lightning.

Chaworó or Chaguoró	(L)	Straps of bells and jingles attached around the heads of the iyá drum.
Chekeré, Agbé, or Agwé	(L)	Percussion instruments; beaded gourds, also called *güiros.*
Clave	(S)	Repeated rhythmic pattern that serves as a point of reference in the music of Santería (chants, drumming, and dancing).
Coartación	(S)	A common system of manumission that involved the payment of a pre-established fee to the master.
Collares	(S)	Necklaces used by santeros. *Ilekes* in Lucumí.
Colonia	(S)	Name given to large farms that were formerly sugar or tobacco plantations.
Congo	(S)	Name given in Cuba to slaves and cultural practices of Bantú origin.
Controversia	(S)	Literally: controversy. Duel or competition among singers.
Conversación	(S)	Literally: conversation. Name given to the rhythmic dialogue that takes place between the iyá and the itótele.
Criado	(S)	Literally: servant. In Palo, the initiates who have been ritually prepared to become possessed, also called *perros* (dogs).
Cuarto	(S)	Literally: room. See *igbodú.*
Cumpleaños	(S)	Literally: birthday. Annual celebration of the initiation as santero/a.
Dadá	(L)	Oricha of the newly born.
Dilogún	(L)	System of divination that uses cowry shells.
Egbó or Ebó	(L)	Sacrifice or offering to the orichas.
Égun	(L)	The spirits of the dead, the ancestors.
Ekón	(A)	A bell used in the Abakuá drum ensemble.
Ekue	(A)	The sacred drum of the Abakuá that incorporates the power and voice of Tanze. See also *fundamento.*
Ekuelé	(L)	Necklace of Ifá used by the babalaos for divination.
Ekueñón	(A)	One of the four symbolic drums of the Abakuá. Used by the dignitary that "bestows justice."
Eleguá or Elegguá	(L)	Oricha, guardian of the crossroads, guardian of the door, trickster, the messenger of Olofi. Has to be honored first in any ceremony.
Empegó	(A)	One of the four symbolic drums of the Abakuá. Called also *tambor de orden,* it is used to open and close all rituals and to impose discipline within the temple.
Enkomó	(A)	Generic name given to the three smaller drums of the Abakuá drum ensemble used for public celebrations.
Enkríkamo	(A)	One of the four symbolic drums of the Abakuá. Used to convene the iremes.
Enú	(L)	The larger head of the batá drums.

Eribó	(A) One of the four symbolic drums of the Abakuá. The ritual sacrifices are placed over this drum.
Erikundí	(A) Two rattles used in the Abakuá drum ensemble.
Ewe	(L) Herbs.
Eyá Aránla	(L) The living room in the house-temple where the public celebrations take place.
Fambá	(A) The sacred room in the Abakuá temple.
Fardela, Fadela, or Idá	(L) Resin placed on the head of the iyá drum.
Fiesta	(S) Literally: party. Used to refer to a celebration in honor of the orichas that includes dancing.
Firma	(S) Literally: signature. In Palo, the magic ritual symbols that represent the spirit that inhabits the nganga. Not only spirits but also paleros have firmas used to identify them.
Fula	(C) Gunpowder.
Fundamento	(S) In all the Afro-Cuban religious practices, the fundamento stands for a thing that is the object of cult because it incorporates a god or a spirit: in Santería, the otanes; in Palo, the nganga; in Abakuá, the ekué.
Güemilere	(L) See *bembé*.
Güiro	(S) A type of celebration for the orichas, where beaded gourds (chekerés) and conga drums are used instead of the batá ensemble. Also the name given to the chekerés. The word is also used to refer to a kind of rattle used in secular dance music.
Ibeyis	(L) Orichas. The holy twins, the mystical twin (*jimagua*) children. They bring good fortune.
Ifá	(L) Also Orula. The oricha of divination. Name given also to a divination system.
Igbodu	(L) Sacred room of the house-temple where most of the important rituals are performed. Sometimes referred to using the Spanish word *cuarto*.
Ikú	(L) Death.
Ilé or Inle	(L) House.
Ilekes	(L) Necklaces used by santeros.
Ilé-Oricha or Ilé-Ocha	(L) House-temple.
Inle	(L) Oricha. The holy physician, owner of the river and of fish.
Ireme or Diablito	(AS) The "little devil," the spirit of the deceased. Well known by the general population for their participation as street dancers in the carnival held on January 6, the Day of the Three Kings. Also called *ñáñigos,* a name used to refer in general to the members of the Abakuá society.
Irongo	(A) See *fambá*.

Isué	(A) Abakuá dignitary. The priest the ñáñigos call the Bishop. Swears the new members in. Responsible for the symbolic drum called the seseribó.
Isunekue	(A) Abakuá dignitary. He accompanied Sikán to the river where Tanze appeared. The husband of Sikán.
Italero	(L) A santero knowledgeable in reading the dilogún.
Itótele	(L) Second largest drum in the batá set, also called *segundo*.
Itutu	(L) Funeral rite in Santería.
Iyá	(L) Mother. The largest drum in the batá set, also referred to as *caja*.
Iyalocha	(L) Name given to a female initiate in Santería.
Iyamba	(A) A dignitary of the Abakuá. The highest priest of the Abakuá, the one that plays the sacred drum. He confirms the newly initiated members.
Iyawo, Yaguó, or Yawó	(L) Name given to initiated santeros during the first year after their initiation.
Iyesá or Yesá	(L) Name given to the liturgical practices, the ensemble of drums, and a repertoire of chants of the Iyesá, a subgroup of the Lucumí.
Juego	(S) *Potencia, tierra, plante,* and *partido* are the other names used to refer to this confraternity of ñáñigos or Abakuás.
Korikoto	(L) Oricha associated with food taboos.
Kpuátaki	(L) Leader of the batá ensemble. Usually the iyá player and owner of the set of drums.
Kuchí Yeremá	(A) The medium-pitched enkomó drum of the Abakuá drum ensemble used for public celebrations.
Libreta	(S) Notebook used by santeros to write chants and myths.
Licencia	(S) Permission.
Llamadas	(S) Literally: calls. The calls made by the iyá drum that have to be answered by the other drums.
Lucumí	(L) Slaves and tradition of Yoruba origin.
Madrina or Yubbona	(SL) Godmother.
Makuta	(C) A set of drums, a dance, and type of music of Congo origin.
Mambo	(S) Congo ritual chants.
Mariwó or Maribó	(L) Ritual ornament made with palm fiber. Skirt made of coconut palm or raffia that is placed around the upper rim of the bembé drum.
Mayombero	(C) Palero. One who practices Palo, the religious practice of Congo origin.
Mokongo or Mokuire	(A) Abakuá dignitary. Represents military power. According to a version of the origin myth, he was the father of Sikán.
Monte	(S) The meaning for santeros and paleros goes beyond the literal translation of forest, woods, or wilderness. For Afro-

Cubans, el monte is a sacred place inhabited by the spirits of the dead and the orichas. It is also the place where all the herbs, plants, and trees that are so important for the ritual practices of santeros and paleros are found.

Mpaka	(C)	A horn embellished with exquisite beadwork, where the vititi mensu is placed.
Mpungu	(C)	Spirits that inhabit the cauldron of a palero.
Muñones, Chécheres, or Beromos	(A)	The ornaments made with feathers that represent the hierarchy of the four main posts or chiefs (obones) in the Abakuá society and the spirits of the four obones of the first Abakuá potencia.
Nación	(S)	Slaves who were considered to share the same ethnic or geographical origin.
Ñáñigo	(A)	Member of the Abakuá society. See also *ireme/diablito*.
Nasakó	(A)	Abakuá dignitary. The diviner.
Nganga	(C)	The spirit of the dead that a palero works with. The recipient or cauldron this spirit inhabits. Also known as *makuto, prenda, nkisi*.
Ngombe	(C)	Medium in Palo practices.
Nsambi, Sambi, or Sambia	(C)	The supreme creator of the world in the Palo religious system.
Oba or Obba	(L)	Female oricha, one of Changó's wives. Owner of lakes. Symbolizes devotion and fidelity.
Obatalá	(L)	Father of the orichas, creator of mankind. King of white cloth; wisdom, justice.
Obi	(L)	Coconut.
Obíapá or salidor	(A)	The lowest-pitched enkomó drum of the Abakuá drum ensemble used for public celebrations.
Obonekue	(A)	Name given to a member of the Abakuá society.
Ocha	(L)	Saint. Regla de Ocha is the name given to Santería.
Ochosi	(L)	Oricha of hunting.
Ochún	(L)	Seductive female oricha of love, beauty, money, fortune. Owner of the rivers. One of Changó's wives.
Ogún	(L)	Mighty warrior, oricha of metals, iron. Knows the secrets of the monte.
Oké	(L)	Oricha of the mountain.
Okónkolo or Omelé	(L)	The smallest drum in the batá set.
Olodumare or Olofi	(L)	The supreme creator of the world for the Lucumí.
Olókun	(L)	One of the roads of Yemayá, the bottomless sea.
Olúañá	(L)	Initiated batá drummer. He who knows the secrets of Añá.
Omiero	(L)	A liquid used ritually in Santería, made with various herbs.

Omo	(L)	Child.
Omóañá	(L)	Son of Añá. Name given to batá drummers who have undergone the ritual cleansing of their hands that authorizes them to play consecrated drums.
Omó-oricha	(L)	Child of the orichas.
Ori	(L)	Head.
Oriaté	(L)	A ritual expert and trained diviner. Plays an important role in all the initiation rituals in Santería.
Oricha	(L)	A Lucumí deity.
Oricha Oko	(L)	Oricha of agriculture, farming, land, and crops.
Oro or Oru	(L)	A liturgical sequence of rhythms and chants for the orichas. *Oro cantado* or *oro del eyá aránla* includes songs, *oro seco* or *oro de igbodu* only drumming.
Orula, Orúmila, or Orúnmila	(L)	Oricha of divination. Owner and master of Ifá, patron of the babalaos. Syncretized with Saint Francis of Assisi.
Osain	(L)	Oricha of herbs and plants, the one-legged and one-eyed lord of the forest, patron of osainistas. This oricha has to be rendered tribute before one takes away plants and herbs. Osain is also the name given to a talisman.
Osainista	(L)	A man with a vast knowledge of the curative and religious applications and uses of plants and herbs. He is the one who visits el monte to collect the plants that are to be used in the various ceremonies. It was traditional for each casa de santo to have its own osainista.
Osun or Osu	(L)	Santeros disagree as to the meaning of *osun*. For some it is an oricha. However, it is never given to anyone (there are no priests of Osun), and it never possesses any adept. It is represented by a ritual object made in lead or any other white metal—a cock or sometimes a dog or a dove—that perches on a pillar given to santeros in the ceremony when they receive the *guerreros*. The guerreros, a series of sacred objects that represent the orichas Eleguá, Ogún, and Ochosi, are given to the initiate to strenthen the bond with and obtain the protection of these orichas. Osun is also the name given to the paints used for ritual purposes.
Otanes	(L)	The sacred stones in Santería.
Oyá	(L)	Female oricha, the wind, fire, and death. One of Changó's wives.
Padrino	(S)	Godfather.
Palero	(S)	Priest of the Afro-Cuban religion Palo Monte or Mayombe. Known also a *mayombero*. The paleros specialize in work with the spirits of the dead.
Palo or Palo Monte	(S)	Literally: stick. An Afro-Cuban religious practice of Congo origin.

Pataki or Appataki	(L)	Lucumí myths and legends. Stories about the life and attributes of the orichas that were transmitted orally, many of which have been written by santeros in private books; some have even been printed. These patakís are also used in divination as advice to the consultant.
Plantar	(S)	Literally: to plant. Word used by both paleros and Abakuás, meaning to "celebrate a ritual."
Potencia	(S)	See *juego*.
Prenda	(S)	See *nganga*.
Puya	(S)	Taunt.
Rama	(S)	Literally: branch. The line of descent based on ritual kinship.
Rayar	(S)	Literally: to scratch. To initiate into the Regla de Palo.
Regla	(S)	Generic name given to the different Afro-Cuban religious practices: *Regla de Ocha*—Lucumí, also known as Santería; *Regla de Palo*—Congo, also known as Mayombé or Kimbisa; *Regla Arará*—from Dahomey.
Santería	(S)	The Afro-Cuban religious practices of Lucumí origin wherein the Catholic saints are syncretized with the African deities known as orichas.
Santero, Santera	(S)	Practitioner of Santería.
Santo	(S)	Saint.
Segundo	(S)	Literally: second. Used to refer to the second-largest drum in an ensemble; in the batá ensemble, the itótele. The drummer who plays it is called *segundero*.
Seseribó	(A)	See *eribó*.
Sikán	(A)	In the Abakuá myth, the woman who found the secret embodied in the fish Tanze.
Sopera	(S)	Tureen. In Santería, the sacred stones are kept in soup tureens.
Tambor	(S)	Literally: drum. See *güemilere* and *bembé*.
Tambor de Fundamento	(S)	Consecrated drum.
Tambor Judío	(S)	Literally: Jewish drum. Unconsecrated drum, also known as *aberikulá*.
Tanze or Tanse	(A)	In the Abakuá myth, the fish that embodied the sacred power.
Tata-Nganga	(C)	Male head of a house-temple in Palo.
Tierra	(S)	See *juego*.
Toque	(S)	Drummed rhythmic patterns. Also used to refer to a ceremony where drums are played, as in the expression "to go to a toque."
Viros	(S)	Literally: turns. Changes in the rhythmic patterns played by the batá ensemble.

Vititi Mensu	(C)	A divination system used by paleros. It is a small mirror placed in the opening of a horn (mpaka).
Yamboki	(L)	An apprentice batá drummer.
Yeguá	(L)	Female oricha, owner of the cemetery.
Yemayá	(L)	Oricha of the sea, salt waters, maternity.
Yesá or Iyesá	(L)	Name given to a subgroup of the Lucumí in Cuba; also to the religious practices and ritual music that originated in this group and to the drum ensemble used in their rituals.
Yuka	(C)	Music and drum ensemble of Congo origin.

INDEX

203

Morales, Beatriz, 137, 145
Moreno Fraginals, Manuel, 172 n. 5
Morrison, Toni, 165
mozambique, 71
mpaka, 15
mpungu, 12
Murphy, Joseph M., 48, 152
Museum of African Art, New York, 133
museums: politics of representation, 133–34; transformation of ritual objects into museum pieces, 134
music theory. See *orichas:* and music theory
música bailable, 71, 72
Myerhoff, Barbara, xvii

naciones. See slave groups
ñáñigos. See Abakuá
Nasakó. See Abakuá: myth of origin
ndungui, 15
nganga. See prenda
nso nganga (house temple), 15

obi, 14
obonekues, 18, 173 n. 25
ochiché añá, 49
O'Farrill, Arturo, 37
okónkolo, 39, 44
Olodumare (Olofi), 13, 28, 139. *See also* Santería
Olofi. *See* Olodumare
olókun drums, 61
olúañá, 3, 49, 51, 126, 171 n. 1
olúbatá, 47, 49
omelé, 39, 44
omóañá, 3, 49, 51, 171 n. 1
Organizaciones Revolucionarias Integradas (ORI), 73, 176 n. 7
oriaté, 14, 123, 125
orichas, xiv, 11, 12, 24–25, 172 n. 10, 173 n. 18; Babalú-Ayé, 11, 62; *caminos* or *avatares,* 12; Changó, 149; Eleguá, 13, 28, 43, 50, 149, 150; Korikoto, 40; and music theory, 40, 174 n. 30; in New York, 149–50; Obatalá, 28; Ochosi, 13, 40; Ochún, 26, 61, 129–30; Ogún, 12, 13, 26, 27, 28–29, 61, 124, 129, 130; Olókun, 61; Orula, 14, 17; Osain, 101, 120, 124, 128, 139, 159; Oyá, 25–26, 42, 97, 99, 100, 127, 150; ritual objects, 182 n. 16; Yemayá, 150. *See also* Santería
Orquesta de Rafael Ortega, 145
Ortiz, Fernando, xi, 10, 19, 20, 40, 50, 53, 58, 59, 61, 93, 126, 146, 147, 152, 172 nn.

4, 11, 174 nn. 33, 35, 175 nn. 40, 45, 48, 50, 177 n. 9, 180 n. 32, 183 nn. 35, 38, 41
osainista, 47, 52
otanes (sacred stones), 13, 118
Otero, Lisandro, 74, 177 n. 11

pachanga, 71
palero(s), 16; Benigno García as, 4, 30–34; and cult of the dead, 31; Felipe's initiation as, 4, 30–31; Felipe's training as, 4, 31–32, 34, 64; misrepresentation of, 31; and secrecy, 31; transmission of religious knowledge among, 31–33
Palo, 10, 11–13, 15–17, 30–34; altars in New York, 132, 143; in Cárdenas (Matanzas), 30; *chamalongos,* 15; communication with spirits, 15; deities (*mpungus*), 12; deities in New York, 143, 150, 151; divination systems, 15; *firmas,* 16; focus of religious practice, 13; *fula,* 15; initiation (*rayamiento*), 15, 30; *mayordomo,* 17, 32; *el monte,* 11; *mpaka,* 15; *mpungu,* 12; *ndungui,* 15; nonorthodoxy of, 16–17; *nso nganga* (house temple), 15; possession or trance, 15, 150, 151; religious practices, 13; ritual experts, 16; ritual music, 16; Sambia, 13; and secular dances, 65; supreme creator in, 12, 13; *vititi mensu,* 15. *See also* Congo origin; *prenda;* slave groups
Pan-Africanism, 115, 138. *See also* Cuban revolution
pataki, xiv, 12
Paz, Octavio, 134
Pedraza-Bailey, Silvia, 85, 108, 109, 180 n. 1, 181 nn. 2, 3
Peña, Lázaro, 87–88, 90. *See also* Arcadio; Cuban revolution: and Afro-Cuban religion
Pérez, Jesús, 147, 174 n. 35
Pérez de la Riva, Juan, 172 n. 3
Pérez Prado, Dámaso, 37
plante, 18, 83
plazas, 18
Portes, Alejandro, 109
possession: and music, 14, 15, 25, 43–44. *See also* memory; Palo; Santería; Santería music
prenda (nganga), 15–16, 32–34, 173 nn. 19, 21, 22; Mariamunda, 16, 32–34; Rompe Monte, 16, 33. *See also* Palo

Rabkin, Rhoda, 89
Raúl "Nasakó," 145

Raymat, Juan "El Negro," 126, 147
recontextualization and secularization of
Afro-Cuban ritual music: in Cuba, 76, 77,
78, 80–82, 85–87, 101–4; in the U.S.,
115–17, 148
Regla Conga. *See* Palo
Regla de Ocha. *See* Santería
repression of Afro-Cuban religions: of
Abakuás, 22–23, 83–84; in early years of
Cuban Republic, 173 n. 23; in Matanzas
27–28, 54; of *paleros,* 33–34. *See also*
Cuban revolution: and Afro-Cuban religion
Rios, Orlando "Puntilla," 117, 126, 147, 148,
182 n. 29
ritual parties (*bembé, tambor,* or *toque*), 14,
25, 28, 40–41, 50
Robbins, James, 75, 79, 176 nn. 5, 8
Roche, Andrés, 53
Roche, Pablo, 147, 174 n. 35
Rodríguez, Arsenio, 145, 183 n. 30
Roldán, Amadeo, 100, 177 n. 9
Romeau, Armando, 37
Rouget, Gilbert, 122
rumba, 36, 37, 85

Salazar, Max, 183 n. 30
Sambia. *See* Palo
Santería, 11–15, 23–30; *aché,* 48, 118, 119,
120, 125 (see also *fundamento*); altars or
thrones, 42–43; *asiento* or *kariocha,* 13,
54; *babalao(s),* 14, 17, 28, 29, 123–24,
125, 126, 136–37, 142; *casa de santo* or
ilé ocha, 8, 9, 19, 24–25; *dilogún,* 14, 125;
divination systems, 14; *ekuelé,* 14, 28–29;
egbó (offerings), 14, 140; *eyá aránla,* 24;
focus of religious practice, 13; *guerreros*
or warriors, 13; *igbodu,* 24, 42–43, 81,
178 n. 19; *ilekes* or *collares,* 13; initiation,
13, 54; *italero,* 17; *itutu,* 14; *iyawo,* 13;
nonorthodoxy of, 16–17; *obi,* 14; *omiero,*
120, 121; *oriaté,* 14, 123, 125; *osain,* 121;
osainista, 47, 52; *osun,* 123, 125; *otanes*
or sacred stones, 13, 118; *pataki,* xiv, 12;
possession or trance in, 14, 25, 43, 44,
149, 150, 155, 167, 168, 174 n. 31, 184 n.
5; religious practices, 13; ritual experts,
16; ritual music, 15, 25; santeros, 11; *soperas,* 13, 118; supreme creator in, 12, 13.
See also Lucumí; *orichas;* Santería in New
York; Santería ritual music; Santería ritual
singing; slave groups
Santería in New York, 134–38; and arrival of
marielitos, 137, 142–44, 147–48; behavior

of *orichas,* 149–53; and Cuban immigrants from "freedom flights," 137; and
Espiritismo, 136; Havana and Matanzas
practices, 109, 182 n. 23; ideological differences, 135, 136; Oyotunji, 135; power
of babalaos, 136–37, 142; and Yoruba religion, 135–36, 182 nn. 20, 21; and
Yoruba Revisionism, 136; Yoruba Theological Archministry, 136
Santería ritual music, 12, 15, 25, 39; African
diaspora and, 116; *bembés* or *toques* (ritual parties), 14; David Byrne and, 117;
ensembles, 39; jazz and, 116; *oro de eyá
aránla,* 43; *oro de igbodu,* 42–43; and
possession or trance, 15, 25, 39, 43, 44,
149, 155, 160; *toque de egún,* 142, 143;
toque de muerto, 142; in the U.S., 116–17.
See also Santería ritual singing
Santería ritual singing, 158–62; call and response in, 158; classification of chants,
159; competence of singers, 160; *controversias,* 159, 160; in New York, 159,
160, 161; payment of singers, 161;
puyas, 159; role of chorus, 161; signifying and *puyas,* 159; *suyeres,* 159; training of singers, 161; translation of
chants, 128, 181 n. 15. *See also* Santería
ritual music
Sarabanda, 12; from altar to museum, 133,
182 n. 17. *See also* Palo
Scott, Rebecca J., 7
Scull, Ornelio, 146, 183 n. 31
Serrano, Sunta, 181 n. 4
signifying. *See* Santería ritual singing
Sikán. *See* Abakuá: myth of origin
Silveira, Juan "Candela," 112, 146
Simmons, Renard, 112, 113, 181 n. 4
slave groups (*naciones*), 8–12; Arará, 10–11;
cabildos and, 8, 9; Carabalí, 9, 10, 11, 17,
34; Congo, 9, 10–12; Lucumí, 8–11, 172
n. 6
slavery in Cuba, 6–8, 172 n. 3
Somavilla, Rafael, 37–39, 41
Somodevilla, Miguel, 40
soperas, 13, 118
Sosa, Enrique, 17, 22, 172 n. 2, 177 n. 11
Stubbs, Jean, 72, 176 n. 3
Suárez, Ricardo (Fantómas), 56, 57–58, 175
n. 42
syncretism, 12, 139–42, 172 n. 11, 182 n. 27

tambor. See ritual parties
Tanze. *See* Abakuá: myth of origin